A PATH TO RESILIENCE

Small Steps to an Unshakable You

Maria Sabio & Lourdes Laifer

A Path to Resilience Small Steps to an Unshakable You

Published November 2025

ISBN: 979-8-9939538-0-9

Edited by Isabelle Laifer

Book design by Lauren @Grafixgurl

To Cheryl , my family and friends, thank you for your love and support.

To Steve, Isabelle, Cassandra, and my entire family. With love and gratitude beyond measure.

Table of Contents

Introduction

The concepts, thoughts, and guidance you'll encounter in this book come from Stoicism, a philosophy born in Athens and tested in Rome, yet completely at home in our modern lives, whether in boardrooms, classrooms, or those quiet moments of doubt we all experience. Stoicism teaches that peace doesn't depend on perfect circumstances, but on practiced perspective. It's not about ignoring pain or pretending to be emotionless, it's about learning to steady yourself when life gets messy. The core principles of Stoicism will give you the grace to appreciate your life and the resilience to face the challenges that life presents.

Stoic philosophy has offered guidance on living with integrity, courage, and calm amidst life's challenges for centuries. This book applies Stoic principles to the complexities of the modern world. Here, we weave that ancient wisdom with modern psychology, mindfulness, and coaching insights. Together, they form a toolkit for resilience: a way to quiet your mind, strengthen your focus, and live with calm confidence no matter what's happening around you. The ultimate goal of this book is self empowerment.

Each day begins with a quote, inspired by the wisdom of Stoic philosophy, followed by one interpretation and one takeaway: the interpretation to help you reflect, and the takeaway to help you apply that wisdom and principle to your life. One invites understanding, the other calls for action. Wisdom doesn't transform us through reading alone — it's more easily absorbed when we live it.

How to Use This Book

This is a book you live with. It isn't meant to be read in one sitting.

Start with one small and deliberate action. Each morning, read one quote and its interpretation. In the evening, return to the takeaway. Reflect, journal, or simply notice how the message showed up in your day. Treat it like a daily ritual.

Whether you're a parent juggling too much, a student searching for direction, an executive under pressure, or simply someone trying to stay grounded, you'll find yourself somewhere in these pages.

The goal isn't perfection, it's practice. Over time, these small, consistent steps will build something bigger than motivation: a resilient core that no storm can shake.

Concept 1: The Love of Fate (Amor Fati)

This isn't happening to you. It's happening for you. Love the plot twist. It's part of your becoming. Whatever happens in your life has been waiting to happen since the beginning of time. The twining strands of fate wove both of them together: your existence and the things that happen for you.

January 01

If it's right for the universe, it's right for me, every season, every twist. I trust the timing, even when it's not my plan.

Whatever the universe throws your way, own it. If it's meant to happen now, it's not too soon or too late, it's exactly on time. Life's seasons bring their fruits, whether sweet or bitter, and you don't get to pick or postpone the harvest.

Everything you experience comes from the same source, flows through you, and eventually returns back. So why fight it? Why act like you're separate from the grand flow?

Stop wishing for a different timeline or a different set of circumstances. Say yes to what life is giving you, not despite it but *because* it's the universe's gift. When you love your fate – *Amor Fati* – you live free, no longer trapped in resentment or regret.

Challenge yourself: can you fully embrace what's happening as exactly what you need? Because that acceptance is the foundation of true peace and power.

Your Takeaway

Life doesn't run on your schedule, it runs on the universe's. Every season, every change, every challenge is fruit that life offers you, so lean into it with love and acceptance. When you accept life, you can confront reality and then take the appropriate action.

Reflect:

- Where are you fighting the timing or circumstances of your life instead of trusting them?

- What would it look like to welcome every experience as part of your growth?

- How can you practice saying "yes" to the season of life you're in, even if it's not what you'd pick?

- Are you willing to believe that if it's for the universe, it's for you, too?

Trust the process. Love your fate. It's all happening for you, not just to you.

January 02

You've seen things from one perspective, now try this: don't get worked up or overcomplicate your life.

You've been spinning your wheels, caught up in all the noise, but now it's time to take a step back and see life from this angle. Don't let yourself get tangled up in drama or make your life harder than it needs to be.

If someone is treating you poorly, that's their problem, not yours. And whatever happens to you, good or bad, was set in motion long before you even showed up. The universe has your back, whether you believe it or not.

Life's too short to waste on resentment or confusion. Your job is to show up, own the moment, and act with reason and fairness. Don't get sloppy when you're off the clock – instead, stay clear-headed and true.

Can you stop fighting the current and flow with it? The only power you truly have is how you respond *right now*. Use it wisely.

Your Takeaway

You can see life as a series of random hassles, or you can flip the script and treat every experience as part of your own custom training program, designed just for you. That's *Amor Fati* – loving your fate, not just surviving it.

The real win is living each day wide awake and meeting each twist with purpose, justice, and even gratitude.

Reflect:

- Where are you overcomplicating or resisting your current circumstances?

- How can you see today's challenges as something that's 'for' you, not just happening 'to' you?

- What would shift if you stopped blaming others and started owning your response?

- Are you ready to use every moment – good, bad, or boring – for your personal evolution?

Don't fight your fate, use it. This is your story. Make every chapter count.

January 03

Life's a blur, the world is unpredictable, but nothing happens outside the bigger plan. Ride the chaos, trust your inner compass, and make peace with where you are.

Life is messy and confusing. Even the great philosophers admit we can't really know everything for sure. Our perceptions flip-flop like the weather – what we believe today might be totally different tomorrow. And all of the things we think matter are often held by the worst of the worst: perverts, thieves, liars, you name it. The truth is, we're all a little hard to deal with at times.

So what's left to hold onto in all that chaos? Honesty, virtue, reason. Don't let the nonsense swirling around destabilize you or throw you off balance. Instead, console yourself with this truth: everything that comes your way fits into the grand design of nature. Nothing is random, nothing is unfair. And the one thing no one can mess with is your own inner compass – that guardian spirit inside you.

No one can force you off your path but you. So why waste energy struggling against *what is?* Lean into the flow. Accept your place in the story, whatever part you're playing, and keep showing up for your own truth.

Don't allow impatience to seep in as you wait for things to unfold. Instead, stand steady, knowing that in this wild, ever-changing world, your inner harmony is what truly lasts and matters. The choice is yours.

Your Takeaway

Amor Fati means you trust that whatever happens, it fits into a bigger design, even if you can't see the full blueprint right now. Don't take it all so seriously. Don't get obsessed with 'figuring it all out' or controlling every outcome.

Your real anchor isn't certainty about the outside world, it's your commitment to living by your own inner guide, your best values, your guardian spirit. No one can make you act against your own integrity. Allow the rest to come, let it go. You don't have to have all the answers. You just have to show up, play your part, and trust the process.

Reflect:

- Where are you getting lost in doubt or trying to control the uncontrollable?

- How can you focus more on following your inner compass, even when life is unclear?

- What would change if you treated uncertainty as a natural part of the journey and not a flaw to fix?

- Are you willing to trust that your story fits into the big picture, even when you can't see the ending?

When the world feels foggy, love your fate anyway. Show up, stay true, and let the rest unfold.

January 04

Whatever comes your way, trust that it's part of a bigger plan, and choose to make it work for you and your world.

If you believe in a universal intelligence and that your fate is destined then trust that it is for the best. Trust the grand plan and the greater good.

Even if you're not the star of the show, your life's a part of the bigger picture, the common good. Believe that whatever is coming your way is not just random chaos. It's part of the plan, and your job is to lean into it, welcome it, and find your place within it.

If you believe that there is no universal intelligence, then it's likely you don't partake in rituals or traditions that some hold sacred. Even so, you have one thing you *do* control: your own mind, your own nature.

Remember, your nature is rational and social. You belong to your community and, ultimately, the entire universe. So focus on what benefits your circle, your community, and the world.

At the end of the day, your true power is in alignment with *your* nature, whether the universe is intelligent or not. That's the real freedom and the real responsibility. So stand up, embrace your role, and keep showing up with integrity. That's how you turn fate into your ally.

Your Takeaway

Fighting what happens is fighting the flow. Your job is to take what lands in your inbox – good, bad, or bizarre – and turn it into something that helps the world around you. You're part of something bigger, whether it's your local community or the whole human family. What's good for you is what adds value to the whole system.

Amor Fati is about loving your fate, not because it's always what you'd pick, but because you trust it has a place in the master design, or at the very least, you choose to make it meaningful. Whether you think your path is written by destiny or just by chance, your move is the same: embrace it, work with it, and use it to benefit the larger whole.

You get to decide how you show up.

Reflect:

- Where are you resisting what's happened instead of seeing how it might fit in the big picture?

- What would shift if you trusted every experience could serve you and the people around you?

- How can you turn today's challenges into a win for your wider community?

- Are you ready to see yourself as a contributor to the world, not just a recipient of random luck?

Love your fate, trust the bigger plan, and use whatever comes your way to make the world better.

January 05

Own your experiences — they're the destiny made just for you.

Your life, every single experience, has been woven together like a tapestry. That whole pattern is made *just for you*. It is made to fit your soul perfectly, even if it doesn't always feel comfortable.

Denying or resisting it is like trying to swim upstream against a current that's way stronger than you. Instead of fighting what's been handed to you, or wishing things were different, try fully embracing it. Own your story: the good, the messy, the painful, and the beautiful.

There's nothing more perfectly suited to you than the life you actually have. Stop wasting energy on "what ifs" and "why me?", and start working with what's *here*. You don't have to like every twist or turn, but you *do* have to lean into them like they're part of your rhythm, because they are.

Own your destiny. It's yours, uniquely tailored, and it's waiting for you to step up and say, "I'm ready."

Your Takeaway

Life might seem random, but every experience you have fits you perfectly. Stop resisting and start embracing what comes your way, stop fighting and start living with ease. That's the heart of *Amor Fati*: loving what life hands you, because it's yours alone. In this, you'll find freedom.

January 06

Embrace the chaos. Your power isn't in control, it's in the 'yes' to what is.

Your mind, that rational human system, runs best when it's optimized.

First, stop just hitting auto-accept on every piece of false or fuzzy data that pops up. Instead, vet your info. Second, start directing your instincts only toward actions that benefit the whole network, i.e. society. No more chasing quick clicks, focus on genuine value. Third, be realistic about your 'wants' and 'avoids', and limit your desires to what's actually achievable or genuinely avoidable. There's no point stressing over things fundamentally beyond your control.

Welcome everything the universe's algorithm hands you. You're an intrinsic feature of that intelligent, fair system. Don't expect your life to mirror or be identical to someone else's, but know that the total sum of your life's value is equivalent to everyone's. It's about the entire unique journey.

This isn't about being passive. This is deep, strategic self-mastery that lets you truly love your fate, not as a resignation, but as an active, rational, and totally liberating engagement with your specific destiny. Live in the flow of life and say 'yes' to all of it.

Your Takeaway

Life moves forward when you stop fighting reality and start working with what you have. Growth isn't about making everything perfect, but about staying clear-minded, cutting through the noise, and putting your energy where it actually matters: helping others, focusing on what's in your control, and letting go of the rest.

Amor Fati means loving your fate, not just tolerating it. That's seeing every twist, setback, or random event as something you can use, not as something to resent. You're part of a bigger ecosystem, like a single leaf on a giant tree. Some things are yours to shape, others are just part of the plan. And while every leaf is unique, the whole tree shares in the same life force, same sunlight, same storms.

Reflect:

- Where are you resisting your current situation instead of welcoming it as part of your path?

- How would things shift if you saw every challenge as an invitation to grow?

- What's one thing you can accept or work with today, instead of wishing it away?

- Are you ready to trust the process and find peace, no matter what life hands you?

Loving your fate means owning your story, and making it count.

January 07

Everything that happens to you was woven into your story from the very beginning.

Whatever arrives or happens in your life right now, whether it's pleasant and unpleasant, was spun into the fabric of your existence *long* before you took your first breath. The universe wasn't scrambling – it was weaving a detailed plan. Every thread, every twist and turn, was meant for *you*.

So when life throws you a challenging curveball, don't waste energy fighting it or wishing it away. That struggle is just you resisting a pattern woven from eternity itself. Instead, lean into it. Own it. Every single moment, especially the hard ones, are part of *your* story, crafted to shape you, challenge you, and push you into the person you're meant to become.

Whatever you're currently facing, right here, right now, is yours to meet head-on. You can either rail against the current or swim with the flow, knowing that this path isn't random – it's your destiny. So choose to embrace it, because it was custom-made for you.

Your Takeaway

Even tough moments are threads in your unique tapestry. When you see life this way, you stop fighting the flow and start embracing your path, no matter what it looks like.

Loving your fate means loving the whole story, the light and the dark alike. That's how you find peace in the now.

January 08

To nature, the giver and taker, a wise person says: 'Give what you will, take what you will', not with defiance, but with respect.

Nature is the ultimate giver and taker, the original source of everything in your life. When life hands you gifts or takes things away, don't act like you're the victim or like you own the world. Instead, say this quietly but firmly: "Give what you want, take back what you wish."

The key here is to say it without arrogance or anger, but with the respect of someone who knows they're part of a bigger system. You're a loyal player in nature's game, not a rebel throwing a tantrum when things don't go your way.

It's about showing up with humility, accepting the flow, and trusting that what comes and goes is exactly as it should be, because you're living *in harmony* with the rhythm of the universe. That's real strength. That's real freedom.

Your Takeaway

A truly educated and humble person accepts nature's gifts and losses with grace, knowing they're part of a bigger plan. It's not about rebellion or resistance, it's about loyalty and trust in the natural order.

When you live like this, you find peace in the rhythm of giving and receiving. That's *Amor Fati*: loving your fate, no matter what it brings.

January 09

Running from life's rules is like being a fugitive on the run. When you let fear, anger, or grief control you, you lose your freedom.

When you run from what's set by the universe, the master law, you're not freeing yourself. You're actually running away like an emotional prisoner who's scared to face reality. Breaking the law, that's one way to be a runaway. Letting grief, anger, or fear control you is another form of running away.

Every moment of resistance to what's ordained — whether it's the past you can't change, the present you're stuck in, or the future you're dreading – makes you less free, not more. It's like putting yourself in chains while pretending you're breaking free.

Learn to stand your ground. Own what's assigned to you by universal law. Feel what you need to feel, but don't let it make a slave out of you. Freedom isn't about escaping hardship, it's about facing it head-on, with calm and courage. That's where your real power lies.

Your Takeaway

Life has its laws, its order – call it fate, nature, or the universe's design. When you break those laws, whether by actions or by letting emotions run the show, you're no longer the master of your own mind, you're a slave to your feelings.

True freedom comes from accepting what's assigned to you, facing it head-on, and owning your responses. That's *Amor Fati*: loving your fate and standing tall, no matter what comes.

January 10

History's just the same story with new actors. Whatever's happening now has played out before, and will again. Own your scene.

Everything you're going through right now isn't new. It's been played out countless times before, like reruns of the same old play. Every drama, every power play, every success or heartbreak you see on your feed has all happened before. Empires rise and fall, companies boom and bust, love is found and lost, and egos flare up on every stage, ancient or modern. Think of world leaders throughout the ages: they all dealt with the same drama and challenges, just different actors on the stage.

So why act like you're the first to face it? Why get caught up in the shock or the drama? Learn to recognize the patterns. The universe isn't throwing curveballs your way, it's running the same script. Once you see that, you can stop reacting like it's a surprise and start mastering your role.

Own your part in the play. Don't let the familiar scenes trip you up. You're not a victim of the story, you're the lead actor who chooses how to show up. Breathe, step up, and perform with purpose. This isn't about fighting the script, it's about embracing your role and playing it with grace.

Your Takeaway

Life feels new, but if you zoom out, it's just a reboot of the same script with different faces and fresh costumes. *Amor Fati* is about loving your role in the story and knowing that you're not the first or the last to face these plot twists. The pressure lifts when you realize this is just another season in a show that's been running forever.

Don't fight the script, or wish for a different genre. Play your part with heart, bring your best to your scene, and trust that you're exactly where you're meant to be. That's how you find peace in the chaos and joy in your unique chapter.

Reflect:

- Where are you treating your challenges or triumphs like they're one-of-a-kind, when they're really part of a bigger pattern?

- How would your perspective shift if you saw your story as one scene in a much bigger play?

- What would it look like to fully embrace your moment, instead of wishing for a different script?

- Are you ready to love your fate and play your part, knowing you're both unique and part of something timeless?

You're here for your scene. Step in and love the role you've been given.

January 11

If someone despises or hates you, that's on them. Your job is to remain kind, true, and focused on what's right.

If someone's going to despise you, that's their problem, not yours. Your job is to make sure you don't give them a reason. If someone hates you, fine. Continue to be kind and generous. Show them who you are, with real grace and respect, instead of being snarky or acting superior.

Inside, that's how you stay: solid, calm, unshaken, and without bitter complaints. The truth is that nothing truly bad can touch you if you're doing and following what is aligned with your nature. Accept what the universe gives you, and keep putting your energy into what benefits the greater good.

That's strength. That's peace. That's true freedom.

Your Takeaway

People will judge you, hate you, or misunderstand you. And honestly, that's their problem, not yours. Your responsibility is to act and speak with integrity, kindness, and patience. When someone's off track, be ready to help – not with harshness, but with genuine care and tact. Keep your composure and dignity even when being tested.

This is how you show up for yourself and the universe as a person unshaken by anger or complaints. Your energy belongs to the greater good, and that's a powerful place to stand.

January 12

Nothing's wrong when something ends on time, whether an action, a life, or a whole chapter.

Resist the temptation to label endings in life as bad. Your whole life is just a long chain of actions, but when that chain comes to its natural end, it's not a tragedy. It's just the right timing.

Sometimes life ends because your own nature says so, like dying of old age, but it can also be the universe's rhythm keeping everything fresh and balanced. And anything that serves the universe, that fits and follows its natural flow, is good and timely.

Don't fear the end. Don't be ashamed of it. It's not your choice to make, and it doesn't harm the greater good. In fact, it benefits the whole.

Embrace your path. Embrace the timing. It's all part of the perfect design.

Your Takeaway

Every action has its time to finish. When it does, there's no harm, failure, or shame in ending well. When you live in harmony with this flow, the end of your story isn't scary or bad – it's good and timely.

You're walking the path of the universe itself, moving with purpose and grace. That's the power of *Amor Fati*: loving your fate, start to finish.

Concept 2: Live in Harmony with Nature

Nature isn't just outside you. It's within you. Live like it.

January 13

Know yourself and your place in the whole. Nothing is stopping you from living in tune with nature every day.

Keep these five truths locked in your mind at all times:

First, understand what the *whole* is: the entire universe, nature's grand design, the big picture.

Second, know *your* nature: what makes you tick, your essence, your true self.

Third, see how your nature *connects* with the whole. You're not an island, you're a piece of this vast, living puzzle.

Fourth, understand the *role* you play as a part of this whole. What's your function? What's your place? What are you meant to contribute?

Fifth, know that *no one* is stopping you from aligning your actions and words with your nature and the universe's nature. You *can* live in harmony. You *must*.

Why not start now? Stop fighting the flow and ride the wave with awareness. When you act, ask yourself, "Is this me being true to my nature and the nature of all things?"

You're a part of this cosmic dance, and harmony is your birthright. Don't miss the rhythm.

How will you check in with your nature today and make sure you're moving with the whole, not against it?

Your Takeaway

It's easy to feel lost or out of sync, but your nature is connected to the whole universe like a note in a vast song.

Know how you fit and what part you play in the big picture. You have the power to live in harmony with this natural flow by being mindful of every word you say and action you take.

Show up, live aligned, and let that connection guide you.

January 14

Nature's beauty isn't about perfection: it's in the cracks, wrinkles, and wildness that make life real.

Nature doesn't always fit the neat, polished image we want it to have. Sometimes, it's cracked bread, split figs, or an old man's furrowed brow – things we might call flaws or failures. But those imperfections aren't mistakes, they're part of the whole picture. They add character, depth, and beauty all on their own.

If you're sensitive enough to really *understand* how the universe works, you start to see the charm in all these natural quirks. You'll find wonder in the wild, raw parts of life, see the beauty in aging faces, and notice the allure in places others wouldn't dare look twice.

Most people miss this because they don't truly know nature. They chase an ideal, filtered version of beauty and life. But living in harmony with nature means embracing it all, not just the parts that make us comfortable or proud.

Today, how can you open your eyes wider to the raw, imperfect beauty around you? How can you stop resisting the natural flow and start appreciating the whole unfolding masterpiece – messy edges and all?

What crack or wrinkle in your life might actually be a sign of something real and beautiful?

Your Takeaway

The world isn't perfect and that's what makes it beautiful. A truly tuned-in person sees beauty in the aged, the flawed, the untamed.

Those imperfections aren't mistakes, they're part of the story, adding character and appeal. They're just natural expressions of life.

When you learn to appreciate the raw, honest truth of the natural world, you find a deeper kind of joy.

January 15

We all share the same reason, law, and community, because the universe connects us as one.

Intelligence, reason, and law are not just random traits we each have tucked away inside us. They're *shared.* They come from something bigger, something we're all a part of: the universe itself, this vast, interconnected community we live in.

We're not isolated islands drifting in the void. When you realize this, it changes everything about how you see your role, your actions, and your relationships. You're part of a grand community, bound by reason and law. Your choices don't happen in a vacuum – they ripple out.

Are you living like you belong to this community? Are you acting with the awareness that your intelligence and reason are gifts from the universe, entrusted to you so you can play your part in its unfolding story?

How might your daily decisions shift if you truly felt you were part of something this vast, this connected? How would that change how you treat others, yourself, and the challenges you face?

Your Takeaway

The universe itself is the greatest community, the home we all belong to. It binds us together as fellow citizens, keeping us from existing in isolation.

Everything and everyone is connected. Living in harmony means recognizing this shared nature and acting accordingly.

January 16

If it's true to your values, do it without apologies. Other people's opinions aren't your GPS.

You have every right and are *entitled* to act and speak in ways that align with your nature. If what you're doing or saying is right, then stand firm. Don't let anyone's criticism or clever arguments shake you or make you doubt yourself. People around you have their own drives and distractions, their own messy guidance systems, but that's *their* path, not yours.

Your job is to keep walking your own path, the one that runs alongside the flow of universal nature. These two, your nature and the cosmos, are not at odds. In fact, they share the same rhythm, and when you honor that rhythm, you're in harmony with everything around you. So, trust yourself, stay steady, and keep moving forward. Others will react, but your focus is to live in alignment, not for approval or validation.

How often do you find yourself distracted or derailed by what others think? What would happen if you treated your inner compass like the only true guide it needs to be?

Your Takeaway

You know those moments when you're about to do what feels right, and then the mental chatter creeps in? "What will they think?" "Am I being too much?" Stop.

Amor Fati means loving your path enough to walk it with confidence, even if the crowd's going the other way. Everyone's acting from their own inner guidance system, but you can't and shouldn't live your life by their programming. If it's right by your nature and serves something larger, keep moving forward.

Imagine your life as a GPS route that only you can see. You don't re-route every time someone else yells directions from the sidewalk. Stay in your lane, trust your guidance, and remember: your job is to sync your actions with your own inner compass and with the rhythm of the universe, not the noise of the crowd.

Reflect:

- Where are you hesitating to act or speak up because you're worried about backlash?

- How would your choices change if you focused only on what feels right to you and the greater good?

- Are you letting others' opinions set your direction, or are you following your own internal GPS?

- Are you ready to move forward confidently, trusting your path, even if it's not the popular route?

Love your fate, own your truth, and let the rest catch up, or not.

January 17

Work isn't unnatural when you're doing what you're meant to do — hands as hands, feet as feet, and you as a human.

There's nothing wrong with work when it's what you were made for. As a human being, your job is to do human work — things that use your mind, your reason, your sense of community, your capacity to grow and contribute.

If you're living true to your nature, doing what's proper for *you* as a human, then no matter how hard it feels, it's not unnatural. And if it's not unnatural, then it's not bad. It's exactly what you're here to do.

Stop fighting your role or wishing things were easier just because you feel resistance. Embrace the work that fits you, the labor that makes you *you*. That's where your strength lies.

What work are you avoiding right now because it feels hard or out of reach? What if that resistance is just your mind pulling you away from fulfilling your true nature?

Your Takeaway

Your hands and feet work best doing their jobs – there's nothing weird or out of place in that.

When you live and act according to your nature as a human, your work feels right and good. Doing what's natural for you isn't a burden, it's part of a healthy life.

Don't fight your role or purpose, it's made for you and you're made for it. Lean into it and find fulfillment in the work that fits your true self.

January 18

Good tools do their job and nature is the ultimate craftsman, working within all things to keep them thriving.

Think of a good tool or instrument. It works because it's built for a purpose, but the tool itself doesn't control the work. The maker is gone, leaving the tool to just *be*.

Now compare that to natural things like you. The power that made you isn't gone, it lives inside you. That means your nature is alive and present, guiding you. When your mindset and actions align with this inner power, everything flows the way it should, no surprises, no wasted energy.

The universe itself moves with this kind of harmony, like a well-rehearsed orchestra playing the piece it was meant to play.

Instead of resisting or doubting, trust the design that's inside you. When you live in compliance with your nature, things fall into place. It's not about forcing or controlling, but about being who you were made to be.

What parts of yourself are you resisting that, if embraced, could help you flow more naturally with life's rhythm?

Your Takeaway

A tool is good when it does what it was made to do, but nature's creations are different: the power that made them still lives within them, guiding their path. That's why respecting nature is so important. When your mind and actions align with nature's will, things flow the way they should.

The universe moves with purpose, and when you move with it, everything falls into place. It's the foundation for a good life.

January 19

Nothing can stop your life from aligning with your rational nature, because the universe moves with reason, and so do you.

No one can block you from living in line with your rational nature. Your ability to think clearly, make wise choices, and act with purpose are *yours* and yours alone.

Nothing that happens to you can ever truly go against the rational flow of the universe. Every event, challenge, and surprise is part of a bigger, reasonable whole that you're built to navigate.

So why waste energy fighting what *is*? Align your mind with that rational current. Stop swimming upstream against the natural order, and instead move with it: calmly, composed, and confident.

You *can* live in harmony with this universal reason. It's already there in you, waiting for you to step into it.

What's one way you can start trusting your own rational nature more today, especially when life throws you curveballs?

Your Takeaway

Reason and nature aren't enemies, they're your greatest allies. Whatever happens fits into the larger plan, even the challenging stuff.

When you accept this, you can live with confidence and calm, knowing you're exactly where you need to be. Lean into that, and nothing can throw you off your path.

January 20

Everything's connected. Nature's not just scenery, it's your network. Play your part, and keep the whole system healthy.

Everything around you is connected, every creature, element, and moment. This isn't just some vague idea, it's a sacred bond. Nothing stands alone. Nothing is truly separate.

The universe is one big network, with one source code running underneath: connection, balance, reciprocity. If you work against that, if you isolate, pollute, or only take, you're breaking the code, and it backfires every time. You can't be out of sync with the universe without being out of sync with yourself.

This unity is powered by a single reality: one law, one reason, and one truth. If we want to be fulfilled, we have to recognize that we're part of this whole, part of this great connected flow.

So stop trying to fight the natural order or act like you're separate from everything else. You *are* part of this magnificent, interwoven whole. The sooner you accept that, the more peace and purpose you'll find.

How can you remind yourself today that you're part of this bigger whole, and let that shift the way you relate to the world around you?

Your Takeaway

You're not an island, and nothing in nature runs solo. What you do ripples out. Living in harmony with nature is about recognizing you're a part of a collaborative ecosystem. That includes both caring for the planet and treating other people, animals, and even your own body as if they're part of your team. Because they are.

Reflect:

- Where are you acting like you're separate from the bigger picture?

- How could you 'sync up' with nature today, through your choices, your relationships, or your routines?

- What's one habit you could change to play your part better in the whole ecosystem?

- Are you ready to treat nature not as a background, but as your actual community?

Plug in, live connected, and help keep the whole system thriving.

January 21

Just as you breathe the air around you, breathe in the universal intelligence that flows through all things.

You breathe in the air around you without a second thought. It's natural, effortless. But another vital thing you can breathe in every moment is *intelligence*: a universal intelligence that flows through everything and everyone.

This intelligence isn't locked away or scarce. It's everywhere, all around you, ready for anyone who's willing to tune in and draw from it. Just like breathing sustains your body, tapping into this all-encompassing wisdom nourishes your mind and soul.

So, the next time you pause to think or make a choice, remember that you don't have to do it alone. Align with that universal intelligence that guides all things in harmony. Let it flow through you and shape your actions.

How might your day change if you consciously invited this universal intelligence into your decisions and your moments of stillness?

Your Takeaway

Universal intelligence flows through everything. Bringing awareness to this allows you to live in tune with it and connects you more deeply to the world.

January 22

Loving your fate means living in truth and playing your part for the good of everyone, anything less just messes with the whole system.

Any act of injustice is like a cosmic glitch. The universe wired us to help each other, not to cause harm, and to deviate from that universal will is to go against existence's very blueprint. Lying is also an irreverent move, as it goes against the natural, truthful order of the universe.

The second you hurt someone, twist the truth, or act out of selfishness, you're not just breaking social rules, you're fighting the flow of reality itself.

For *Amor Fati* to truly flourish, you must embrace reality as it is, rooted in truth and justice. Stop fighting it and put in the work to understand and embody it in your actions.

Can you honestly say you're doing your part to distinguish falsehood from truth, even when it's uncomfortable?

Your Takeaway

The universe isn't random chaos, it's a system built for connection, honesty, and helping each other succeed. Every time you act with integrity, you're in sync with the bigger plan. This is about showing up in a way that uplifts the whole, playing your role honestly and transparently, and not cutting corners or spreading lies.

You were born with what you need to discern truth from lies and to work for the common good. Loving your fate means you accept responsibility, knowing that helping others and living honestly keeps you in harmony with everything around you.

Reflect:

- Where are you tempted to fudge the truth or look out for yourself at the expense of others?

- What would shift if you saw your words and actions as part of a bigger, interconnected plan?

- How can you align your choices with the flow of honesty and service, even when it's tough?

- Are you willing to trust that living honestly and helping others is the fastest way to real peace?

Love your fate by loving the truth, and by being a positive force in the bigger system.

January 23

You're part of a greater whole, connected to those like you. When you act for the common good, your life flows with ease and contentment.

Whether we break it down to atoms or see it through the grand scheme of nature, the truth is that you're not separate, you're a part of a greater whole guided by nature's wisdom, which always aims for what's good for the entire system.

Nothing that benefits the whole can truly harm any part, including you. If something happens in your life that feels difficult, remember it's part of a bigger, beneficial flow. Nature doesn't work against itself. When you hold that perspective, frustration and discontent lose their grip.

Act for the common good. Let every impulse and decision be steered towards supporting those around you.

How can you stop resisting what happens and instead lean into the idea that you're part of something bigger? And how will you bring your energy toward the common good, where true harmony and peace live, today?

Your Takeaway

Your impulses naturally lean toward supporting others, because you share a bond with them. When you act with their good in mind, your own life flows smoothly, like a citizen who works for and trusts their community. Living in harmony with nature means living for the greater good, and that's how you find true contentment.

January 24

The earth welcomes the rain, the air moves with love, and the universe delights in creating so I choose to love what it loves too.

Accept the universal flow. Move and love what the universe provides. Stop fighting against the way things unfold. Stop wishing for something else, and align yourself with the natural course of events. When you start loving what happens because it *has* to happen, you're no longer swimming upstream.

The phrase, "This loves to happen" is a call to live in sync with nature's love, to accept life's unfolding with open arms, and to find peace in the certainty that what's coming next is exactly right.

Stop resisting the flow and start loving the moment as it is. Stop struggling and start thriving in harmony with everything around you.

Your Takeaway

Nature isn't cold or indifferent. The earth drinks the rain with joy. The air swirls, moved by a kind of love.

The universe itself loves to bring things into being, unfolding exactly as it should. So why not align yourself with that? When you love what nature loves – growth, change, creation – you step into harmony with the whole.

Concept 3: Use Reason as Your Guide (*The Logos Within*)

When you follow reason, you follow your true nature.

January 25

Don't live on autopilot, let your inner wisdom call the shots. Respond, don't just react.

The body feels, the soul reacts, but the mind is where your power lies. Everyone has feelings, impulses, and gets pulled around by their urges. Plenty of people get lost in their feelings or fooled by outside hype. What sets a mindful person apart is using their mind as the true guide.

A mindful person embraces whatever life throws at them, knowing it's all part of the plan, woven by fate. They don't let the noise of feelings or distractions mess with their inner calm, center, and true self. This tranquil mind follows reason, speaks the truth, and does what's just.

If the whole world refuses to believe in your simple, honest, peaceful way or calls you naive or weak, simply respond by keeping your cool and not veering off your path. Keep walking steadily: pure, at peace, aligned with your fate, and ready for whatever comes.

At the end of the day, it's not about others believing you, it's about you living true to reason, true to your soul's purpose. That's where real freedom lives.

How can you strengthen your mind's role as your guide today, especially when impulses and distractions pull you away?

Your Takeaway

Using reason as your guide means letting your inner CEO run the company, not just your senses or emotions. It's about pausing, checking in with your deeper principles, and making moves that line up with your best self.

You don't need to prove your worth to the world, just keep following your own inner compass, and arrive at the end of your story with a clean heart and a clear mind.

Reflect:

- Where are you living on autopilot instead of checking in with your inner wisdom?

- How could you let your reason, not just your reactions, lead the way today?

- What's one area where you can practice more pause, less impulse?

- Are you ready to make decisions that align with your core values, even if no one else sees it?

Let reason lead, let the noise fade, and walk your path with intention.

January 26

Stick to your principles and reason, and soon those who see you as less than will see you as something greater.

Right now, some people see you as less than you truly are, like an animal. Maybe they don't respect you, maybe they mock or underestimate you. But that's their problem, not yours.

You can turn it all around by coming back to your core, principles, and the steady light of reason that lives inside you.

When you follow reason without wavering and when your actions and thoughts align with it, others won't just respect you, they'll be in awe of you. You become a force of true wisdom and integrity.

Focus on mastering your mind and your reason. This dedication is enough to rise above the noise and step into your true greatness. Let that be the thing that transforms you.

What's one small step you can take today to realign with your reason and start that transformation?

Your Takeaway

Some people might look down on you now and judge you unfairly, but don't let that unsettle you.

If you commit to living by your values and reason, you'll rise above their opinions and stand tall with integrity, wisdom, and the kind of strength that commands respect.

January 27

Check in with yourself: Who's driving right now, your higher self or your old habits?

Pause for a moment and ask yourself, "Is this activity truly aligned with my deepest purpose?" Keep this question close as your personal compass.

What's occupying the seat of power inside you? Is it clarity and reason or is it chaos and distraction? Is your soul acting like a child throwing tantrums or a teenager caught up in drama? Is it ruled by fleeting emotions or wild impulses?

You have the ability to choose. Steer your soul toward wisdom, patience, and strength. Guide your mind with reason, instead of letting feelings run the show.

Every moment is your chance to check in and course-correct. What kind of soul do you want to live with?

What's your soul showing you right now? How can you bring more reason and calm to that inner guidance system?

Your Takeaway

Most people never pause to ask, "Who's really behind the wheel of my decisions right now?" Is it the wise, future-focused you, or are you letting your inner kid, your ego, your hunger, or your stress run the show?

Maybe today your mindset feels a little childish and impatient, or maybe it's chasing comfort and avoiding pain. No judgment, just notice it. Ask, "Is this the mindset I want leading my life?" and choose to step out of autopilot when you need to.

That's how you build a life you're proud of, one honest check in at a time.

Reflect:

- Who's running your mindset right now: your wisest self, or some lesser version of you?

- How can you pause and course-correct when you're not loving who's in charge?

- What would change if you made these check-ins a daily habit?

- Are you willing to let reason, not just impulse, guide your choices?

Keep asking, keep choosing, and let your best self take the lead.

January 28

Reason is a self-contained system. It starts with clear thinking and leads you straight to the right path.

Reason is like your internal GPS. It starts from where you are – your values, your knowledge, your current situation – and guides you where you need to go, using clarity, virtue, peace.

When you act from reason, your actions are aligned with your true nature, your purpose, your path. Every time you pause and choose to respond thoughtfully instead of reacting blindly, you're recalibrating your GPS. You're making sure you don't get lost in the chaos of impulse or emotion.

Trust your reason, it's designed to lead you home. When you let it, it keeps you steady, grounded, and moving forward on the right path.

How are you tuning your internal GPS today? Are you letting reason map your way or letting distractions steer you off course?

Your Takeaway

Reasoning isn't random, it's a process with a beginning and an end. It keeps you on track, steady and sure, even when life gets confusing.

Trust your mind's ability to lead you. Follow it, and you'll walk the path that's best for you and those around you.

January 29

Live like you're walking with universal intelligence: content, obedient, and guided by your inner reason.

What does it mean to live with universal intelligence or a power greater than you? It's not about temples or rituals, it's about living so that your soul is always ready for divine inspection. The part of you that matters most – your mind, your reason, your inner guide – is content with what life gives and obedient to its own highest self and inner wisdom.

It's the voice that tells you when you're aligned with your true nature and when you're not. When you live this way, you're living alongside this intelligence, not as a distant fantasy, but as a present reality.

Stop waiting for permission or a sign. Start living like your soul is on display, knowing it's your reason that keeps you honest, steady, and aligned with the universe's flow.

How often do you check in with that guardian spirit inside you? Are you living with its approval or running on autopilot?

Your Takeaway

Listen to your inner voice. Allow it to align you in a sense of calm, clarity, and steadiness. This is your guide to living well and in harmony with the universe.

January 30

Most admire things that stick together or grow naturally. But true respect belongs to those who nurture their rational, social soul.

The crowd's awe goes to what's visible and tangible, things that are tied to life but still about possession or control.

Then there are those who admire intellectual or artistic skill. But the true value is in the rational and social soul, the core of who you are. Your focus sharpens to maintaining your own soul's health, making sure your mind stays rational and that your actions are aligned with reason and kindness.

When you find your tribe, those who value the same things, you move forward together, cultivating wisdom, cooperation, and true growth.

Are you still caught up in chasing the applause for the outside stuff? Or are you tuning your soul to the deep, steady rhythm of reason and social harmony? What does your inner guidance want you to focus on today?

Your Takeaway

The truly wise focus on what matters most: the rational, social soul inside themselves. They care about keeping their mind clear, their heart connected, and their actions aligned with reason. They seek out others like them, building community based on shared values.

When you prioritize your soul's health over shallow things, you tap into real respect and true living.

January 31

Make it a habit to really listen and try to see things from the speaker's perspective.

Learn to really listen. Active listening is not just about hearing words, but really tuning into the mind behind them. Step into the speaker's world, try to understand where they're coming from, what's driving their thoughts and feelings.

It's not about agreeing blindly or reacting emotionally. It's about training your own reason to grasp the whole picture, even when it's different from yours. This practice sharpens your judgment, deepens your empathy, and keeps your guidance system steady.

When you truly understand others, you control your responses rather than being controlled by the noise. Listening well is one of the smartest moves your rational mind can make.

How often do you listen to understand, not just to reply? What might change if you started practicing this right now?

Your Takeaway

Too often, we hear people but don't truly listen. Listening well means stepping into their shoes, understanding their thoughts and feelings. It helps you respond wisely, not just react emotionally.

Being present for others is part of using your reason as a guide, deepening connection and clarity. So slow down, listen with intention, and watch how your mind and relationships grow.

February 01

When you see life and time from a higher perspective, human life feels small and death loses its sting.

When you really focus your mind on the big picture – seeing all of time, all of existence – human life shrinks down to its rightful size. It's impossible to get all tangled up in small, fleeting dramas when you're holding the vastness of everything in your view.

And guess what? Death loses its sting. It's just part of the natural flow, nothing terrifying or personal. When your reason guides you to this truth, fear falls away because you understand life as it truly is: temporary, interconnected, and meaningful only when lived with wisdom.

So instead of fearing the end, focus on living your values right now, because that's where real power lies.

How might stepping back to see the big picture shift how you feel about your daily worries or fears?

Your Takeaway

When you look at all time and existence, individual life seems tiny by comparison. That perspective makes the fear of death shrink, and seeing life this way helps you live with calm and courage.

You're part of a vast story and death is just one chapter. Let reason guide you to this bigger picture, and you'll find peace in the face of endings.

February 02

Just like a tree bears fruit, so does the human mind: producing more reason, growth, and wisdom in its time.

Everything has its own natural time to produce what it's meant to produce. Don't get caught up in narrow, surface-level definitions.

Your reason, the part of you wired for wisdom and truth, is like a tree that grows more trees of reason. The fruit it produces is more clarity, more good judgment, more aligned action. When you lean into your rational mind, you're not just surviving, you're actively creating the kind of life that mirrors the order and purpose of the universe itself.

Stop seeing yourself as separate or less than. You're part of a bigger flow, meant to bear your own unique fruit of reason. Your role is to cultivate it daily.

What kind of fruit are you nurturing in your own life right now? How can you feed your reason so it grows stronger?

Your Takeaway

Everything that lives and grows produces something. Your mind is no different – it's a source of reason, wisdom, and clarity that lead to better living. This growth happens naturally when you nurture your capacity to think and reflect.

Focus on cultivating your mind's fruits – they're the real harvest of a meaningful life.

February 03

If you know the next step, take it, don't overthink it. If you're unsure, pause and get advice. Let reason, not panic, set your course.

When the path forward is clear, when you know what needs to be done, stop overthinking and just do it. There's no room for second-guessing here. But if things become fuzzy, if you hit a wall, don't panic. Step back, get some wise counsel, and recalibrate.

Obstacles are part of the deal. Use what you have, proceed carefully, but never lose sight of what's right. Justice isn't just a fancy ideal, it's the true measure of success. Fall short of that, and you've truly failed.

When you let reason lead every step, no outside pressure can shake you. You become light, joyful, and steady – unfazed by chaos or noise. That's real freedom.

Are you trusting your reason to guide you through the confusion today? Where could a calm, just decision change your course for the better?

Your Takeaway

Reason isn't about cold logic, it's about clarity, integrity, and steady progress, no matter the mess around you. As long as you're chasing what's fair and honest, you can walk through chaos and come out steady, unbothered, and genuinely joyful. The only real failure is selling out your values for comfort or approval.

Reflect:

- Where are you overcomplicating a choice you already know is right?

- Who are your 'advisors', and how often do you check in with them or your inner wisdom?

- How can you use reason to move forward, even when you hit obstacles?

- Are you willing to trust clarity over confusion, and justice over comfort?

Let reason set your course. Move when you know, pause when you don't, and never trade your values for shortcuts.

February 04

Nature is the ultimate artist, nothing we create can outdo its perfect design. Justice arises from this natural order and grounds all virtues.

Nature is the original master artist. Every skill, every craft, every art we admire is just a copy, an imitation of how the universe itself works. No human ingenuity can outdo that perfect design.

All these arts serve the higher purpose of nature. Just like the farmer cultivates the soil to grow food, nature works for something greater: balance, order, justice.

Justice is the cornerstone of all virtues. But justice slips away the moment we start treating unimportant things as if they really matter, when we get fooled, or when we waver and change our minds like the wind.

If you want to live wisely, start by grounding yourself in justice rooted in reason and in tune with nature. Only then can all your virtues stand firm.

Are you letting your reason guide your sense of justice, or are distractions and doubts pulling you off course? What small step can you take today to stand firm in what's right, no matter what?

Your Takeaway

Everything in nature works together, and from this harmony comes justice, the foundation for every other virtue. Keep justice central, and your reason will guide you toward true integrity.

February 05

Not every thought deserves attention.

Your mind, your reason, your inner guidance, is the real captain here. But it can go off course in four big ways, and you have to be on constant alert.

First, catch those unnecessary thoughts, they clutter your mind and steal your focus. Repeat this to yourself, "This thought is not needed."

Second, watch for thoughts that tear apart the bonds between people. When those come up, remind yourself, "This is breaking us apart, and I'm better than that."

Third, beware when you're about to say or do something that doesn't feel like you, whether it's something forced or fake. That's one of the worst things your mind can fall into. Call it out and remind yourself, "This isn't me."

Fourth, never let the lower, mortal part – the body with all its cravings and discomforts – take the wheel from the higher, divine part of you. That's how you lose control and lose yourself.

This is a daily mental workout. When you see these four threats, stop them dead in their tracks. Your reason is your strongest ally so always let it lead.

Are you noticing any of these off course thoughts creeping in? How will you catch them next time and remind yourself who's really in charge?

Your Takeaway

The more you monitor your mental feed and filter out the junk, the more you show up as your best, truest self. Don't let your most divine, rational self get hijacked by old habits or emotional autopilot.

Reflect:

- What unhelpful thoughts keep popping up on your mental screen?

- Where do you need to hit 'mute' on impulses that don't line up with who you really want to be?

- How can you practice pausing and filtering before you speak or act?

- Are you willing to be the moderator of your own mind, not just a passive scroller?

Keep your inner software clean and let reason run the show, and the rest will fall in line.

Concept 4: See the Bigger Picture (*Cosmic Perspective*)

Zoom out. There's wisdom in distance.

February 06

Everything fades fast. Your true connection is to the part of you that touches the divine.

Look around. Everything you see, every body, every person, everything that grabs your attention with promises of pleasure or threats of pain — it's all fading fast. Not just the physical forms, but even memories that people have of them vanish into the vastness of time. What we chase after, what we brag about, and what scares us is all temporary. Bodies turn to dust, memories fade into nothingness, and all that remains is the endless flow of the universe.

So why get caught up in the chase for fame, wealth, or comfort? These are just corpses in the cosmic scheme: lifeless, fleeting, and often petty. The wise see death for what it truly is: a natural process, as ordinary as night turning to day. There's nothing scary about it. Fear of death is like a child afraid of the dark, holding onto illusions instead of seeing reality clearly.

Death isn't an end, but a part of the whole — it nourishes nature's cycle. It's also the moment where the human spirit touches something greater, connects with the divine. Let go of the illusion and choose to connect now. Be clear within yourself: pure, calm, and free from illusions.

Ask yourself, "Am I living trapped by illusions about life and death? Or am I stepping back to see the whole picture: my place in the vast universe, the impermanence of all things, and the chance to live fully in that truth?"

What illusions can you let go of today? How might embracing this *cosmic perspective* change the way you live, love, and let go?

Your Takeaway

Death isn't against nature, it *is* nature, and it actually helps the cycle continue. That spark, the part that touches the divine, is where your true self lives. Keep that connection strong, and nothing in the world can shake you.

February 07

The universe is ordered whether by design or by natural balance. You can't be calm inside if everything outside is chaos.

The universe either runs on order, like a perfectly mixed cocktail where every ingredient plays its part, or it's chaos that somehow still manages to create a kind of order.

Everything around you – every star, every wave, every person – is connected, interacting, and blending together in this massive web, including you. You can't expect to be this rock of peace while everything around you is chaos, because you *are* the universe, in a sense. Your inner world reflects the outer world.

Will you flow with that order, accept how things connect, and move, or will you fight against it, trying to hold on to control where there is none? The universe has your back, it's all tied together. When you recognize this, you can relax into the flow, knowing that your peace and purpose are part of something much bigger.

What if, instead of resisting the world's chaos, you leaned into the greater order that it's part of? How would that change the way you see your challenges and your role in life?

Your Takeaway

Everything is connected – distinct yet intertwined, and always influencing each other. If you want peace, start by aligning yourself with this order. When you see the bigger picture, you realize that your calm isn't separate from the world.

Bring order inside first. It's where your power lies.

February 08

History repeats itself. Don't waste your energy on what fades, focus on what truly matters.

Look back at time and you'll find the same old story. People got married, had kids, got sick, died. They made war, celebrated, traded, schemed, loved, and chased after power and wealth. People hustled, struggled, lived their lives just like anyone else, then faded away. And now, not a trace of their lives remains.

Zoom out even more, through all history and all people, and you'll find the same pattern repeating over and over: sweat, toil, ambition, and then the end. Even people you knew personally probably got caught up in their own busy dramas, failing to live true to themselves and satisfied with what they were.

The hard truth and the great relief is that what you focus on and how much energy you give to any one thing needs to be measured. Not everything deserves your time or your sweat. When you see life from the *cosmic perspective*, it's easier to stop exhausting yourself over trivial stuff and focus on what truly aligns with your nature and your purpose.

Ask yourself, "Am I spending my time on what lasts? Or am I burning out chasing shadows?"

If we all disappeared tomorrow, what would really matter? How would you want to spend your energy right now?

Your Takeaway

Don't burn yourself out chasing things that vanish. Put your energy into what aligns with your nature and lasts beyond the moment. That's where your time is well spent.

February 09

Remember the vastness of existence, the brief moment you live, and your small place in the grand scheme.

Pause for a moment. Picture the entire universe, vast beyond your imagining, stretching out in every direction, filled with stars, planets, galaxies, life beyond measure. Now, zoom in on your life, your time here. It's tiny. Just a blip, a drop in the enormous ocean of existence.

Then consider time itself. It's been flowing for billions of years and you've been granted only a brief moment, a fleeting breath in which to live, to act, and to be. Fate is this vast river, carrying everything along, and you're just one small leaf on its surface. No matter how much you want to control it, you're part of something much greater, something ancient and immense.

What's the point of getting caught up in little dramas, daily annoyances, and transient pains? When you see your place in the grand scheme, it's easier to let go of petty worries and focus on living in harmony with this huge, unfolding whole.

You're a tiny part of an enormous, interconnected cosmos, so why not play your part with calm, courage, and clarity?

What if your problems looked small from the eyes of eternity? How would you face today differently?

Your Takeaway

The universe is huge – far beyond what you can imagine. Your life is just a tiny flicker in the endless stretch of time. Your role in fate is even smaller, it's a single thread woven into a vast tapestry. That awareness helps you live with humility, calm, and focus on what really matters.

February 10

The elements rise and fall in cycles, but virtue follows a higher, mysterious path beyond all that.

Think about the world around you: water flows down, fire rises up, the seasons turn in endless cycles. Everything moves in repeating, predictable patterns. But virtue doesn't follow those visible cycles.

It's something deeper, more profound, almost divine. It moves in a way that isn't easy to see or understand at first. Its path isn't a straight line or a circle you can trace on a map. It advances slowly, sometimes imperceptibly, through the complexity of life and time.

This isn't just about good or bad days, wins or losses. Virtue is a lifelong journey that defies the usual ups and downs of the world. It grows in ways that matter far beyond the immediate and obvious.

So when life feels like it's looping or you're stuck in a rut, remember that virtue is on a higher track. Its progress is steady, even if invisible and it's leading you to something truly worth your effort.

What if you trusted that your growth was happening, even when you couldn't see it? How would that change how you handle life's cycles?

Your Takeaway

Everything physical moves in patterns, but virtue isn't caught up in those cycles. It moves along a deeper journey, one that's not easy to fully understand. Virtue is about steady progress on a path that transcends the everyday. When you focus on cultivating virtue, you align with something eternal.

February 11

Oceans are droplets. Time is a blip. Everything's small and fleeting, but it all comes from the same great source.

The continents, the oceans, and even the towering Mount Everest are just specks in the vast universe. Time itself, the whole stretch of it we know, is just a fleeting instant in eternity. Everything we get caught up in, all the noise and drama, is small, fleeting, and always changing.

And yet, all of it — the good, bad, beautiful, and ugly — comes from the same source. The universe's universal guidance sends out everything: the majestic and the harsh, the noble and the cruel.

Don't let the ugliness of the world make you forget the common origin we all share. Even the toughest, darkest things are part of the same whole that holds beauty and goodness. Seeing this bigger picture grounds you and helps you tap into reverence for the whole cosmic dance.

How might your frustration or fear soften when you remember that even the hardest moments are part of something vast and shared? What space does that open up inside you?

Your Takeaway

Everything in existence is derived from the same source. Being mindful of this allows a greater reverence for the universe and peace with whatever life brings. Remaining connected to the big picture is a grounding force.

February 12

Step back and look at life from above. See the combination of all things; the chaos and order, birth and death, festivals and grief.

To really understand human life, you have to picture it all: herds of animals, armies marching, farmers working the land, weddings and divorces, births and deaths. The chaos of courts, the serenity of the deserts, celebrations, grief, bustling markets.

At first glance, it might seem like a mess, a wild jumble of opposite forces clashing. But when you step back, you see the order in it all. Opposites dance together, each playing its part in the vast story.

When you remember this, it's harder to get stuck in the petty frustrations or dramas of daily life. You start to see your own struggles as part of this vast, interconnected flow, an important note in the grand symphony. That perspective brings peace, even when things feel out of control.

What happens inside when you remind yourself to step back and see life from this higher view? How can this help you lean into the flow rather than fight against it?

Your Takeaway

When you view life from this higher vantage point, the noise quiets, and the patterns emerge. You start to see how everything fits and harmonizes together. That perspective helps you make sense of the chaos and find your own peace within it.

February 13

Don't let the big picture overwhelm you. Focus on what's right in front of you and handle that with strength.

It's easy to get overwhelmed when you try to take in your whole life all at once: the past messes, the future worries piling up like a storm on the horizon. But none of that actually needs your attention except for this very moment, right now.

Stop spinning your wheels in "what ifs" and 'what was'. Instead, zero in on what's right in front of you. Is the task you're facing *really* unbearable? Would it be shameful to admit it? If your answer's no, then you have no excuse to crumble.

The past is gone. The future isn't here yet. Only the present demands your energy, and this present moment, stripped of all the noise, is far easier to carry than your mind lets on. So when your mind starts to fold under pressure, call it out. Remind it: "This is simple, manageable, and it's all I have to deal with."

Mastering life isn't about wrestling with every storm all at once, it's about standing firm in the calm eye of the present.

How might grounding yourself in the present shift the way you handle stress? What small step can you take now to rebuke that overwhelmed mind?

Your Takeaway

Thinking about your past mistakes and future worries can make your mind spiral. But only this moment matters. You're stronger than you think: focus on the present and handle it with grace. That's how you keep your peace amid the chaos.

February 14

Clear your mind. Master your impulses. Let go of craving. Keep your inner captain steady.

Clear your mind. Stop letting every fleeting impulse or craving hijack your focus. When desire pops up, don't just react: watch it, let it go, don't let it own you.

Your mind is like the captain of a ship navigating vast, sometimes stormy seas. Your inner guidance holds the bigger picture, the cosmic view. It's the calm in the storm, anchored in reason.

When you hold on to that self-mastery, you're no longer tossed around by petty wants or distractions. You're grounded in the vastness of time and space where impulses are just small ripples, and you're the ocean.

Mastering yourself isn't about denying life's experiences. It's about seeing beyond them, staying steady, and steering your ship with clarity.

What's one impulse you can catch and calm today, seeing it as a ripple, not the storm? How would that shift your sense of control and perspective?

Your Takeaway

Clarity comes when you stop giving in to every desire or impulse. In this grand cosmic journey, it's this calm inner guide that keeps you steady and on purpose. So clear the clutter, hold your course, and sail with confidence through life's vast ocean.

February 15

Your worries, reputation, and status are here today, forgotten tomorrow.

Step back, like you're standing on a mountain looking down at the endless flow of life. Countless ceremonies, journeys braving storms and calm, births, lives, deaths – an endless tide moving without pause.

Your life is just a single thread woven into this vast tapestry. Memory, fame, applause are all fleeting, empty noise. They don't hold real meaning.

Why waste your energy chasing shadows? Focus on what truly matters: the substance of your actions, your character, and your peace of mind in this vast, ever-moving cosmos.

The next time you feel overwhelmed, rejected, or desperate to impress, pull back. Get some perspective. The world is massive, and you're just passing through, so let go of the need to control how you're seen or remembered. Find your freedom in that.

What small shift can you make today to stop feeding the hunger for fame and start nourishing your true self?

Your Takeaway

Memory fades. Fame is fickle. The universe has been spinning long before you arrived and will keep spinning long after. What really matters is living truthfully, seeing past your own worries, and appreciating how little any of this stress really counts in the big picture.

Reflect:

- Where are you letting your reputation, worry, or ego take up more space than it deserves?

- How might your stress change if you zoomed out and saw the big, wild world you're a part of?

- What could you release today, knowing it won't matter in the long run?

- Are you willing to trade the chase for significance for the peace of perspective?

You're a part of something huge. Don't let small stuff shrink your view.

February 16

Time is short. Live boldly and honorably, no matter where you are, as part of one human family.

The time you have left is short, much shorter than you think. Stop shrinking to fit anyone else's expectations or hiding your values because you're worried about how you'll be received. Start living fiercely, grounded, and loyal to what's real and right. It doesn't matter where you are, whether it's your hometown or halfway across the world. Treat every place like it's one big community, one nation where honesty and nature's law rule.

Let people watch you live with integrity, in harmony with your true nature. And if they can't handle it or if they push back or try to tear you down, just let them. Standing tall and true – even if it costs you everything – is better than shrinking into a life that's anything less than real.

You owe it to yourself and to this vast, interconnected world to live like you belong: honestly, boldly, and with purpose.

What small act of integrity can you claim that sets you apart from the noise?

Your Takeaway

Your time here is limited, so live with honor, stand tall, rooted, and proud of who you are. Be living proof that you can exist in alignment with nature with your own sense of right and wrong.

Cosmic perspective means refusing to play small. If the world isn't ready for what's real, that's still better than joining in with a crowd that's lost its way. Show the world what's possible.

Reflect:

- Where are you playing small to fit in, instead of living out your values?

- What would it look like to treat the world as your home, and everyone in it as your neighbor?

- How can you let your actions be guided by the bigger picture, not just the immediate crowd?

- Are you willing to live your truth, even if it means standing out?

Don't let the size of the world make you shrink. Let it remind you: this is your stage, own it.

February 17

Check your perspective. Most of what causes stress is small in the cosmic timeline.

Keep these three truths close because they'll ground you when the world tries to shake you.

First, don't just act for the sake of acting. Let every move you make have purpose. Don't waste your energy blaming the universe or railing against chance over things that are beyond your control.

Second, remember what you are, how you came to be, what you're made of, and where you're headed. Your body and soul are part of a cycle, born from the earth and air, and eventually returning there. It's natural. Embrace that flow instead of resisting it.

Third, imagine looking down at human life with fresh eyes. See the same chaos, the same drama, the same endless cycles of birth, death, joy, and sorrow. All the things we think matter so much appear tiny and fleeting from this distance, like dust swirling in a breeze.

Why sweat the small stuff? Why get caught up in the noise when the bigger picture shows you how small and temporary it all is? Ground yourself in what lasts: your purpose, your justice, and the calm that comes from seeing the world as it really is.

What's one way you can step back today and remind yourself of this cosmic view? How might it change the way you respond to what feels overwhelming right now?

Your Takeaway

Keep three things in mind if you want to live above the noise.

First, act with intention, don't just go through the motions or cut corners.

Second, remember that some things happen by pure chance, others by a bigger plan. Accept what comes, do what's right, and keep it moving.

Third, realize most of what eats at us is the same drama, same patterns, looping over and over.

The *cosmic perspective* means asking, "Is this really as big as it feels, or am I caught in the close-up? Will this even matter in a year, or a thousand?"

Reflect:

- Where are you letting the small stuff pull you off course from your real purpose?

- How can you act more intentionally, instead of just reacting to what's around you?

- What would change if you accepted chance and chaos as part of the cosmic flow?

- Are you ready to see your problems in the context of the whole, and focus on what truly matters?

Remember: You're a part of something much bigger. Don't let the little things make you forget it.

Concept 5: Recognize the Oneness of All (*Interconnectedness*)

You're not separate from life, you're woven into it.

February 18

You're not disconnected from the whole, unless you shut yourself off from the world and the shared mind that connects us all.

If you don't understand the world you live in, you're a stranger to it. Even worse would be closing yourself off to how everything flows and connects around you. If you reject the basic principle that we're all part of one big system or community, you're basically homeless in this universe.

It's as if you're blind when you close off your mind, or like a beggar if you rely on others without trusting yourself. You become like a tumor, a harmful growth that separates itself from the natural order. Your bad experiences aren't a reason to disconnect – those experiences are just as much part of nature as you are.

Cutting yourself off from the shared mind of humanity is like tearing out your own roots. You're not just alone, you're fragmented and missing the point of why you're here.

The truth is, your life and well-being are deeply linked to the whole. When you embrace that connection, you find your real home, not somewhere out there, but right here, in the flow of life itself.

Your Takeaway

If you're feeling like an outsider, it's not about not knowing the world, it's about ignoring how everything and everyone is connected. If you close off your mind, refuse to trust yourself, or reject the community, you're cutting yourself off from your true home, standing apart only because life's challenges have hardened you. But these experiences are part of nature, just like you.

You're never truly alone.

February 19

See the universe as one living being, a connected network in every part, moving as one, sharing one consciousness.

The universe isn't a collection of random things. It's one living, breathing whole: one 'body', one 'soul', one vast consciousness. Everything you see and everything that happens is part of a single, massive flow. It moves together, acts together, feels together.

Imagine that every event, every action, and every breath is tied to something else, like threads weaving an enormous, intricate tapestry. No one part is isolated. When one thread moves, the whole fabric shifts.

That means you're never truly alone. Your thoughts and actions ripple through this living being. And just as the universe acts with one impulse, you're called to move in harmony with it, recognizing your role in the grand dance.

This awareness doesn't just bring peace, it demands responsibility. When everything is connected, every choice you make matters beyond what you see. So today ask yourself, "How am I contributing to this vast whole? And how can I move with the current instead of against it?"

Your Takeaway

Everything around you is one whole, alive and connected. You're connected to everyone and everything.

Everything that happens is the result of this deep connection. When you truly see this, you start to understand your place as part of a vast, interwoven web. Let that realization change how you live, with more care, purpose, and compassion.

February 20

We're all connected: every system, every being, every role.

The universe is fundamentally social, interconnected and seamlessly working together. It's designed like a giant, interlocking web where everything has its place and purpose, from the tiniest cell to the biggest leader.

This powerful insight gently challenges us to recognize that we're all intricately woven into a vast, collaborative network. Our purpose comes from understanding and embracing this deep *interconnectedness*, aligning our actions with this universal principle.

Find your place, play your role well, and remember that your actions affect the whole. When you see yourself connected like this, cooperation becomes natural. Conflict fades because we're all notes in the same song.

Explore how this understanding changes the way you live and relate to others.

Your Takeaway

Nothing in this universe works alone.

It's not about hierarchy or competition. It's about everyone and everything doing their part so the whole can thrive.

Connection isn't optional, it's the design. Your well-being and your impact are always tied to how you show up for the whole.

Reflect:

- Where do you forget that your actions ripple out and affect the bigger picture?

- How can you lean into teamwork, family, or community instead of going it alone?

- What's one way you can honor the role you play, and support someone else in theirs?

- Are you willing to see your daily life as part of something much bigger than just you?

We're all in this together. Play your part, and trust the web to hold.

February 21

Everything in the universe is connected, woven together in a dance of breath, tension, and unity.

Take time to reflect and meditate on how everything in the universe is linked and interconnected. It's not just random, it's a vast web where every thread is connected to every other. There's a pulse, a breath, a tension that holds it all together, creating a loving, living whole. Things hold together because they depend on each other, support each other, and move in harmony.

This isn't just poetic. The breath of life flows through all things, keeping them in a dance of tension and release, a constant flow that knits everything into one living whole. Every part matters, and nothing stands completely alone.

When you hold this in your mind, life stops feeling isolated or random. Your challenges and your joys are all woven into a bigger fabric. You start to act not just for yourself but for this greater unity. That's where true compassion and purpose come from.

If you want to feel that deep sense of belonging and know that you're not just *in* the world but *of* it, then this is how it begins.

Your Takeaway

Nothing in the universe stands alone. Everything is linked like threads in a giant tapestry, moving in harmony. When you meditate on this connection, you start to see your place not as separate, but as deeply part of the flow. This awareness brings compassion, peace, and a sense of belonging. You're not alone – you're woven into everything.

February 22

What harms the whole harms the part, just as what is bad for the community is bad for the individual.

The individual and the community aren't separate. What hurts the community, hurts each individual; what helps the community, helps the people. You and the world around you are the same. You can't thrive alone. Your well-being is tied up with the people, environment, and community you're part of.

This isn't about losing yourself or giving up your individuality. It's about realizing that your life and purpose are woven into something bigger. When you nurture the whole, you're nurturing yourself.

Next time you think you're just one small person facing the world solo, remember that your actions matter because they ripple through the whole. Take care of your community in the same way you care for yourself, because they're one and the same.

How can you show up for your community today?

Your Takeaway

You're not an isolated island, you're part of a bigger community. If the group suffers, you suffer too. When you act for the common good, you're really protecting your own well-being.

See yourself in the bigger picture, and live in harmony with those around you.

February 23

We're all threads in the same fabric — what happens to one part touches us all.

Everything is intricately interwoven, like threads in a cosmic tapestry, a massive, collaborative system where every part contributes to the smooth operation and order of the universe. There's one world, one shared reality, and one truth that we all participate in, even if we see it from different angles.

The universe itself is one unified whole, so see beyond superficial divisions and recognize your place in the vast network that is aligned with this fundamental unity. Here, you will find genuine fulfillment.

So, when you feel disconnected or like your actions don't matter, remember this: you're part of something greater, inseparable and essential. Your life contributes to the harmony of the whole.

Are you living in a way that honors this unity? How can you tune in today to the oneness that connects us all?

Your Takeaway

Nothing in this universe stands alone. There's a bond holding everything together, and it's deeper than any difference or distance. Community, collaboration, and mutual respect are built into the design of the universe.

Next time you feel disconnected, remember that everyone is working in the same ecosystem. *Interconnectedness* isn't just a spiritual idea, it's a survival skill.

Reflect:

- Where are you acting like you're separate or above the system, instead of part of the whole?

- How would your choices change if you really believed everyone (and everything) is connected?

- What's one way you can strengthen the bond at work, at home, or in the world today?

- Are you willing to see yourself as part of a bigger story, not just the main character?

We're all in the same network. Keep the connection strong.

February 24

We're limbs of one body made to work together. Helping others is helping ourselves.

You're not just a random person on this earth, you're an essential part of a larger body.. We're designed to cooperate and support each other. This isn't just about obligation or *duty*. It's about deep, genuine love for your fellow humans because when you do good for others, you're really doing good for yourself.

If you see yourself as merely a part instead of a limb, you're missing the point. You're stuck in the "I have to do this" mindset rather than the "I get to do this" mindset. Loving others and acting kindly isn't just a task, it's a source of real joy and fulfillment.

Stop thinking small. See yourself as an active, living piece of the whole. When you do, the way you treat others changes. It's no longer a chore – it's life-giving, because you're nourishing the very body you belong to.

How can you embrace your role today as a vital limb in the greater whole? What small act of kindness or cooperation reminds you that we're all in this together?

Your Takeaway

Each of us is connected with a shared purpose, meant to support and care for one another. True connection comes when you love others deeply and find joy in doing good simply because it's right. See yourself as part of this whole, and you'll live with more kindness, purpose, and joy.

February 25

Every part of nature feels fulfilled when it grows well, and human nature thrives by focusing on what's real, good, and shared.

Every living thing is naturally content when it's moving forward, growing, learning, and doing what it's meant to do. That progress looks like not just accepting every thought or feeling that pops into your head. Question what's false or confusing. Aim your energy at things that actually help others and make the world better. Keep your wants and fears focused on what you can realistically change or avoid. And, most importantly, acknowledge whatever life hands you as part of the bigger universal plan.

The universe treats everything fairly, giving each thing its time, its chance, and its role. That doesn't mean every person or thing gets the exact same share in every way, but the overall balance is there, like pieces of a puzzle fitting together.

Find peace in knowing you're part of this grand design. Trust that your progress, however small, is part of the whole moving forward.

What's one way you can steer your impulses today toward something socially beneficial? How can you welcome your current circumstances as part of this universal flow?

Your Takeaway

Every living thing is content when it's growing and moving in the right direction. For humans, that means mastering reason, controlling your impulses, managing your desires and dislikes, and accepting what life hands you as part of a greater whole.

Not everything is equal all the time, but everything balances out in the big picture.

February 26

Injustice and lying go against the natural order because we're meant to help, be truthful, and live in harmony with each other.

When you act unjustly, you're going against the very order of the universe. We are wired to help and uplift one another, not to cause others harm. When we break that rule, we're going against the oldest, deepest laws of nature.

Lying is another form of disconnection. Truth is baked into the fabric of reality itself and is universal nature. So when you lie on purpose, you're actively working against that natural order and harming others. Resisting the truth is a fight you're starting all on your own, even though nature gave you everything you need to see clearly.

The problem isn't that the truth is out of reach, it's that you haven't done the work to use the tools you were given to recognize it.

Start living in alignment with the truth and justice that bind us all. It's not just about being a good person in isolation, it's about being part of a vast, interconnected whole where your actions ripple outward. Every time you uphold truth and fairness, you're reinforcing the harmony of the universe, not breaking it.

What truth are you holding back from seeing or speaking today? How can you step into your role as a guardian of justice within this vast interconnected web?

Your Takeaway

Universal nature created us to support and care for one another, not to harm or deceive. Truth isn't just a nice idea, it's the foundation of all that exists. Living with integrity means aligning your actions and words with this universal truth. That's how you honor the *interconnectedness* of all things.

February 27

All living things share one soul, just like we share the same earth, air, and light. Animals rely on instinct, humans on reason.

The world isn't a collection of isolated islands, it's one big, interconnected organism. We humans share an intelligent soul, a collective consciousness that links us in ways deeper than any surface-level differences.

The sunlight that lights your path is the same light illuminating everyone else's. We're not separate beings colliding into each other by chance, we're threads woven into a single, vast tapestry.

So when you feel alone or disconnected, remember that your life, your mind, and your soul are part of this greater unity. The health of the whole is tied to the health of each part and your actions matter not just for you, but for the entire living web we all share.

How might embracing this oneness change the way you treat others and yourself? What does it mean to you to be part of one intelligent soul?

Your Takeaway

We're all connected, part of one big living system. That connection means your actions ripple out beyond yourself. Recognizing this oneness helps you live with respect, care, and purpose for all life. You're not alone, you're part of everything.

February 28

Everything naturally seeks its own kind. Humans are drawn to each other by nature's powerful pull.

Everything in nature has this built-in magnetism. Things that share the same essence naturally come together. This is the way the universe holds itself together. It's the natural order to come together, to merge and unite with what's like us.

But somewhere along the way, many have forgotten this truth. Humans, the very creatures made for connection, often act like islands: shutting down that urge to unite, pushing others away, and choosing separation over belonging. Still, no matter how much we resist, nature has a way of pulling us back to each other. We are wired for unity, for relationship, for community – even if we sometimes forget.

What walls might you be putting up that separate you from others? How could recognizing this natural pull toward connection help you open up and build bridges?

Your Takeaway

We're all meant for connection, and it takes effort to keep these natural bridges apart. For humans, this urge to unite is even stronger. Today, many people try to deny this natural urge for connection, but no matter how much you run from it, connection catches up to you because it's part of who you are.

February 29 (Leap Year Bonus)

Sunlight is one even when split by walls. Soul and mind are one: even when they seem apart, they naturally seek to unite.

Even when a ray of sunlight touches different places, with their own shapes and colors, or gets split by hills, walls, windows, and spreads out in countless rays, it is still one. The same goes for everything around us. The matter that makes up all things is shared, even if it looks different in every object.

Our souls are all part of one big whole, even if they seem scattered across millions of people and creatures. The intelligent soul – the spark of reason and awareness – is one, even if it feels broken up by all the different minds and personalities.

Like attracts like, unity holds it all in balance. Our minds naturally seek out what's like them, pull together, create community, and keep that sense of belonging alive, even when it feels hard.

You're part of that one intelligent soul, connected to everything else that shares this spark. So when you feel separate or alone, remember: like sunlight, you're a ray of a greater whole, naturally drawn to reconnect and belong.

What parts of your life are calling for that deeper connection? How might seeing yourself as part of a greater whole shift the way you relate to others and to yourself?

Your Takeaway

Sunlight shines as one light, even if it's diverged by obstacles. Souls are one, even if they seem scattered among different beings, and minds naturally reach out, unite, and keep a sense of belonging alive. This deep connection is what binds us all, no matter how separated it looks on the surface. Recognizing this unity helps you see your place in the bigger story and live with more empathy and purpose.

Concept 6: Practice Compassion and Forgiveness

Stop obsessing over others' faults; instead, focus on keeping your own spirit clear and kind.

March 01

It is part of human nature to err. Why be angry when someone makes a mistake?

Nothing's more exhausting than a person who's always poking around in everyone else's business, trying to figure out what's really going on inside their heads. They're missing the whole point – their real work is to care for their own inner self, their guardian spirit.

Taking care of this spirit means keeping it clean from needless drama, bitterness, and frustration with how the world or people behave. People are connected, part of one big human family, so their actions should be met with kindness and acceptance.

Sometimes people make mistakes because they can't tell right from wrong, just as someone who is colorblind can't distinguish red from green. It's not evil, it's ignorance or a lack of ability. That's when compassion and forgiveness matter most.

You can't control others, but you can control how you respond and keep your own heart steady and kind.

Your Takeaway

All you need to do is care for your own inner self, your guardian spirit. We're all connected by humanity, so we should welcome each other, flaws and all. Compassion and forgiveness are your best guides. Focus inward, be gentle, and let go of the need to judge others.

March 02

If it doesn't harm the whole, it doesn't truly harm you. Respond with understanding, not anger.

If something doesn't hurt the whole, it can't really hurt you either. Next time you feel wronged or harmed, pause and ask yourself, "Did this damage the bigger picture?" If not, then it's not worth getting worked up about.

If it *did* harm the whole, don't rush to anger against the person who caused it. Try stepping back and consider what they might be missing. Maybe they don't see the full impact of their actions. That's where compassion steps in. Instead of lashing out, help them understand what they're overlooking.

Holding onto anger only weighs you down, while forgiving and guiding others helps the community and lightens your own heart.

Your Takeaway

When you feel hurt, take a second to look at the bigger picture. Assess whether real harm has been done, and if it has, don't rush to anger at the person who caused it. Instead, help them see what they've missed or misunderstood. Respond with patience and compassion. That's how you practice real forgiveness and keep your peace.

March 03

Becoming angry because of someone's flaws doesn't help. Use your reason to guide, not to judge.

What good does it do to get angry at someone because of their nature? If their body odor offends you, know that their smell is just a fact of their body, it's how they are right now. They have reason, and they *could* change it if they wanted..

Don't waste your time and energy stewing in anger. Instead, use your reason to engage theirs, talk to them and gently point it out. If they understand, then holding onto anger becomes unnecessary. If not, remember that it only reflects badly on them. You don't have to become bothered or stoop to pettiness over it.

Keep your dignity. Be real, be kind, and leave the anger out of it.

Your Takeaway

Stewing in annoyance over someone's flaws never fixes anything, and judging from a distance just makes you bitter. Compassion isn't about pretending not to notice issues, it's about choosing understanding over irritation. Forgiveness is deciding to let go of the judgment, even if someone doesn't change.

Don't waste your life holding grudges or playing the critic. Be the one who brings truth and kindness to the table, without making it a performance.

Reflect:

- Where are you holding on to frustration instead of speaking up or letting go?

- How could honest, gentle feedback change a situation, for you and for them?

- What would shift if you chose compassion over anger, especially when it's not easy?

- Are you ready to be real, not perform, and move forward with a lighter heart?

Lead with humanity. Choose forgiveness, choose candor, and let that be enough.

March 04

Don't stop people trying to get what they think is right for them. Teach with patience, not anger.

It's cruel to stand in the way of someone pursuing their dreams and desires, even if you think they're misguided. It's the same concept when you get angry at their mistakes and flaws.

Remember, they're drawn to what feels right and useful to them, just like you are. Instead of letting anger block the path, use your head and your heart to calmly explain, teach, and guide. Real change happens through patience and kindness, not fury.

When you drop the anger, you stop being an obstacle and you become a light that helps them find a better way.

Your Takeaway

Everyone chases what they believe is best for themselves, even if they're wrong. Getting mad at them for their mistakes only makes you part of the problem. You can't control their choices, but you can guide them calmly with kindness.

Real compassion is helping others grow without adding more pain. Keep your cool and lead with understanding.

March 05

Show grace. Most people who make mistakes aren't villains, just humans working with blind spots and limited info. Life's short, don't let their flaws infect your peace or compromise your own values.

It's human to care for those who mess up, because deep down you recognize them as family, as fellow travelers lost to ignorance, and not as villains by choice. You remember that life's short for both of you. And crucially, if they haven't damaged the core of who you are, your mind remains unshaken.

Their mistakes can't change who you are, unless you let them. Your mindset, your values, are yours to protect. Don't let someone's ignorance or misstep become the thing that takes you off your game.

Don't hold grudges that weigh down your spirit. Extend compassion instead. Forgive the stumbles, knowing they're part of being human. It's not about excusing wrongs, but about protecting your peace and recognizing the shared journey we're all on.

Your Takeaway

People are going to make mistakes. Forgiveness isn't letting people off the hook. It's letting yourself off the hook from resentment. Compassion is strength, not weakness, and it's always an option, no matter what went down.

Reflect:

- Who are you struggling to forgive, and how is it affecting your own peace?

- How can you practice seeing people's mistakes as human and not personal?

- What would shift if you focused on protecting your own mindset, instead of taking on someone else's error?

- Are you ready to move forward with more lightness and less baggage?

Choose compassion, keep your center, and let the rest go. That's how you free yourself.

March 06

Understanding someone's motivation makes forgiveness easier.

When someone wrongs you, pause and ask, "What idea of good and bad is driving their behavior?" Understanding this helps you see them as someone limited by their own beliefs and misunderstandings. It softens your shock and melts away anger.

Maybe your own view of what's right or wrong hasn't strayed that far from theirs yet. In this case, forgive because you recognize your shared humanity. Maybe you recognize that you've grown beyond those basic judgements, and with that knowledge it becomes easier to show leniency, knowing they simply haven't caught up yet.

Forgiveness isn't weakness. It's clarity and a refusal to let someone else's confusion poison your peace. You stay clear, kind, and rooted in your own growth, no matter where they are on their journey.

Your Takeaway

When someone behaves poorly, your first impulse might be to react in anger. However, their behavior often comes from their own distorted beliefs about what's good, bad, fair, or necessary. When you frame it this way, it's easier to understand that their actions say more about them than about your worth.

Compassion doesn't mean you let things slide or become a doormat. It means you choose understanding over escalation.

Reflect:

- What belief or story might be driving the other person's

behavior?

- Where have you been stuck in your own old patterns, and how did you move forward?

- How can understanding someone else's perspective help you let go of anger or resentment?

- Are you willing to forgive, not because they're right, but because you're ready to move on?

Practice compassion, keep perspective, and let growth – not grudge – be your guide.

March 07

No one willingly rejects truth or goodness. Keep this in mind, and you'll find more compassion for others.

No soul ever willingly turns away from the truth. The virtues of justice, moderation and kindness aren't foreign to anyone's heart. They're natural aspirations, even if sometimes buried under confusion or pain.

When someone acts out or stumbles, remember that deep down, they're not choosing harm or unkindness, they're simply misled.

With that awareness, you can soften your judgment and open space for compassion, which allows you to see the struggle underneath someone's mistakes. Forgiveness isn't just mercy, it's wisdom knowing that beneath every flawed action is a soul still seeking truth.

Your Takeaway

People lose their way because they haven't shifted their negative perspectives. Everyone is doing the best they can with what they know right now. Keeping this in mind, you're more likely to respond with empathy than with judgment. Forgiveness is letting go of the idea that everyone should know better all the time, including yourself.

Reflect:

- Where are you expecting perfection from someone who might just be lost or learning?

- How can remembering your own struggles with truth or virtue make you gentler with others?

- What would shift if you led with understanding instead of frustration?

- Are you willing to offer compassion, knowing everyone's on their own messy learning curve?

Keep it gentle. We're all learning as we go.

March 08

Stop procrastinating being your best self. Don't wait for tomorrow to show up with kindness and forgiveness.

It's completely human to feel resistance to change today, and instead want to put it off until tomorrow. Restlessness and hesitation is normal, don't berate yourself for it. Instead, pay attention to what's in front of you: the task, the principle, the meaning behind it all.

Compassion starts with recognizing your own struggle without judgment. Forgiveness means cutting yourself some slack while still gently encouraging yourself forward. The best you can do is show up today, imperfect but willing. Tomorrow will take care of itself when you practice kindness to yourself in this moment.

Are you making excuses for staying stuck, or are you leaning in and choosing to be kind, to forgive, to grow today?

Your Takeaway

It's easy to put off compassion and forgiveness, to wait for the right time, but all you ever really have is right now. Practicing compassion means paying attention to what's really happening, to how you're showing up, to the bigger principle behind your choices.

Show up with grace for yourself, no matter how far along you are in the process. That's how healing starts.

Reflect:

- Where are you putting off compassion or forgiveness, hoping it'll be easier someday?

- What's stopping you from choosing to be good, right now?

- How can you pay closer attention to the moments where you could lead with heart instead of habit?

- Are you ready to stop postponing your best self and bring that energy into today?

No more waiting. Compassion is a 'now' thing. Step in.

March 09

I act for the good of all, and when things happen, I accept them as part of a greater whole.

When you take action, remember that it's not just about you, it's about the good of all people. This mindset shifts your focus beyond the small stuff and into something bigger, something meaningful.

When life presents you with challenges, don't waste energy resisting or resenting. Instead, accept them as part of a vast, interconnected whole – a design you may not fully see, but that holds everything in balance.

This acceptance isn't about passivity, it's about compassion for yourself and for the whole human experience. It's about forgiving the messiness of life and moving forward with grace. You're part of something greater, and living with that awareness brings peace and purpose.

Your Takeaway

Every time you make a choice, actively consider how it affects others. When life is challenging, accept what comes with openness, trusting that everything plays its part. This mindset helps you stay compassionate and forgiving, not just toward others, but toward yourself.

March 10

When people judge or dislike you, look past the surface level and see their humanity. You don't have to change for them, but you can still choose kindness.

Not everyone is going to like you, support you, or make an effort to get along. When people disapprove of you or express hatred, don't get caught up in their words or let them shake your peace. Take a moment to look deeper and see who they really are. Look past the surface and see what's driving them, whether fear, pain, or their own insecurities.

There's no need to scramble or twist yourself to win their approval. Your energy is better spent on kindness, because even if they don't show it well, they're part of your human family and primed for connection.

The universe doesn't abandon anyone. It nudges people in quiet ways — through dreams, signs, or moments of clarity — to help them find what they truly need. Learn to extend that same grace and benevolence. Compassion is not only for the easygoing or the kind, but for those who challenge you as well.

Your Takeaway

Although you may feel an impulse to win the approval of someone who dislikes you, that shouldn't be the goal. You don't need to struggle for their validation, but treating others with basic decency is important. Show others compassion, even if they don't treat you kindly in return.

Reflect:

- Who are you letting get under your skin right now, and what's it costing you?

- How would things shift if you saw their behavior as about them and not about you?

- Where can you show kindness without expecting approval or a change in their attitude?

- Are you ready to let go of the need to be liked, and lean into real compassion instead?

Compassion doesn't mean being a doormat. It means keeping your peace and your kindness, no matter how the world reacts.

March 11

When someone's flaw offends you, pause and ask "Do I share this flaw too?" Understanding this can dissolve your anger.

When someone rubs you the wrong way, don't react right away. Ask yourself, "Do I struggle with the same thing?" Maybe you also indulge in the chase for money, the hunger for pleasure, or the craving for fame.

When you take a moment to think about it, letting go of your anger becomes easier. You realize they're not acting out of sheer willfulness, but instead caught in the same patterns, trapped by the very things you yourself wrestle with. It's about letting go of blame and understanding that they're not fully in control of their actions.

Real compassion is helping to change the conditions that keep us all stuck.

Your Takeaway

It is possible that the same mistakes that irritate you, are ones that you are guilty of. Recognizing this helps you see that others are caught in the same struggle. Let go of your anger and extend compassion, which starts with understanding that we all share flaws and none of us are perfect.

March 12

Stay firm in your purpose, but never lose kindness toward those who stand in your way. Being tough and being gentle aren't opposites, they're both signs of real strength.

When someone tries to block your path or mess with your progress, don't let them shake your resolve. Hold steady in what you know is right.

Kindness isn't weakness. It's strength wrapped in compassion. Staying gentle with those who push back shows you're in control, not just of the situation, but of yourself.

Becoming bitter or harsh is no better than giving up and letting them win. And remember: we're all connected. Fighting against others, who by nature are our family and allies, is just running away from your responsibility.

Hold your line, hold your heart, and let both be unshakable.

Your Takeaway

You need to develop a backbone to stay true to your values and decisions, but don't let that make you harsh. True power is when you can keep moving forward, no matter the resistance, and still treat people with basic decency, no matter their behavior.

Reflect:

- Who's testing your patience or trying to throw you off your game right now?

- How can you stand firm in your choices while still leading with empathy?

- What would real strength look like in this situation? More understanding, or more open-heartedness?

- Are you ready to let kindness and courage run together, not in competition?

Keep your standards high and your heart open. That's next-level compassion.

Concept 7: Virtue Is the Highest Good

Character is the only true wealth. Build that.

March 13

Live every moment as if it could be your last. What truly matters is who you are, not what happens to you.

Every move you make, every word you say, and every thought you think should be guided by the truth that this day could be your last. Stop grading your life by what you have or what happens to you. Good luck, fame, and success might be desirable, but you can't use any of it as proof of your own value. Bad luck, obscurity, and struggle might be hard to deal with, but you can't use it as an excuse to slip from your path.

Start measuring your life by who you're becoming and how you treat others. The real measure of your life, the true good, is virtue: how you act, how you treat others, and how you hold yourself to your principles. Virtue isn't just the highest good, it's the only thing that can't be taken from you.

Your Takeaway

Stop drifting through life on autopilot. Start developing your sense of virtue. Being a better person is the only thing that really matters, because nothing outside your control can make you worse than you already are.

Reflect:

- Where are you letting circumstances define your worth, instead of your character?

- What's one 'bad' thing you could see as just neutral, a chance to show up with virtue instead of fear?

- Are you ready to start living like today could be your last, and let virtue lead the way?

- If you stopped chasing what the world calls 'good', what kind of person would you become?

Virtue is the only scoreboard that counts. Live it, breathe it, and let the rest sort itself out.

March 14

Don't let someone who disrespects you control your thoughts. See things clearly and stand by what's true.

Every part of you – your spirit, your fiery energy, your true nature – naturally wants to rise, to soar upward, but it's held here, grounded inside your body, tied down by gravity.

So why is it that your mind, the one part that's free and unrestrained, refuses to accept its place? Why does it resist by straying into anger, selfishness, sorrow, and fear? It is this resistance that cuts you off from nature's flow, from what you were made to be.

Your mind wasn't made to rebel. It was designed to honor justice, to live with reverence, and to exercise humility. When you resent what happens or act out of selfishness, you're stepping away from your *duty*, abandoning your proper place.

Come back to your role. Stand firm in your place in the grand design. Fulfill your *duty* with respect, fairness, and humility. That's where true peace and purpose live.

Your Takeaway

Holding onto your own integrity is the real strength. Your virtue shines brightest when you refuse to stoop to someone else's level. Stay clear-headed, stand tall, and keep your values in focus.

March 15

Fame fades fast. What lasts is a just mind, truthful words, and actions that serve others.

In the blink of an eye, the fame of celebrities, CEOs, and other icons of the era will become buried under new headlines, new faces, and new stories. What seems so grand today will soon be forgotten, lost to the endless flow of time. Everyone, no matter how brilliant, ends up the same way, stories told and then buried in oblivion.

Vanity isn't worth your energy and devotion. The struggle to be remembered forever is fruitless. The only things truly worthy of your focus are:

- a just mind, one that is fair and clear

- actions that benefit the community and work that makes a difference
- words spoken honestly, with truth as your constant companion
- the courage to accept everything life presents to you as part of a bigger, rational design

Keep your eyes on what lasts, not the applause or the fleeting fame, but the steady light of virtue, the highest good that never fades.

Your Takeaway

Stop living for the vague notion of being remembered. Who you are when the spotlight's off is what really matters. Show up with virtue and make a difference in your life and others. That's the best version of yourself.

Reflect:

- Where are you spending energy chasing recognition instead of living with real integrity?

- What would your choices look like if virtue, not vanity, was your highest priority?

- How can you practice being useful, honest, and open-minded today?

- Are you ready to let go of the fear of being forgotten and focus on what's truly meaningful?

Virtue is the only legacy that sticks. Everything else gets swept away. Make yours count, moment by moment.

March 16

Remind yourself that you were born to do work that matters, not to just chase comfort.

Trees grow, ants build, and bees work. Everything in nature follows the natural order of their species without question or concern. It is only humans that procrastinate their work, put off their role.

When your alarm goes off and you want nothing more than to stay under the covers, stop and remember that you're here to accomplish, to show up as the human being you were born to be. Why resent that or spend your days wasting your gift on comfort instead of contribution?

When it comes to action, are you really giving your all? Or are you holding back because you don't fully love who you are and what you're made for?

A master craftsman sacrifices comfort for his art, a dancer lives and breathes her movement, a driven entrepreneur chases their vision without pause. Your nature should not be devalued compared to theirs.

It's time to stop playing small. Your highest good and virtue are in how fully you engage with your purpose. Own your role like the remarkable human you were meant to be.

Your Takeaway

Comfort isn't your purpose. You were created to contribute and to do your part. The real challenge is in showing up, even when you'd rather not. Learn to value your purpose and treat yourself with the same respect you give to others. That's the virtue that moves your life forward.

March 17

Wisdom sees the whole story from start to finish and trusts the natural order of things.

A truly informed mind isn't just about having facts or clever ideas. It's about seeing the whole picture, it's about knowing the start, the finish, and the meaning that runs through everything in between.

This kind of mind understands the grand design, that the universe isn't chaos but a carefully ordered system, cycling through time with purpose and balance. It sees that everything happens for a reason, and that reason is woven into the fabric of all existence.

So, when the uninformed challenge the knowledgeable, they're really wrestling with a truth that's bigger than their limited view. But the understanding of virtue and reason guiding all is the highest good. It's what grounds us, keeps us steady, and lets us play our role in the world with clarity and grace.

Your Takeaway

People who don't understand often misjudge those who do. But a wise mind isn't just smart, it sees the big picture, the patterns and cycles of life. When you hold this perspective, you're less rattled by confusion or ignorance around you. You stay grounded in the flow of life and your role within it.

March 18

No one grows tired of kindness. Helping others is who you truly are, so keep giving and receiving with an open heart.

Receiving feels good because kindness, support, and comfort is natural for us, but so is giving back and doing things to benefit others.

Ask yourself, if it feels good to be helped, why would you ever get weary of helping? The two go hand in hand. When you benefit others, you're not just acting out of goodwill, you're living in alignment with your true self. You're fulfilling your role as a human being who's part of a greater whole.

This is virtue in action: kindness, generosity, and the willingness to contribute without keeping score. When you embrace this, you become a source of good in a world that desperately needs it, and that is the highest good you can offer.

Your Takeaway

Don't hold back when you can give, and don't resist receiving the good others offer you. On this two-way street both sides gain from kindness and generosity. Keep your heart open and your actions generous. That's living in alignment with your highest good.

March 19

Regardless of the behavior of others, my job is to stay real and unaltered.

People may cast aspersions on you or behave badly in your presence, but you don't have to let that affect who you are at your core. Your goodness isn't a reflection of others, it's a constant you carry inside.

When chaos swirls around you, remind yourself that you are not defined by others' noise. You are steady, honest, and kind, no matter what. Your power stems from your virtue, the truest form of strength there is: to remain unchanged by the actions of others and the circumstances that surround you.

Your Takeaway

The world will test you, but your worth isn't measured by the behavior of others. Real value is in consistency. Virtue is about creating a baseline of your values, holding your ground, and being who you say you are.

Reflect:

- Where are you letting other people's behavior pull you away from your values?

- How can you stay consistent in your character, even when it's not easy?

- Are you ready to let virtue, not the crowd, set your standard?

Stick to who you are. Let virtue be your true color, no matter what's happening around you.

March 20

Every challenge you face has been faced before, and those who became stuck in anger are long gone. Focus on how you grow from it, not how you react.

Every challenging experience you face has happened to countless others before you. They felt anger, shock, or frustration and then they faded and were forgotten. Don't follow their path by allowing yourself to be trapped by emotion. Instead, keep your focus sharp and ask yourself "How can I use this moment?" and "How can I turn this into something good?"

Build your life not by reacting to every upset, but by shaping your response. Make every action you take the kind an honorable person would take. That's what matters.

The actions you take are important, but the context around them is simply a distraction. Don't give it more power than it deserves.

Your Takeaway

Why let your mood be tossed around by what life throws at you? Rise above, using your experiences as fuel for growth. Focus on living honorably in every action you take.

Your actions matter. Own your response. That's where true virtue shines.

March 21

Everything happens as it should, and none of us lasts forever. Focus on the task at hand with kindness and integrity.

Don't allow life circumstances to unsettle you. Nothing happens outside the flow of universal nature. All of us, every living being on earth, is just passing through the same cycle. Soon enough, none of us will be here.

Instead of worrying or becoming upset, focus on what's right in front of you, clear and unfiltered. See it for exactly what it is, no more, no less.

Remember who you are and what you owe to yourself, to others, and to your own humanity. Step up and handle your business. Do what you know deep down is the right, just thing.

Do it with kindness, with humility, and without pretending to be anything you're not. That's where true virtue shines.

Your Takeaway

Life unfolds according to nature's rhythm, and your time is limited. Look at what you need to do right now, and see it clearly, without exaggeration or drama. It's your responsibility to act without hiding your true self. That's what living with virtue looks like: steady, honest, and respectful, no matter the circumstances.

March 22

True happiness comes from living like a human: being kind, seeing clearly, and appreciating the world as it is.

Happiness is not about chasing fleeting pleasures or sensory thrills, but instead is found in doing what we're truly made for.

That means being kind and generous to others, your tribe, your people. It means tuning out the impulses that pull you off course and focusing on what's real and trustworthy.

It's about sharpening your mind to spot what's true and reliable and to question what's false or misleading. It's about spending time reflecting on the vast, interconnected universe we're part of: its rhythms, its patterns, and its meaning.

This is the kind of happiness that lasts. The kind that builds you up, grounds you, and connects you deeply to those around you and the world. That's virtue and that's the highest good.

Your Takeaway

Happiness is about being benevolent toward others, training your mind to trust what's true, and stepping back to see the bigger picture. Live like the thoughtful, social creature you are, and you'll find lasting joy.

March 23

True good comes from wisdom, justice, courage, and moderation, not from the clutter of wealth and luxury.

Most people chase after wealth, luxury, and status, all things they think of as good. They pile up possessions like they're trophies, thinking it will fill the void. But if you actually understood what *true* good is – wisdom, moderation, justice, courage – then you wouldn't get stuck trying to juggle so many things that you can't even manage your own peace.

When you chase the wrong kind of good, you just end up overwhelmed, stuck, and frankly, miserable. Ask yourself, "Is it really smart to value things so much that you have no room left for the basics, for your own dignity, for peace of mind?" True good is different. It's about cultivating what truly matters inside you, not piling up what the world tells you to want.

Your Takeaway

Focus on virtues like wisdom, fairness, courage, and self-control, instead of wealth, luxury, or praise. True good is found in living virtuously, not in how much you have. That's where lasting fulfillment lives.

March 24

Real freedom comes from seeing things as they are, acting with integrity, and telling the truth. Make your life a chain of good moves, one right action after another.

Salvation, real peace, and freedom come from seeing things clearly by breaking down everything you experience into what it really is: matter and its cause. When you know the truth behind things, it stops confusing you or pulling you off track.

From there, it's simple. Focus on doing what's right, speak honestly, and live authentically. Make your life a seamless chain of good deeds without any gaps or excuses. Each act of goodness builds on the last, and that's how you create a life worth living.

The real power is in showing up, day after day, doing the right thing even when no one's watching.

Your Takeaway

If you want peace and meaning, investigate the driving force behind your experiences.

Virtue is about being honest with yourself and others and living true, one decision at a time.

You save yourself from regret and chaos by showing up, telling the truth, and doing the next right thing. Make your character your anchor, and let your days be filled with integrity.

Reflect:

- Where are you not seeing things, or yourself, as they truly are?

- What's one small action or truth you can step into today?

- How can you keep the good deed chain going, even when no one's watching?

- Are you willing to let virtue, not shortcuts, be your success story?

You don't need saving from the world. Just link your days with honesty and right action. That's the life that lasts.

Concept 8: Fulfill Your Role and Purpose (Duty)

You're here for a reason. Act like it.

March 25

It's foolish to focus on fixing others' faults, as they are out of your control, and even more so to ignore your own, since they are within your control.

You can change yourself and escape your own vices if you choose to, but trying to control the flaws and mistakes of others is absolutely impossible.

Your real *duty* is to own your part, clean up your own act, and do the work on your own mind and character. Don't waste your energy on the failings of others, they're not yours to carry or fix. Focus on what's actually within your control.

Stop looking outward for problems you can't solve. Step into your role fully, take responsibility for your own growth, and trust that it's enough. That's how you live your *duty*.

Your Takeaway

Trying to change the faults of others is a losing battle. Let others do their own work. Focus on your own growth and responsibility. That's where real progress and peace begin.

March 26

Your soul loses honor when it rejects nature, others, or purpose. Stay focused on your role and act with intention.

Your soul disrespects itself in five big ways and you have the power to stop each one.

First, when you resent what happens, you're putting yourself above nature instead of being a part of it. That's a fundamental betrayal of your role.

Second, when you reject or actively harm another human being out of anger or malice, you're dishonoring your own soul, because your purpose is to live in harmony, not conflict.

Third, when you give in to pleasure or pain, you're losing control over your own nature and the dignity of your soul.

Fourth, when you pretend or act dishonestly, you're abandoning your true self and your responsibility to live authentically.

Fifth, when you drift through life without purpose or attention, failing to direct your actions toward a goal, you're ignoring the very reason you exist.

Your highest purpose is to follow reason and serve the greater community, the universal city of all rational beings. Ask yourself, "Am I living aligned with honor? Or am I letting distractions, emotions, and chaos pull me off course?" Your soul's honor depends on stepping into your role and fulfilling your *duty* with intention in every moment.

Your Takeaway

Your soul is part of the bigger universe, like a thread in a vast tapestry. You're not here to wander aimlessly, you're here to live by reason and to serve your community well. Keep your eyes on that goal and let every action, big or small, have meaning and direction. That's how you fulfill your role and honor yourself.

March 27

Show up fully, without hesitation or selfishness. Be the steady leader of your life, ready for whatever comes.

There's no room for half-hearted, selfish, or confused actions in the life you're meant to live. Don't embellish your intentions with elaborate speech to puff yourself up.

You're not just anyone – you're a citizen of this earth, someone who's been entrusted with a role and responsibility. But you're also on a temporary assignment, fully aware that your time here is limited. There's no need to boast, swear oaths, or seek external validation.

Find your joy deep inside. Don't depend on others to hand you peace or approval. Stand tall on your own two feet and don't wait for life to straighten you out. Own your role fully and walk your path with pride, clarity, and unwavering purpose.

Your Takeaway

Fulfilling your purpose means doing what's right. Do your *duty* with presence, not with pretense. Real purpose is quiet and grounded. Stay humble, let your integrity set the tone, and keep your ego in check.

Let your inner compass be what holds you upright, not external validation or outside pressure. Stand tall on your own terms.

Reflect:

- Where are you holding back or letting self-interest cloud your purpose?

- How can you bring more presence and intention to your daily work?

- What would it look like to let your values, not the crowd, guide your actions?

- Are you ready to stand tall from within, knowing your *duty* is enough?

Purpose isn't about performance. It's about showing up true, no spotlight needed.

March 28

Let your craft or calling be your steady companion: lean on it, trust it, and walk through life with integrity.

The skills you've developed and the path you've chosen aren't just ways to pay the bills: they're your allies, your support system, and part of your bigger purpose. Let it be your anchor and your rest in the storm. When life gets noisy or uncertain, return to what you've learned and built. Let your work, your practice, or your mission ground you and keep you steady.

Move through the rest of your days fully committed, not holding back, not half-in, but wholeheartedly surrendered to your purpose and to what's bigger than you.

Fulfilling your *duty* means trusting your path and showing up for it every day, not getting lost trying to dominate others or shrinking to please them. You don't have to play the tyrant or the pushover. Do your job, honor your commitments, and trust that you're where you're meant to be. Hand over what you can't control, focus on your role, and let the rest play out.

Stand firm in your role, with integrity and balance. That's how you fulfill your *duty* – not just to yourself, but to the whole.

Your Takeaway

Treat your craft, skill, or calling like a trusted friend, someone you can lean on when life gets heavy.

Your calling isn't just a job: it's a friend, a resting place, and a reminder of who you are. When you lean into that, you're free from the ego games of trying to be 'above' or 'beneath' anyone else. You simply live your purpose, day by day.

Reflect:

- Where are you forgetting to lean on your own strengths and skills?

- How can you trust your training or purpose to guide you, especially when things get tough?

- What would it look like to walk through life without needing to dominate or defer to anyone?

- Are you willing to let your craft or calling be enough: no status, no comparison, just purpose?

Fulfill your role, trust your journey, and let your purpose be both your anchor and your freedom.

March 29

When your actions follow reason and nature, there's nothing to fear. Doing your part moves you forward.

When the task before you aligns with the reason, when what you're doing moves you forward in a way that fits your nature, then there's nothing to fear. No harm can come from moving forward with purpose and integrity.

This is the space where growth happens, where your actions serve your true self and the greater whole. Lean into that. Focus on progress that's right for you, rooted in reason and purpose.

Trust that stepping up in alignment with your nature is not just safe – it's your calling.

Your Takeaway

Fear fades when you focus on what's right and natural. If your task aligns with reason shared by all humans then you're on the right path. Step into your role with confidence. You're exactly where you need to be, doing what you're meant to do.

March 30

Do good quietly and without keeping score, because true duty is in the action, not the applause.

Fulfilling your role isn't about trading favors or collecting thank-yous, it's about showing up and doing what you're here to do. There's a common trap in wanting others to see and acknowledge your contributions, but that misses the profound truth. When you act from genuine purpose, your service becomes as natural and uncalculating as a bee crafting honey. It's a spontaneous outflow of who you are, deeply integrated into your very being.

This isn't about neglecting your social responsibilities, it's about elevating them. By shedding the need for external validation, your actions become purer, more impactful, and truly selfless. Your *duty* transcends mere obligation and transforms into an effortless, continuous expression of your best self. Enrich the community not for your recognition, but simply because it is your nature to contribute.

Your Takeaway

Duty means you act because it's your responsibility, not because you're fishing for validation. Your true purpose is natural. You serve, help, and contribute because that's your role in the bigger system. You're part of a team, a community, a world that needs you fully present, doing your job for its own sake.

Reflect:

- Where are you letting the need for recognition distract you from your real responsibilities?

- How would your mindset shift if you saw your contribution as a *duty*, not a favor?

- Are you showing up for your purpose, or for the applause?

- What's one way you can recommit to your role: no scoreboard, no audience needed?

Duty is about consistent service. Show up, do your work, and let that be enough.

March 31

Everything in life was designed for a reason. Your life is about more than chasing fame, comfort, or entertainment.

Everything has a specific purpose for existing. The sun generates light and warmth, trees produce oxygen, and rain replenishes the soil.

Humans, on the other hand, have the tendency to overindulge in pleasures and comforts, neglecting their design. But in order to fulfill your *duty* and purpose, you must look beyond gratification and seek fulfillment. Your life has purpose built in. It's important to live not just in enjoyment, but to show up for what needs doing, make a difference, and leave something better behind.

Your Takeaway

Fulfillment comes from knowing your role and playing it with heart. When you put your energy into living your purpose, pleasure becomes a side effect. Focus on identifying and acting upon your role, and actively contribute to the larger community in a way that aligns with your deeper capabilities.

Reflect:

- Where are you settling for comfort when you could be leaning into your purpose?

- What unique gifts or strengths are you meant to bring to the table?

- How would your daily choices shift if you focused on *duty* and meaning instead of just pleasure?

- Are you willing to dig deeper and discover what you're really here for?

Pleasure fades. Purpose fulfills. Step up and live for what matters most.

April 01

Destiny hands you certain people and events — embrace them sincerely and adapt with grace.

Life has handed you a set of events — your destiny. You didn't choose the deck, but you *do* get to play your hand. Your job is to adapt, be flexible, and roll with what comes by owning it, not by just putting up with it.

The people you cross paths with are part of your journey too. Care for them genuinely, because they matter in your life's story. Come from a place of doing it because you want to, not because you have to.

Your role is to live fully in the moment, to meet your fate with open arms, and to show up for those around you with sincerity. It's not about changing destiny, but owning how you respond to it. When you do that, you're not just surviving — you're fulfilling your purpose.

Your Takeaway

Life's dealt you a specific hand filled with people and situations that are part of your journey. Your job isn't to fight what's given but to accept it and make the best of it. Adapt with kindness and openness, even when it's tough. That's how you fulfill your role and live in harmony with what's meant for you.

April 02

Don't get sidetracked by others. Focus on your own path, what life asks of you, what your nature calls you to do, and serve the greater good with your best effort.

The first principle is to not let your attention get hijacked by other people's inner guides or opinions. The universe is unfolding, putting things in your path, and your responsibility is to show up for your own assignments.

Your second principle is resisting control of fleeting bodily sensations, ensuring your rational mind remains the leader, only using impulses for higher purposes.

The third principle is to avoid deception by not rushing into assent or agreement, critically evaluating all information. Thus, if your own inner guidance system stays true to these core principles, it will fulfill its purpose.

Fulfilling your role and purpose means leading with your higher self:

- Serve the common good, not just your ego
- Don't let cravings or comfort run your day, let your mind guide your actions
- Don't rush into judgments or decisions, stay clear, grounded, and thoughtful.

Your Takeaway

You're wired for a purpose, and it isn't to copy or compete with anyone else. In the big picture, we're here to support one another, not to jockey for the best position or succumb to every feeling that comes along.

You're a rational, powerful human being designed to serve, grow, and do meaningful work. When you keep your mind steady and your heart on your *duty*, that's where you find fulfillment.

Reflect:

- Where are you distracted by other people's choices instead of focusing on your own path?

- How can you show up today for what's truly yours to do?

- Are you letting impulses or comfort make decisions for you, or are you letting your higher self lead?

- What's one way you can serve the common good, right now, just by fulfilling your unique role?

Stay in your lane, do your part, and let the rest unfold. That's *duty* in action.

April 03

Before you act, tune into your sense of integrity. If your actions honor your nature, what else do you need?

Every time you take action, hit pause and ask yourself, "Is this how I want to show up? Will I look back and regret this?" Life is short. One day, you won't be here, and everything you've done or wanted will be gone.

Ask yourself, "Is what I'm doing right now in line with what a rational, social human being should do?" If yes, then you're exactly where you need to be. What else could you possibly want?

Let that question guide your choices daily. It's about living with integrity, with purpose, owning your role and playing your part with honor. That's the work. That's what matters.

Your Takeaway

Every choice you make shapes your story. Focus on doing work that fits your role as a thoughtful, social being; a part of a greater whole. When your actions align with that, you don't need anything else. That's how you live with purpose and peace.

April 04

You either keep living your role, step away when your work is done, or pass on. There's no need to worry about the timing.

Stop wasting energy worrying about things you can't change. There's no point stressing about the 'when' or 'how'. Focus instead on showing up fully in the life you have because whatever stage you're on, it's yours to own. Your *duty* is to live with purpose, whether that means continuing the grind, knowing when to rest, or accepting when it's time to move on. When your work is complete, you'll know it's time to let go peacefully and without fear.

There's peace in understanding these simple facts. No need to resist the natural flow. That's how you honor your role and find calm.

Your Takeaway

Life gives you three clear choices: keep playing your part, walk away when you're ready, or let life take its course. Focus on doing your *duty* well while you're here. Worry doesn't help, but living with purpose does.

April 05

Like the elements held in place by nature, your mind belongs where it is. Resisting that is resisting your true role.

Your body, your spirit, even the smallest piece of you is following the rules of nature, doing what it's meant to do, holding its position, waiting for the right moment to shift. The water in you wants to go down, the fire in you wants to rise up, but everything stays put until it's time. That's order. That's purpose.

Your mind – your inner guidance system – is often the only part discontented with its proper function, despite being under no external constraint. Any movement toward unjust, self-indulgent, angry, sorrowful, or fearful behavior is a direct disconnection from your true nature and purpose. And every time your inner guide resents something that happens, it's abandoning its rightful place, as it was built for reverence and connection to the universal order. Don't abandon your post, don't run from what you're here to do, just because it's uncomfortable or inconvenient.

Therefore, to fulfill your role, *duty*, and purpose, you must bring your mind into alignment by choosing just, moderate actions, accepting the universal scheme without resentment, and recognizing that your well-being is intrinsically linked to your harmonious participation within the larger cosmic and social order.

Your Takeaway

Every time you let your thoughts wander into anger, self-pity, or avoidance of your real duties, you're stepping away from your true purpose. You're breaking formation while everything else in you is holding steady. Fulfilling your role and purpose is about letting your mind line up with the rest of you.

Don't let your mind be the only part slacking off. Step up, hold your ground, and honor the role you're here to play.

Reflect:

- Where are you letting your mind wander off instead of stepping up for your purpose?

- How would your days look if your thoughts were aligned with your highest responsibilities?

- What's one *duty* you've been avoiding that you can recommit to today?

- Are you ready to let your mind fulfill its post, just like every other part of you does?

Duty isn't just about action, it's about aligning your whole self, mind included, with your purpose. That's how you make your life count.

Concept 9: Don't Seek Fame or External Approval

The crowd is loud. Your soul is quiet. Follow the quiet.

April 06

So many public figures who were once household names are now forgotten – and all of those who lauded and applauded them are gone, too.

How many influencers, celebrities, and viral sensations from just a few years ago have faded into total silence? They were once featured everywhere, but now their 15 minutes have expired, and the world's moved on.

People who previously had crowds chanting their names are now just memories, lost in the endless scroll of new faces and fresh content. Fame is a moving target. The minute you think you've arrived, the world turns the page.

If you're living for external approval or hoping the world will remember your name forever, you're betting on a short memory. That doesn't mean your life can't matter, but it means your meaning can't come from other people's spotlight.

What if you focused less on being remembered, and more on making this moment count? Focus on what lasts, the quiet work you do when no one's watching, and the integrity you hold when it's just you and your reflection.

Let go of the pressure to be legendary. Legacy isn't built on applause, it's built on authenticity

and impact, whether the world remembers your name or not.

Your Takeaway

Chasing fame is a losing game. People move on, the applause always fades. Instead of seeking something fleeting, focus on doing good work, living by your values, and being present for the people who matter now, not just the audience out there somewhere. Real value doesn't need a spotlight.

Reflect:

- Where are you spending energy trying to be seen or remembered, instead of just living true?

- How would your choices shift if you stopped chasing attention and started chasing meaning?

- What impact do you want to have today, with or without recognition?

- Are you ready to let go of the spotlight and focus on what's real?

Fame fades. But a life lived with purpose? That's unforgettable, even if no one's keeping score.

April 07

You don't need to escape to faraway places. Your mind is the true sanctuary, calm and unshaken by fame or praise.

You've probably caught yourself daydreaming about running away to some perfect place – a cabin in the woods, a quiet beach, or a mountain retreat – but the real retreat, the real peace you're searching for, is already inside you. Any time you want, you can pull away from the noise and chaos by simply turning inward.

The mind, when it's trained right, is the most peaceful, unshakable sanctuary you can have. It's a place that, once you know how to access it, can wash away any frustration or stress that life throws at you, no matter how tough things get out there.

Stop holding onto anger that people aren't living up to your standards. Most people aren't deliberately trying to mess things up, they're just doing their best. Keep reminding yourself that we're all wired to help one another. Let go of the resentment that just weighs you down.

The moment you realize your mind's power, you'll stop letting fame and vanity pull you off balance. People who praise you now will forget you soon enough. The world is vast, time stretches out infinitely before and after you, and your big moment will soon be just a whisper.

So settle into your own little estate, the calm center within you. Don't let the world's chaos shake you. Own your space, own your peace. Be the master of your mind and soul, and never forget these two truths: First, the outside world can't touch your soul unless you let it. Second, everything that you see and think matters will soon change and fade. The universe is in constant flux, and life is just a fleeting moment.

Live like you know that. Because when you do, you're unstoppable.

Your Takeaway

Your mind is your real sanctuary. Whenever you want, you can step back into it and find calm in a peace that comes from within, a place you carry with you, no matter the chaos outside.

Be your own master. Look at life clearly as a human with a role in a changing universe.

Remember, the world can't shake your soul unless you let it. Change is constant. Life is short. Find your peace inside, and hold on tight.

April 08

Memories fade, and relying on the approval of others wastes your chance to live fully now.

Chasing after fame and trying desperately to establish a legacy that will remain after you're gone is like trying to catch smoke with your bare hands. Anyone who might remember you is going to die, too. Eventually, your name, your stories, your legacy will all vanish like a candle flickering out in a windstorm.

Ask yourself, "What does this even do for *me* right now, while I'm still alive?" Praise from others, compliments, and applause all feel good, but do they really serve you? Or are they just distractions that keep you hooked on approval you don't actually control?

By tying your sense of worth to what others think, you're basically handing over your life's power to someone else. You're throwing away the one thing that's truly yours: the gift of living fully and freely, here and now, in line with nature's design.

Stop worrying about how you'll be remembered and start focusing on how you're living *today*. That's the real gift. Fame is just a hollow echo, but your life, your choices, your actions – that's where true meaning lives.

Your Takeaway

Wanting to be remembered forever is a trap. Praise means little if it doesn't help you grow or live better today. When you depend on others' opinions for your worth, you throw away the greatest gift nature has given you: the power to live fully in the moment.

Stop waiting for applause from the future. Start owning your life and your worth right here, right now. That's real freedom.

April 09

It's not about how others remember you, it's about the quiet strength of your soul.

What truly matters is the quality of a person's soul. Can you find satisfaction simply in living rightly, treating others with justice and not letting the darkness in the actions of others drag you down? Can you face ignorance without bitterness? Can you accept whatever life hands you without seeing it as an unbearable weight? Can you keep your mind steady, without being affected by passing bodily pain or fleeting pleasures?

This calm, resilient integrity is what outlasts fame, glory, and stories. It's what keeps your soul steady when the world throws punches. So, forget the applause and the reputation. Focus on building the kind of inner strength, where you don't need anyone else's approval to know you're doing what is right. That's real greatness. That's real freedom.

Your Takeaway

People often judge greatness by fame, courage, or the stories others tell, but real greatness is about something deeper, about the quality of your soul. That's what really counts, not the glory, not the applause. Focus on building that quiet strength.

That's a legacy worth leaving.

April 10

True value lies in doing your work well and living according to your nature.

You've already said no to chasing fame and empty praise. Now it's time to focus on what really matters: living according to your nature and doing what you were made to do. Like a farmer tends his crops, a doctor treats a patient, or a teacher guides a student. The value is in fulfilling your role well, not in the applause that comes from doing your best.

If you focus on being true to your nature and your purpose, you won't need to linger in the emotional quicksand of envy, jealousy, or mistrust. If you respect your own mind, if you hold a modest but steady regard for your character, you'll find true happiness. You'll be at peace with yourself, easy to be around, and in harmony with the universe. You'll see that everything you've been handed, whether you think it's good or bad, is exactly what you need.

Let go of what others think, tune out the noise, and focus on being the person you were made to be.

Your Takeaway

What really matters is doing what you're made to do, indulging in your true nature, gift, and value that you uniquely bring to the world. Real value lives in your purpose, your craft, and your work. When you focus here, other things lose their pull. You become self-reliant, at peace with yourself, and in harmony with the world around you. That's how you live with true respect for your mind and true freedom from needing others' approval.

April 11

Stop chasing approval and understand where people's judgments come from. You'll free yourself from needing their praise.

If you're constantly chasing people's approval, you're signing up for a lifetime of frustration. Investigate the inner workings of how people think and act the way they do. Look at their inner guidance system and dig beneath the surface of their opinions and impulses.

When you understand where their beliefs come from, you'll firstly stop judging them for their mistakes, because you'll see that most of those missteps aren't even fully in their control. They're caught up in their own stories, biases, and blind spots.

Secondly, you won't be desperate for their endorsement anymore. You won't depend on the applause or approval of people who themselves are just trying to navigate their own mess. You become your own authority, your own true north. You stop handing over your power to the opinions of others and start focusing on what *you* know to be right.

That's real freedom. That's maturity.

Your Takeaway

When you really look at why people think and act the way they do, you see they're not perfect. Everyone makes mistakes, often without meaning to. Focus on your own values instead. That's how you break free from the endless need for external validation. And that freedom is real power.

April 12

Being afraid of death just means you're scared of the idea of nothingness or of a new unknowable chapter. But if death is nothing, you won't notice — and if it is something new, you'll still be present, just in a different way.

A lot of the race for fame or approval comes from fear: the fear of being forgotten, fear of disappearing, fear that you won't matter when you're gone. But death is either a total lights-out – in which case you won't care or know about any missed applause – or it's a new kind of existence, and you'll still be part of the story, just in a different way.

Either way, death isn't the enemy, it's just a transition, so why waste energy chasing clout or approval like it's your eternal ticket? None of that follows you past the final curtain. Focus on living with integrity right now, because that's the real legacy you control.

Your   Takeaway
Fear of death is just fear of the unknown. All that matters is how you live

now: the choices you make, the love you give, and the integrity you hold. Don't let fear of being forgotten or a hunger for applause run your life. Do what's meaningful for you, and let go of what you can't control.

Reflect:

- Are you chasing attention or approval because you're scared of being forgotten?

- What would change if you trusted that 'now' is enough, no matter what happens later?

- How would you live if you weren't afraid of the end or of not being remembered?

- Are you ready to release fear and focus on your present impact?

Fame fades. Death is just the next unknown. But how you live today is fully in your hands.

April 13

Give yourself the gift of this moment. Future opinions don't belong to you.

This moment right here is yours. Life is a gift — why waste it chasing a legacy you'll never witness? The posthumous praises and critiques of the people who come after you will be just like those you already find frustrating in the present, because they're flawed, mortal, and distracted.

What's the point of sweating over what they might say or think about you once you're gone? You won't be around to hear it, and they won't be around for long either. Instead, give yourself the freedom to live fully now, without the chains of future approval or reputation.

Your worth isn't measured by the whispers after you leave, it's in how you choose to live this very moment, with authenticity and self-respect.

Your Takeaway

Worrying about what people will say about you after you're gone is just a trap. Their opinions aren't your burden to carry. Instead of chasing some distant legacy, focus on living well right now. This moment is your real gift. Own it. That's where your true worth lives – not in the echoes of others' words.

April 14

The commodities that impress the world are not as valuable as you think.

Everything around you – every shiny thing you chase, every status symbol – is just dust and water mixed with a bit of stardust. Marble is simply hardened dirt, gold and silver are earth's leftovers, dressed up in finery, and your favorite designer clothes are processed animal parts and crushed shells stitched together.

Chasing fame or external approval is like collecting trophies made out of sand – it might catch the light for a moment, but doesn't mean much in the long run. Stop letting yourself get distracted by the packaging. The real value is never in what you own or how the world sees you. It's in how you show up, how you treat people, and what you stand for when no one's looking.

Focus on what really animates you: your character, your choices, your integrity. That's the only thing that can't be bought, sold, or replaced. Everything else is just noise. Keep your eyes on the source.

Your Takeaway

We waste so much energy trying to stand out, chasing what glitters, and trying to impress others with titles, brands, and finery, but your breath, body, and possessions will all break down and return to the same old elements someday. Why waste your one wild and precious life chasing other people's approval or trying to look important? You're here to live true and make an impact.

Reflect:

- How would your choices shift if you stopped letting the world's 'sparkly' standards set your goals?

- What legacy do you want to leave that can't be measured by stuff or status?

- Are you ready to focus on real value, the kind that outlasts dust and trends?

Fame fades. Approval is fleeting. But living with real meaning? That's solid gold, no filter needed.

April 15

Stay calm no matter what life throws at you. Act with fairness, because that's who you truly are.

Stay unshakable when the world throws its noise and chaos at you. Let the outside stuff bounce off you without messing with your peace. Keep your cool, stay balanced, and don't let external chaos rattle your peace. Your real power is in how you act, especially when your actions come from a place of justice and serve the common good. That's what your nature is wired for.

Don't get caught up chasing applause or worrying about who's watching. Focus on doing right by others because it's the right thing to do, not because it'll earn you fame or approval. True strength is quiet, steady, and unwavering. Own that.

Your Takeaway

The world outside will toss all kinds of challenges your way. You can't control that, but you can control how you react. When it comes to what you do, make sure it's fair, just, and meant to help others. That's your nature, where real strength and freedom live.

April 16

Your body and your image are just tools, it's your inner drive that makes you truly alive.

The real puppet master pulling your strings isn't the opinions of those around you or your ever-scrolling feed. It's the power inside you: that quiet, steady force that sparks your thoughts, your choices, your life itself. Without that, none of the external noise, or even your physical self, means a thing.

Your devices are just tools. The latest smartphone, a fancy keyboard, or a sleek laptop are useful instruments, but pointless without the person scrolling, typing, and creating behind them.

Never mistake your worth or power for the vessel or the instruments you use every day. You're not your profile picture, your follower count, or the likes on your latest post. You're the one who holds the pen, moves the strings, and writes the story.

Own that power. Let it lead, not the spotlight or the noise. Your life's energy comes from within, not from external applause.

Your Takeaway

We live in a world obsessed with the surface, but the part of you that actually matters is your drive, your intention, and your mind. Your worth isn't tied up in how you look or how you're seen. What makes you you is what's happening inside, the choices, the character, the real motivation. The outside will fade. The inner spark is what gets things done, what builds meaning, and what stays, even when no one's watching.

Reflect:

- Where are you putting all your energy into how you're seen, instead of who you actually are?

- What would change if you invested more in your character than your image?

- How can you remember today to honor the 'puppet master' within, not just the outer appearance?

- Are you ready to live from the inside out, and let the rest be just tools?

Don't let the world confuse you, the real power is always on the inside. Lead from there.

April 17

Most people claim to love themselves, but deep down they care more about what others think of them than about their own opinion of themselves.

We talk a big game about self-love, but most of us hand over the keys to our confidence the minute someone else's opinion comes into play. We scroll through social media feeds, craving the dopamine hits from approval and validation. But all that external noise is fleeting and shallow. The real connection that matters is the one you have with yourself: the respect, love, and trust you build inside.

When you chase fame or approval, you're giving away your power. You start living by other people's scripts, losing sight of what genuinely fulfills you. The danger isn't in wanting to be seen, it's in making your worth depend on it.

Stop measuring yourself by likes or retweets. Ask yourself, "Am I living to impress, or am I living to respect the person in the mirror?" It's time to love and honor the person you are behind the scenes: the one who's showing up, doing the work, and staying true to their values, even when no one's watching.

That's where real strength lives. The approval that truly matters comes from your own mind and heart. Tune out the crowd. Be your own champion.

Your Takeaway

We crave acceptance, we want to fit in, we keep changing ourselves to please the crowd. Stop letting other people's judgments outrank your own. If you put your opinion of yourself first and trust your own voice more than the outside noise, you'll be freer and a lot happier.

Reflect:

- Where in your life are you putting more weight on what others think than on your own truth?

- How would it feel to trust yourself more, even if not everyone gets it?

- What's one decision you can make today that's for *you*, not for someone else's approval?

- Are you ready to let your own opinion of yourself be the loudest voice?

Self-respect starts with putting your opinion in the driver's seat. Stop chasing applause. Start owning your worth.

Concept 10: Practice Moderation and Self-Control (*Commitment*)

Power isn't in excess. It's in restraint.

April 18

Endings are just as natural as beginnings – nothing's ruined just because it's over. The same way a ball thrown up must come down, every part of the cycle matters. It's all about balance.

We love the high points, new starts, big wins, and the feeling of things going our way. But life isn't just about the rise. Every ball thrown up comes down. Every bubble that forms will pop. Even the brightest lamp eventually burns out. That's not tragedy, that's the natural flow.

Practicing moderation and self-control means accepting this ebb and flow without letting yourself get attached to just one phase, the launch, the peak, or the constant 'more'. There's no shame in endings – they're not failures, just part of the cycle.

Commitment is about being steady, appreciating beginnings, riding out the middles, and accepting the endings with grace. You don't need to overdo, overreach, or fight what's natural. Let things rise, let things fall, and know you're okay in every phase. That's how you find peace and power in the flow of life.

Your Takeaway

This powerful perspective helps you practice moderation and self-control by detaching from specific outcomes, fostering emotional stability, balancing your efforts without obsession, and accepting life's impermanence. It allows you to find value in every phase and engage fully with the present moment, understanding it as part of a complete and natural design.

Reflect:

- Where are you clinging to what's ending, instead of letting the cycle complete?

- How could you practice more balance, enjoying the ride without needing to control every outcome?

- What would change if you saw endings not as failures, but as natural, necessary parts of your growth?

- Where can you let go a little and trust the rhythm of beginnings and endings?

Moderation means being okay with the full story, not just your favorite chapter. That's real self-control.

April 19

You're one piece of a much bigger puzzle. It's about being part of the cycle, not the center of it.

You didn't put yourself here, and you won't be here forever. You're a part of something larger: nature, the universe, the flow of life itself. Just like everything else, you'll change and eventually return to where you came from.

Practicing moderation and self-control is about remembering your place in this bigger picture. It's easy to get swept up in ego, thinking your story is the only one that matters, or clinging to what you have as if it's permanent. But when you step back and see yourself as one chapter in a much larger book, you gain the freedom to live with more balance and less anxiety.

Commitment means letting go of the urge to overdo, overown, or over-identify with what's temporary. It's about appreciating your moment, playing your part, and then moving on, just like every other piece in the great design.

Your Takeaway

Everyone is a small part of the universe. You are born from the cycle of nature and return to it at the end of your life. Cultivate moderation and self-control by reminding yourself that you are just one part of a vast, interconnected whole. This allows you to release attachment to external outcomes and possessions, which prevents anxiety and fosters humility.

Reflect:

- Where are you holding on too tightly, forgetting you're part of a bigger cycle?

- How could remembering your place in the whole help you practice more moderation?

- What would shift if you accepted transformation as a natural, healthy part of life?

- Are you willing to release the pressure to control everything and simply play your part well?

Moderation is knowing you're not the whole story, but you are an important part of it. Practice presence, self-control, and trust the cycle.

April 20

Even if life pulls you in different directions, always come back to your core values — that's where you can find balance and recharge.

Your inner moral compass – your personal philosophy – is your sanctuary. To practice moderation and self-control, you must frequently return to these core principles and inner calm, especially amidst the demands of the modern corporate grind or public life.

This consistent grounding makes even the most draining responsibilities tolerable and transforms you into a more composed and effective presence. Prioritizing this internal well-being prevents burnout and enables you to navigate external pressures with grace.

Commitment isn't about saying no to life's challenges, it's about not letting them define you. Do what needs to be done, but always come home to what matters most.

Your Takeaway

Practicing moderation and self-control means making a habit of returning to your personal philosophy. No matter how busy or chaotic things get, keep checking in with what grounds you. When you make space to regularly reconnect with your values and self-awareness, even tough situations become manageable, and you show up better for everyone, including yourself.

Reflect:

- What are the core values, practice, or mindset you need to return to for balance?

- How can you build in regular check-ins with your true self, even on the busiest days?

- Where are you letting outside demands pull you away from your inner stability?

- Are you willing to return, again and again, to what restores your self-control and calm?

Moderation is about remembering what centers you, and choosing to return, no matter what else is going on.

April 21

Strip away the fancy stories and see things as they really are. Vanity will lose its grip.

Whenever you're sitting down to enjoy something grand – a rich wine, your finest clothes – pause. Remember what it really is: squashed grapes and dyed wool.

This is about breaking through the illusions that vanity casts. The stories we tell ourselves that inflate the value of things, that make us chase after fleeting pleasures or status. Vanity loves to trick you into thinking you're dealing with something monumental when it's really just superfluous.

Keep this practice as your steady habit, to strip away the fluff and see things exactly as they are. The clearer you are about the real nature of things, the less power they'll have to control your mind or your choices.

Because when you understand what's truly valuable – justice, self-control, kindness – everything else falls away. You free yourself from getting swept up by surface distractions and stay anchored in what actually matters.

Your Takeaway

Getting into the habit of seeing things stripped down helps you stop getting caught up in all the drama and vanity that inflate their importance. Keep your mind clear by seeing past the shiny surface. Real self-control and *commitment* keeps you grounded.

April 22

Pain has limits. It doesn't break the mind that steers your life, and your judgment is what gives it power.

Pain can't weaken the part of you that steers the ship: your rational mind. It can't touch your capacity to think clearly or care about what's right.

Pain always has a limit, and is either bearable or temporary. It's only when you give it more power in your head that it only becomes unbearable.

Take a moment to notice how many things feel like pain but are just discomforts: soreness, feeling overheated, or losing your appetite. When you feel burdened by them, bring awareness to the fact that you're giving in to pain.

Recognizing this puts you back in control. You don't have to let pain run the show. You can endure, keep your balance, and choose how you respond. This awareness is real *commitment* – mastering yourself, even in discomfort.

Your Takeaway

Pain is part of being human, but it's not a reflection of your strength or worth. Your mind stays intact even when the body protests. Most pain isn't unbearable or permanent. It comes and goes, and you get to decide how much power it has over you. When these feelings hit, remind yourself: "I'm feeling pain, but I don't have to be ruled by it."

April 23

True contentment comes from living simply and staying humble. Focus on what's real.

Much of what we experience is just a social construct or a digital overlay, and very few things are truly what their packaging makes them seem. The world will always try to convince you that happiness is found in chasing more: more material objects, more status, more validation. Strip all that away, and you realize how little is truly essential.

Find your bliss in simplicity, genuine humility, loving humankind, and following the universe's lead. By consciously cultivating these attitudes – valuing simplicity, practicing universal love, accepting the flow of the universe, and seeing through societal illusions – you gain profound moderation. Through that self-control, you'll simplify your desires, calm your reactions, and shift your focus to your inner state and ethical conduct.

Your Takeaway

Practicing moderation and self-control is about making simplicity your superpower. Stay rooted in your values, treat others with genuine love, and let your choices be about what matters. Let that guide you, let yourself be free from the urge to impress or outdo. Find joy in being enough, doing enough, and letting life be a little lighter.

Reflect:

- Where are you complicating your life chasing things that don't truly matter?

- How could practicing more simplicity and modesty bring you more peace?

- What 'rules' or expectations are you ready to let go of, so you can focus on what's real?

- How might you choose moderation and self-control today, just to see how it feels?

Bliss isn't found at the edges – it's found in the middle, in the gentle practice of enough.

April 24

Don't berate yourself for missing opportunities for pleasure. Regret simply means you think you lost something good. But real good isn't found in chasing every moment of pleasure.

Regret is a self-censure, a facepalm moment for having missed a genuine opportunity, from thinking that you missed something good. But if you're chasing pleasure as if it's the ultimate goal, you're setting yourself up to feel like you're always losing.

Practicing moderation and self-control means seeing pleasure for what it is: a nice bonus in the scheme of things, but not the most important in the search for a good or meaningful life. A person who's truly grounded doesn't feel crushed about missing out on a dopamine hit. They know that the best things – integrity, kindness, and growth – don't come from indulgence, but from living on purpose.

Commitment is about knowing what's worth holding onto, and what's okay to let pass by.

Your Takeaway

Opportunities come and go, and with them there's often regret. Let go of the idea that every pleasure is a missed win. Reframe your goals to ensure that true regret aligns with moments when you fail to act virtuously or seize meaningful, character-building opportunities, as opposed to lamenting missed temporary gratifications.

Reflect:

- Where are you confusing pleasure with real value or goodness?

- What regrets do you need to let go of that are only about missing out on momentary fun?

- How can you practice choosing long-term peace over short-term pleasure today?

- What would change if you trusted that true satisfaction comes from moderation, not excess?

Pleasure is fleeting but purpose lasts. Practice self-control, and you'll never regret living in alignment with what matters most.

April 25

It's rare to live without ever falling into vanity or deceit, but it's never too late to turn away and clean up your mind.

Few people leave this world untouched by vanity, lies, or excess. But what matters is that you know when enough is enough, that you don't keep sliding deeper into corruption or indulgence like it's a path with no exit.

Do you really want to dedicate yourself to depravity? To let your mind rot away in selfishness and vanity? Diseases can wreck your body, but corruption of the mind is the worst kind of poison. It destroys what makes you truly human: your reason, your integrity, and your capacity for virtue.

This is about the survival of your dignity, your clarity, and your peace of mind. Choose to guard your mind fiercely. Practice moderation and self-control not just as rules for yourself, but as armor against the slow ruin that comes from unchecked desires and selfishness.

Living well isn't about perfection. It's about knowing when to stop, when to turn away, and when to reclaim your better self. That's how you care for your soul and live well.

Your Takeaway

It's rare to go through life without ever falling into deceit, vanity, or excess, but what really matters is when and how you choose to step back from those things. Experience should teach you to avoid those mental poisons and protect your inner health. It's never too late to choose moderation and clear thinking.

April 26

Ask not for what you want or don't want, but for strength to stop fearing, desiring, or being hurt by anything.

Let's reframe the idea of imploring the universe for what we want. If we are guided by an intelligent universe doesn't it make more sense to ask for strength: the strength not to fear, not to crave, not to be hurt?

Instead petition for the power to not want things so badly, to not be afraid, to not be ruled by desire or fear. Turn your petitions around, and see how much freedom you actually have.

Try it. See how your life changes. That's where true peace starts, in mastering yourself instead of the world.

Your Takeaway

Some people ask for quick fixes: winning love, getting rid of enemies, holding onto what they cherish. But real power is in flipping the script and asking to want less, to fear less, to be more steady inside.

April 27

Do what nature asks of you: care for your body, honor your mind, and embrace your role in the community. Let go of the rest.

Learn to tune into what nature expects from you. Live as if you are only ruled by nature itself, no excuses, no dodging responsibility. Follow what your body needs, without succumbing to overindulgence, focused on staying healthy and whole.

Then, notice what your rational nature — your higher self, the thinking, feeling, choosing part — asks of you. Honor its capacity for reason, reflection, and wisdom fully, as long as it's still sharp and clear.

Being rational means you're wired to be social. You belong here with others, so respect that.

Keep these simple rules close. Don't let yourself get tangled up in nonsense beyond this. You have a body to care for, a mind to master, and a community to engage with. Do that well, and you're living right. That's how you keep your balance in life.

Your Takeaway

You're both an animal and a thinker, a body and a mind. Take care of your body's needs without letting them take over. You're part of a larger community and living well means caring for others too. Follow these simple rules, and don't stress about everything else that's beyond your control. Moderation and self-control start with knowing what truly matters and focusing there.

April 28

You have three big relationships to manage: one with your own body, one with the bigger universe, and one with the people around you. Finding balance in all three is real self-control.

At your core, you navigate three essential relationships.

First, with your physical body: Are you respecting it, fueling it right, giving it rest, or are you running it into the ground? Moderation here means neither neglecting yourself nor overindulging.

Second, with the universe, that creates all experiences: Are you grounded, grateful, and humble enough to know you're part of something larger or are you trying to control it all yourself? *Commitment* invites you to find peace in not having all the answers, and to live with respect for the mystery.

Third, with the other individuals you encounter: Are you practicing patience, setting healthy boundaries, showing compassion, without burning out or overextending? True moderation means knowing when to step forward, when to step back, and how to keep your interactions honest and kind.

Check in with yourself. Where's the imbalance? Where could you practice a little more moderation, so all three relationships, body, universe, and others, are in harmony?

By consciously managing these three core relationships with moderation and self-control, you cultivate a balanced, resilient, and purposeful life.

Your Takeaway

Commitment isn't just about skipping dessert or limiting your screen time. It's about practicing moderation and balance in your whole life, starting with how you treat your own body, how you relate to something greater than yourself, and how you show up in your relationships.

Reflect:

- How are you caring for your body – are you neglecting or overdoing it?

- Are you staying connected to your sense of purpose and something bigger, or trying to go it alone?

- Where do your relationships need more balance? Are you giving too much, or holding back?

- What's one area today where practicing *commitment* could help you find more peace?

Self-control isn't about deprivation, it's about balance. Bring that energy to every part of your life.

April 29

Making mistakes isn't always about what you do, it's also about the actions you don't take. Sometimes, holding back or staying silent is just as misguided as going too far.

We usually think about self-control as stopping ourselves from overdoing it: don't eat too much, don't lose your temper, don't hit send on that angry text. But on the flip side, moderation also means not disappearing when action *is* called for. Sometimes, it's your lack of courage or your refusal to step up that does the real damage.

Commitment isn't passive. It's about finding the middle ground, knowing when to hold back and when to step forward. If you never speak up, never try, never help out, you're missing the mark just as much as if you went overboard. Doing nothing, when something needs to be done, is its own kind of excess, too much comfort, too much fear, too much "what if".

Practice moderation in all directions. Don't let self-control become self-erasure. Show up, speak up, and act, just don't let your actions or your inaction run your life on autopilot. Choose your response with awareness and courage, whether that means restraint or stepping into the arena.

Your Takeaway

Wrongdoing is not only the outcome of a mistake, but of inaction. Harm can stem from omission and neglect, from remaining passive instead of making an active choice. Developing a higher level of self-control allows you to be mindful of your duties and opportunities to do good, to eliminate procrastination and apathy, and to shift your focus to a more proactive form of personal responsibility.

Reflect:

- Where are you holding back when you know action is needed?

- How can you practice self-control that includes *both* courage to act and wisdom to pause?

- What would shift if you saw inaction as a choice, not just a default?

- Are you willing to use moderation to guide *all* your choices, not just your impulses?

Real *commitment* is active. Find your balance, not just in holding back, but in knowing when to move forward.

Concept 11: Master Your Mind and Thoughts

You can't always control what happens. But you can always control what you make it mean.

April 30

You're more than your body and breath, you're the mind in control. Stop letting impulses pull you around and own your thoughts.

You are a mix of flesh, spirit, and that all-important inner guide.

Your body is nothing more than a fragile shell. Your spirit is the breath you take in and out, never steady, always moving. The inner guide is where your power lives.

Stop letting your mind be jerked around by cravings, old patterns, or fear of what might come next. Your body will age. Your energy will rise and fall. But your mind is your headquarters, your place of real freedom. The sooner you start taking ownership of your thoughts, the stories you tell, the focus you choose, and the complaints you drop, the sooner you stop living life like a puppet and start living as the author.

Own your thoughts. Control your responses. Your inner guidance system is yours to rule, so start acting like it.

Your Takeaway

You are flesh, which is temporary; breath, here one moment, gone the next; and your inner guidance system, your mind, the place where you actually get to choose your direction.

Let go of the urge to run from discomfort or obsess over what's out of your hands. Instead, show up for what's right in front of you, with a mind that's clear, steady, and actually working for you, not against you.

Reflect:

- What are you letting control your mind: old habits, fear, or outside noise?

- Where can you practice leading your thoughts, instead of letting them lead you?

- How would your daily life shift if you stopped complaining and started choosing what you focus on?

- Are you willing to take your mind off autopilot and step into the driver's seat?

Master your mind, and the rest of your life follows. That's where your real power lives.

May 01

Respect your power to choose how you judge things. The freedom you crave starts with your own mind: how you see, interpret, and respond to the world.

Your most powerful tool isn't your talent, your bank account, or even your connections, it's your ability to judge, pause, and decide what's true for you. When your mind isn't clouded by snap judgments, bias, or knee-jerk reactions, you're in control.

Mastering your mind means not just reacting to every thought or emotion that pops up. It's about cultivating an inner guide that can step back, weigh what's happening, and choose a response that's wise, kind, and in line with your values. That's how you stay connected to others, and to whatever higher purpose you believe in.

Don't treat your faculty of judgment like an afterthought. Honor it, sharpen it, and trust it. That's how you protect yourself from getting swept up in the noise, and how you build a mind you can rely on.

Your Takeaway

Your faculty of judgment is sacred. This judgment frees you from rushing to conclusion or falling into emotional traps. It's what connects you with other humans.

Respect this faculty like the priceless tool it is. Mastering your judgment means mastering your life, and that's where real freedom starts.

Reflect:

- Where are you letting your thoughts or emotions make snap decisions for you?

- What would shift if you paused to check in with your deeper judgment before reacting?

- How can you train your mind to see clearly, choose wisely, and act in line with your best self?

- Are you willing to make your mind your strongest ally, not just your loudest critic?

Master your mind by mastering your judgments. That's the first step to true freedom.

May 02

We're all sharing the same life. Some arrive sooner, some later, but in the end, we're all part of the same story.

It's easy to compare timelines, to feel behind or ahead, to measure your worth by where you are versus everyone else. But step back and picture this: just like beads of incense dropped onto one fire, each at a different time, we're all burning in the same world, part of the same bigger picture.

Mastering your mind means letting go of the race. Early, late, or right on schedule, it doesn't matter – everyone's path is equal at the core. The fire treats all incense the same. Your journey is yours, and someone else's starting point or finish line doesn't make you any less worthy or meaningful.

So when you catch yourself spiraling into comparison or impatience, remember: it's not about who gets there first, or who stays the longest. It's about showing up, burning bright, and being part of the whole. That's all you're ever asked to do.

Your Takeaway

Release the pressure of comparing your timeline to others and embrace the impermanence of all things. Focus on the present, on how you can live with purpose, integrity, and peace.

Reflect:

- Where are you comparing your life to others, instead of honoring your own timing?

- How would it feel to let go of the pressure to 'arrive' first or last?

- What could shift if you saw everyone's journey, including your own, as part of something bigger?

- Are you ready to focus on your unique contribution, not just your timeline?

Master your mind: drop the comparison, embrace your place, and know you belong right where you are.

May 03

Be the rock the storm can't break. You can't always stop the waves, but you can decide not to let them shake your peace. Bad luck isn't what happens — it's giving up your strength to it.

Life's waves will crash against you: unexpected setbacks, losses, annoyances, even heartbreaks, but you don't have to let any of it break you. Like a breakwater standing solid while the sea rages, you can learn to stand fast and let the chaos roll past.

When your mind tries to call it bad luck or 'unfair', flip the script. Real luck isn't avoiding problems, it's keeping your cool, your values, and your integrity, *no matter* what comes your way. Anyone can get knocked over by the storm. Not everyone can stand up and say, "This is tough, but I'm still here. Still honest, still kind, still strong."

So, next time something challenging happens, don't get stuck in "Why me?" or "I can't believe this is happening." Instead, recognize your real good fortune, because you get to decide how you show up. And nothing, not even the worst luck, can take that away.

Your Takeaway

What occurred could have happened to anyone, but not everyone could have navigated it without letting it crush their spirit. Whenever something happens that might cause you distress, remember to rely on this principle: this event is not bad luck and bearing it valiantly is good luck.

Reflect:

- When have you stayed steady in the middle of a storm, and how did it feel?

- How could you reframe your next setback as proof of your strength, not your misfortune?

- What qualities can you choose, right now, that no challenge can take away?

- Are you ready to see your resilience as your real good luck?

You can't control the waves, but you can always control your stand.

Master your mind and be the rock, not the wreckage.

May 04

Worried about where everything or everyone 'goes' when it's gone? Nature has a way of transforming and making space, so don't get stuck on the unknown. Seek truth by looking deeper into what things are made of, and why.

Your mind can spin out over mysteries you'll never solve, like what happens after death, or how the world keeps making space for all that's come before. The truth is that nature is built on change and transformation. Everything that comes in eventually goes out in some new form. Bodies become earth. Souls shift, break down, and return to the universe in ways we can't fully see.

If you want to master your mind, don't waste energy getting lost in questions with no clear answer. Instead, focus on the bigger patterns: everything cycles, transforms, and finds its place. That's not just about death, it's about every part of life. When something ends, something else begins. The universe is the ultimate recycler.

So when your mind wants to ruminate on the unknowns, ask yourself, "What's the substance here? What's the deeper cause?" This is how you find clarity, peace, and the freedom to focus on what you *can* know and do, instead of getting stuck in endless speculation.

Your   Takeaway

Profound understanding of life's continuous cycle offers a potent strategy for mental tranquility by encouraging you to distinguish the fundamental matter from the underlying cause of all things. It allows you to release fear of annihilation and embrace impermanence as a natural re-integration into the universal system, rather than resisting change.

Reflect:

- Where is your mind stuck on mysteries or worries that no one can truly answer?

- How could you practice accepting transformation and change, instead of resisting it?

- What would shift if you focused on understanding what's here, now, and what you *can* influence?

- Are you willing to let go of unanswerable questions so you can live more fully today?

A masterful mind doesn't get lost in what it can't know. It seeks understanding, stays curious, and lets the rest unfold.

May 05

As long as you're doing what's right, don't let comfort, popularity, or even fear of death distract you. Every moment – good, bad, or final – is your chance to show up fully.

Life's going to throw you curveballs. Some days you'll be tired, cold, left out, or just plain overwhelmed. Other days you'll feel on top of the world, but none of that should shake your core, as long as you're acting with integrity and intention.

Mastering your mind is about refusing to let your circumstances or even your comfort level, run the show. It means you don't wait for the perfect mood, the perfect conditions, or everyone's approval before you do what's right. Whether you're exhausted or energized, celebrated or ignored, you still choose to show up with your best.

Even dying is just another action you take in life, so own it. Own every moment you're given, whether it feels good or not. Your power isn't in changing what happens to you, but in how you show up and respond. That's how you master your mind and take charge of your life – by making the absolute best of right now.

Your Takeaway

Nothing changes what's within your control. What *does* matter is how you act right now, in this moment. You get to choose how you show up, making the present count, right up to the end. Don't let life's ups and downs steal your focus. You're not here to chase comfort or applause, you're here to live with purpose, every moment you get.

Reflect:

- Where are you letting your mood or circumstances dictate your actions?

- How can you commit to doing what's right, regardless of what's happening around you?

- What would it look like to treat every moment as a fresh chance to show up fully?

- Are you willing to let go of needing everything to be perfect before you give your best?

The present is always yours to use. Master your mind and make every moment count.

May 06

If you're going to ask for something, make it honest, simple, and focused on what really matters, then do your part, too.

So many of us overthink our requests: whether it's asking for support, setting an intention, or putting a wish out into the universe. We pile on specifics, micromanage the details, and then wonder why we feel anxious or stuck.

Real clarity comes from putting your intentions out there, then getting back to doing your part, showing up for your life, and trusting you'll handle whatever comes.

Self-reliance isn't about going it alone, it's about owning your effort while staying clear on what's truly worth asking for. Wish for what matters, put your energy into what you can control, and leave the rest to the universe, fate, or just plain reality.

Your Takeaway

Sometimes we complicate our hopes, wishes, or even prayers with endless details, conditions, or self-doubt. But mastering your mind means keeping it straightforward and asking for what you truly need, nothing more, nothing less.

That's self-reliance in action: making a clear, honest request, then trusting yourself to show up and handle your part.

Reflect:

- When you set a goal, ask for help, or even just hope for something, keep it direct and focused on what actually matters.
- Don't get caught up in controlling every outcome or wishing for things that don't serve you.
- Speak your need, then put your energy into taking the next right step.
- It's like placing an order and then letting the kitchen do its job, you don't hover or stress about every ingredient. You trust the process, and you stay present with what you can actually influence.

Bottom line: Be clear. Be honest. Take responsibility for your part, and let go of the rest. That's where real strength and peace of mind begin.

May 07

Don't just take things at face value, dig deeper. Notice what really matters beneath the surface.

In a world moving a million miles an hour, it's easy to make snap judgments and keep things surface-level. But if you want to truly master your mind, you have to look closer: at people, problems, opportunities, and even yourself.

Look deeper. Pause. Ask yourself:

- What's really happening here?
- Is this situation as good or as bad or as it first seems?
- What's the real value, not just the hype?

Sometimes what's valuable is hidden. Sometimes a setback is actually a setup. Sometimes your mind is running on autopilot, playing old tracks that don't serve you anymore. Master your mind by becoming a little more curious, a little less reactive. Ask questions. Be willing to see beyond your knee-jerk reaction. It's not about being skeptical of everything – it's about being awake and intentional. That's where real understanding, and real wisdom live.

Your Takeaway

Life isn't about getting distracted by appearances. When you train your mind to see deeper, you become less reactive and more discerning. You're not so easily fooled or thrown off track. You can appreciate what's unique and valuable, even if it's hidden from plain sight.

Reflect:

- Where in your life have you been settling for the obvious instead of digging deeper?

- How might your mindset shift if you started searching for what's valuable beneath the surface?

- What can you learn from taking a second look, at a problem, a person, or yourself?

- Are you willing to move past snap judgments and see what's truly there?

A masterful mind isn't quick to judge: it's curious, patient, and always looking for the deeper truth.

May 08

Every time you make a mistake or act out, you're not just hurting others, you're holding yourself back. Every wrong choice chips away at who you want to become.

When you slip up, cut corners, or act out of anger or ego, the first person you actually damage is yourself: your own growth, your own peace, and your own self-respect.

Mastering your mind means recognizing that your actions shape your character, one choice at a time. You're not just building a reputation out there, you're building the person you have to live with every day. And when you ignore your values or let your mind run wild, you're the one who pays for it, even if no one else sees it.

So when you're tempted to make a move you'll regret, remember: this isn't about being perfect, it's about protecting and honoring your own best self. Every right choice, every honest thought, is a deposit in your own growth account. Every misstep is a withdrawal, but the good news is that you always get to choose again.

Your Takeaway

Every wrong move chips away at your own integrity. Acting badly doesn't just hurt others, it rewires your brain toward patterns that hold you back. The real damage of any transgression isn't out there, it's inside you. The path to being stronger, wiser, and more grounded starts with owning your choices, because that's how you build yourself up instead of tearing yourself down.

Reflect:

- Where have your actions or thoughts made you feel less like yourself?

- What would it look like to prioritize your own growth and integrity, no matter who's watching?

- How can you use slip-ups as lessons, not labels?

- Are you willing to make your next choice with your own well-being in mind?

The person you become is built on what you think and do. Master your mind, and you master your future.

May 09

Everything and everyone gets exactly what they need, exactly when they need it – trust that timing, and let your mind find peace there.

Life rarely shows up on your preferred schedule. You might feel behind, left out, or frustrated that you're not getting what you want, when you want it. But what if everything that comes your way – and even what *doesn't* come – is happening at the right time for your growth?

Think of universal nature like the ultimate life coach: it shows up with exactly what you need, exactly when you need it. No early deliveries, no last-minute rushes. Every person, every situation, every moment gets the right stuff, perfectly timed.

Mastering your mind isn't about forcing the universe to meet your deadlines, it's about trusting its timing. Don't stress over what hasn't arrived yet or what you think you're missing. When you drop the urge to rush, control, or compare, you actually free your mind from stress and resentment. Focus on the here and now, knowing that what's meant for you is already on its way, exactly when the universe knows you're ready for it.

Your Takeaway

Learn to trust life's process, knowing that every person, every situation, every twist and turn is giving you something you need: sometimes a lesson, sometimes a blessing, and sometimes both. Gain peace by focusing on what's here, right now, and believing it's enough for this moment.

Reflect:

- Where are you fighting the timing of life instead of trusting the process?

- How can you train your mind to see what's good about the present moment?

- What would change if you believed you're being given what you need, even when it's not what you *want*?

- Are you ready to choose trust over control, and peace over impatience?

Master your mind by mastering your perspective on timing. That's where true growth and calm live.

May 10

Break things down: when you see the parts clearly, distractions lose their power.

In our modern world, where we're constantly bombarded with curated experiences like viral videos and polished influencer content designed to bypass our critical thinking with a seamless, emotionally resonant whole, the wisdom is to master your mind and thoughts by hitting the 'pause' button and zooming in.

The allure often comes from the combination of parts and the illusion of effortlessness, not the individual, often mundane, components. Going straight to the components of everything external, especially what creates a strong emotional pull, reveals the ordinary reality behind perceived glamor or fear.

The purpose of this mental exercise is to cultivate the power of detachment, not cynicism: by seeing the individual – often unremarkable – parts, the emotional charge diminishes. This helps you avoid manipulation, focus on substance, and elevate what truly matters: virtue and virtuous action, which only grow clearer upon deconstruction.

Applying this 'deconstruction' procedure to your entire life means regularly examining your challenges, successes, and identity as a collection of moments and choices, reducing their emotional hold and empowering you to act with clarity and purpose, and becoming the master editor of your own life's script instead of a passive viewer.

Your Takeaway

The things that pull you in lose their magic when you zoom in on every tiny detail. When you analyze closely, what seems captivating often feels less impressive. Apply this same lens to everything in your life, especially distractions or desires. Break big overwhelming moments or emotions into smaller pieces. When you do, you realize how little some things deserve your energy. Focus instead on what really matters: virtue and right action. Mastering your mind means seeing through the noise and choosing what deserves your attention.

May 11

Stay focused, act from your values, and use your mind to reason instead of allowing it to spin out of control or overcomplicate the matter. Stick to what you know is true.

Your mind can wander, get distracted, or chase every "what if" until you're lost in the weeds. But if you want to master your mind, it starts with intention. When it's time to act, check in with yourself: are you moving from what matters most to you, or are you letting impulse or outside noise run the show?

When your thoughts start spiraling, don't let them drag you off track. Stick with what you *know* is clear, true, and certain. If you're just guessing, worrying, or trying to read minds, that's a sign to pause and come back to your center. It's about clarity, not chaos.

Mastering your mind is about discipline, choosing to steer your thoughts and actions, not letting them steer you. It's not about being rigid or robotic and it's about not getting pulled off course by every new feeling, fear, or distraction. Make it a habit to return to what's real, what's important, and what's proven. That's how you build trust in yourself and move forward with confidence.

Your Takeaway

When it's time to act, do what's right, align your choices with your values, and avoid distractions or external pressures. Stick with what's clear and certain, cutting through mental clutter, speculation, and misinformation to base your judgments on facts and clear reasoning. Act with greater effectiveness, peace, and authenticity.

Reflect:

- Where are you letting your thoughts spiral into confusion instead of sticking with what you know?

- How can you act more from your values, and less from impulse or pressure?

- What's one thing you're certain of, and how can you build on that today?

- Are you ready to choose clarity over confusion, and action over distraction?

Keep your mind focused, and your actions honest. That's how you take the reins: one thought, one choice at a time.

Concept 12: Adjust Your Perceptions

It's not the thing, it's how you see the thing.

May 12

Things only have the meaning you give them, your perspective shapes your experience. That's not just philosophy, it's your daily reality.

The world is constantly throwing stuff your way: challenges, setbacks, even surprises that knock you sideways. But what really shapes your experience isn't what happens, but how you *see* it.

Everything is as you take it to be. Your mindset is the lens that colors everything, how you interpret what's happening around you shapes your entire experience. It's not about denying reality or spinning some fantasy. It's about choosing the lens through which you view things. Your story isn't written by events, it's written by your perception of them.

You get to decide if a situation crushes you or teaches you, if a setback is a disaster or a stepping stone. Accept the truth in this, but don't overcomplicate it. The next time life feels overwhelming or unfair, pause and check your lens. You might not control what happens, but you can always choose how you see it, and that changes everything.

Your Takeaway

Your perceptions aren't just reactions, they're powerful tools you can adjust to live better, think clearer, and act wiser. Your reality starts in your mind – own that.

Reflect:

- How are your perceptions shaping your current reality?

- What story are you telling yourself about what's happening, and is it helping or hurting you?

- Where can you adjust your perspective to see opportunity instead of only struggle?

- What's one belief you can challenge today to shift how you experience your world?

Your power is in your perception. Adjust the lens, and see what new possibilities open up.

May 13

If something costs you your integrity, your peace, or your character, it's not worth it. The right mindset keeps you steady, drama-free, and true to yourself, no matter what's happening around you.

Don't ever count something as a win if it forces you to compromise on what really matters: your promises, your integrity, your kindness, or your honesty. If you find yourself hating, suspecting, hiding things, or acting fake just to get ahead, you've already lost the game.

When you put your inner compass first – your mind, your values, your sense of what's right – you stop being pulled around by what's happening outside. No more constant swings between craving and avoiding, no more selling yourself out for a quick hit of approval or comfort.

The person who truly owns their perception doesn't need to escape to solitude, or lose themselves in the crowd. They're good wherever they are, because they're not acting for applause or hiding from criticism. When it's time to move on, they're at peace with it, because they've lived in alignment with who they are. Their one true focus is keeping their mind clear and aligned with reason and the way humans should treat each other. That's how you live free and real.

Your Takeaway

If you want less drama and more clarity, check your motives. If it costs your character, it's not a bargain. Adjust your perception so you can walk through every moment with integrity, no matter what's on the line.

Reflect:

- Where are you tempted to compromise just for short-term gain or comfort?

- What would shift if you started measuring success by your inner alignment, not just outside results?

- How can you stay steady, no matter who's watching or what's happening?

- What's one situation right now where adjusting your perspective could help you act with more integrity?

You don't need to chase or avoid, just live true. That's the mindset that sets you free.

May 14

You can let go of negative thoughts way faster than you think. Peace is just a mindset shift away.

We all get hijacked by unwanted thoughts, regrets, worries, things that just won't quit. But you actually have the ability to choose a new perspective.

We often feel controlled by these thoughts, as if they have free rein in our minds. Most of your stress comes from holding on, replaying old stories, or believing every random worry your mind throws up. But you don't have to engage with every intrusive thought, analyze it endlessly, or let it run wild. You have the power to simply banish and erase it, which leads to immediate and complete tranquility.

It's not about lengthy meditation or therapy at the moment. It's about a swift, decisive act of mental control. By realizing you don't have to entertain an upsetting thought, you instantly reclaim your mental space and restore calm. Challenge the thought, let it float by, and bring your focus back to what's real and within your control.

You can practice this anytime. Notice the next negative thought that pops up. Take a breath. Ask yourself, "Is this true? Is it helpful? Do I have to keep it?" If not, let it go. That's your real superpower: the ability to clear space in your mind and come back to calm, as often as you need.

This isn't about denying reality or suppressing emotions. It's about consciously controlling your inner landscape and adjusting your perception from being a victim of your thoughts to being the operator of your own mind.

Your Takeaway

Tranquility is available, right now, whenever you decide to stop gripping so tightly to what's not helping you. When an unwelcome thought pops up, you don't have to host it – you can choose to dismiss it, clearing the way for instant peace.

Reflect:

- What thought has been taking up too much space in your mind lately?

- How quickly could you let it go, if you stopped believing it was permanent or important?

- What's one new perspective you can choose, right now, to create more peace?

- How would your life feel if you created the habit of releasing and not replaying what's not serving you?

Peace isn't out there. It's a decision you make, one thought at a time.

May 15

Challenges and difficult circumstances can't shake your mind, only your thoughts about them can.

Life's circumstances don't have the power you think they do. The world can't mess with your mind unless you let it. It's not the events or objects themselves that shake you up, it's the story your mind chooses to tell about them.

When something happens, your mind interprets it, decides if it's good or bad, upsetting or fine. When you realize this, you take back control. You become the boss of your reactions, not a victim of circumstance.

So next time something hits you hard, pause. Ask yourself, "Is this really how I want to see it?" Shifting your perspective isn't just an option, it's the key to owning your peace.

Your Takeaway

The world itself isn't what messes with your peace, it's your mind that gives them meaning and power. Change your story and the impact changes too. Your mind is your fortress, so keep it strong by choosing your perceptions wisely.

May 16

Your mind is in charge. It shapes not just who you are, but it also shapes how you see what happens to you.

The most important force in your life isn't what happens to you, it's what you do with it inside your own head. Your inner guide – your mindset, your attitude, your story – gets to decide what anything means. That's not just positive thinking, that's your built-in superpower.

You get to choose the lens. Stuck in traffic? You can see it as wasted time, or as a chance to breathe, reset, maybe even catch up on that podcast you keep ignoring. Got reprimanded at work? You can take it as proof you're failing, or as a sign you're growing, learning, and pushing your limits. Ask yourself, is this setback or a crushing defeat? Or is it a chance to learn, grow, and prove your resilience? Is that criticism a personal attack? Or just someone's opinion you don't have to carry?

This isn't about lying to yourself or ignoring real problems. It's about realizing you always have a say in how you interpret your world. Your mind can make even the toughest situation meaningful, if you let it. You can reframe, pivot, and find purpose, no matter what's outside your control. You don't just react, you respond. That's where real freedom lives.

So next time life throws something unexpected at you, pause and check in with your inner guide. How are you going to see this? What's the story you're going to tell yourself, and is it one that lifts you up, or drags you down?

Your Takeaway

Your mind is your true inner guide. It's not just a passive observer – it shapes everything you see and feel. It decides what meaning to give to every event, every twist and turn life throws your way. You get to choose how things show up in your world. When you fully own that power, you stop being tossed around by circumstances and start crafting your reality with intention.

Reflect:

- How have you been interpreting the events of your life lately? Are your stories helping or hurting you?

- What's one situation where a different perspective could completely change how you feel?

- Are you using your mind's flexibility to empower yourself, or to reinforce old limits?

- What story will you choose today, and how will it shape your experience?

Your mindset is your superpower, adjust it, and you can shift your whole world.

May 17

Life flows fast: what feels huge today is gone before you know it. Everything passes, so don't get stuck on any one moment.

We live in an era of continuous updates and breaking news. Like any feed, information and events are always flowing. One post or trend quickly replaces another, then fades from immediate view. Learn to adjust your perceptions of life's constant movement and where you focus your energy.

This isn't a glitch, it's how existence works. Life moves fast. Everything's temporary. You can't slow down time, prevent new events from appearing, or hold onto old moments. Fighting this flow just leads to exhaustion.

However, you *can* adjust your perception. By accepting that everything is temporary – every joy, sorrow, challenge, or victory – you release the attachment that causes suffering. Since the past is swept away and the future hasn't happened yet, your only point of influence is the present. Instead of being consumed by what just passed or what might come, direct your full attention to the 'now', allowing you to experience life as it is.

Your Takeaway

Time doesn't stop for anyone. Your power lies in adjusting your perspective, in seeing that everything – stress, joy, pain, excitement – is temporary. If you can remember that, you get to move through life with more calm, more courage, and way less drama. You learn to ride the current, not fight it.

Reflect:

- What are you holding onto that's already drifting away?

- How would your stress change if you remembered that "this too shall pass"?

- Where could you let go, move on, or forgive, knowing that time will carry it all away anyway?

- What would it look like to show up for the moment, without getting stuck in it?

Life keeps flowing. Let your perceptions flow with it, and find your peace in the present.

May 18

You have the built-in power to flip obstacles into opportunities, just like nature uses everything, even setbacks, to keep moving forward.

Your ability to change how you see things isn't just about feeling better, it's about actively using every obstacle and turning it to raw material for ourselves. We learn to repurpose every challenge.

When you hit a roadblock, face a setback, or run into a challenge, your first thought might be that it's a dead end. But, by adjusting how you see it, you can start to view that obstacle not as a wall, but as material or fuel. It's not just about 'positive thinking'. It's about asking yourself, "How can I use this?" instead of "Why me?" That little mindset shift is the difference between feeling stuck and feeling unstoppable.

This isn't about ignoring problems or pretending they don't exist. It's about consciously choosing to reframe them. A rejection becomes helpful feedback. A failure turns into crucial data for learning. A limitation becomes a spark for new ideas or different routes. When you do this, you're not just getting through the challenge, you're actively turning its energy into momentum for your own growth and goals.

Your ability to change a problem into a resource is a powerful skill you already have. It means you can keep moving forward, no matter what's happening around you, simply by choosing to see every difficulty as a chance to advance. That can totally change your whole path.

Your Takeaway

Your ability to change the way you see and use obstacles is what makes you powerful. Universal nature doesn't waste anything: it recycles every barrier, every block, into part of the process. You can do the same.

Obstacles are just the universe's way of giving you more to work with, not less.

Reflect:

- What obstacle are you facing right now that could become your next opportunity?

- How would your attitude change if you saw setbacks as useful, not pointless?

- Where can you recycle resistance into growth or momentum?

- What's one small way you can use your current challenge as material for your next step?

You're not here to be blocked, you're here to build, create, and adapt. Use everything. That's your superpower.

May 19

If you change your belief about what's hurting you, the pain loses its grip. Your rational mind can always find peace, even if the rest of you feels the sting.

Most of the time it's not the situation itself that hurts you, it's what you *believe* about it. The story you tell yourself about pain, rejection, or struggle gives it power, or takes it away. Shift that story, and you stand in a place no one can touch.

When something feels like it's tearing you up, pause and check the narrative running through your mind. Is it, "This is unbearable, I can't get through it", or can your reason step in and say, "Yeah, this is tough, but it doesn't have to own me."

Your rational self is always there, ready to steady the ship. It can't be hurt unless you give the pain permission. If you let reason call the shots, the emotional waves lose their punch.

Next time you feel under attack, whether by someone else, your circumstances, or your own mind, try to separate the pain from the story. Let your reason keep you anchored, even if everything else wants to drift.

Your Takeaway

If you can drop that story you're telling yourself about what's hurting you, you'll find a place where pain just can't reach you. Your reason is the part inside of you that is clear and steady.

Reason never hurts itself. Whatever part of you is hurting, let it believe its pain, but don't let that pain drag down the whole of you. You get to choose which voice runs the show. Let reason lead. Pain is just noise, not your truth.

Reflect:

- What belief is making your current struggle hurt more than it needs to?

- How can your rational mind offer you a new, calmer perspective right now?

- What would change if you stopped identifying with the pain and started choosing your response?

- Are you willing to let reason guide you back to solid ground, even in the middle of discomfort?

Remember: Your mind is your safe place. Use it, and watch your perspective and your life transform.

May 20

Today, let go of what is weighing you down: not by changing the world, but by changing your mindset. The real problems were never out there — they were just beliefs you've been holding onto.

Most of what drags you down isn't out in the world, it's living rent-free in your own head. Stress, resentment, fear, old grudges? Nine times out of ten, they're not facts, they're stories and beliefs you've been carrying around. And the good news is that if you put them there, you can kick them out.

Adjusting your perception is about realizing you have the power to clear your own mental space. When you notice yourself weighed down by anxiety or frustration, ask yourself, "Is this really happening, or is it just the way I'm thinking about it?" The moment you call out those beliefs for what they are, you start to become free.

It's not about ignoring reality or pretending you have no problems. It's about taking ownership of the beliefs you're feeding. When you change your mind, you change your world, even if nothing else around you shifts.

Your Takeaway

Freedom isn't about changing the world outside, it's about clearing out the junk inside your own head. What afflicts you is not external, it's in your own stories and judgments. Change your perspective and gain freedom.

Reflect:

- What beliefs are you holding onto that are making your life harder than it needs to be?

- How would things change if you let go of just one limiting story today?

- Are you willing to take responsibility for your own peace, instead of waiting for the world to cooperate?

- What's one new belief you can adopt to help you move forward lighter, stronger, and clearer?

Freedom starts in your mind. Clear out what's holding you back, and watch the weight lift.

May 21

When something ends, it doesn't disappear, it just changes form and becomes part of something new. Even the hardest losses are part of a bigger cycle, not an ending.

Loss, change, and endings are all part of the deal. But nothing is ever truly 'lost'. When something or someone passes, they aren't erased from existence, just transformed. Everything that stays within the universe gets broken down, is recycled, and becomes raw material for what comes next.

When things change, it's just nature's way of remixing the elements, turning endings into beginnings. There's no need to fight the process or become mired in grief, because nothing's *really* gone, it's just living on in a new way.

The next time you're facing loss or change, try looking for what's being made new instead of focusing on what's missing. Notice the cycle. The universe never wastes a thing, and neither should you. You can move through change with acceptance, and even a bit of awe, instead of resistance and regret.

Your Takeaway

The universe breaks things down into the basic building blocks that make up everything. When life shifts or ends, it's not a loss. It's simply part of a bigger cycle and you don't have to fight it. You just have to adjust how you see it, because perception is where the real power lives.

Reflect:

- Where in your life are you grieving an ending, when you could look for what's emerging?

- How does it feel to know you're part of a cycle that never truly loses anything, it just changes?

- What would shift if you saw loss as transformation, not finality?

- Are you willing to let go, trust the process, and let change be part of your growth?

Change is the universe's remix, trust it, and let your perspective open to what's possible.

May 22

Make the most of your life. The power is in your mindset. Most things are neutral, and it's your judgment that gives them power.

Most of what stresses you out isn't the issue itself, it's your judgment about it. Money, status, criticism, trends, even other people's opinions, these are 'indifferents', meaning they don't define your worth unless you let them. You get to decide what's big and what's small, what deserves your focus and what's just noise.

Want more peace and purpose? Break things down. If something is nagging at you, look closer at it. What's it made of? Is it really as important as your mind wants you to believe? Remember, these things don't force their opinions onto you. You're the one giving them meaning and creating judgments. And you can always choose to erase those judgments and see things differently.

Don't waste your short, precious life mired in stress. If something aligns with your nature, if it feels right, and if it helps you grow, embrace it. If not, let it go and focus on what's actually nourishing for you, even if it's not what everyone else would choose.

You're allowed to live your good life by your standards. The key is perception: what you give meaning to, what you let go, and what you decide to focus on.

Your Takeaway

Pursue your wellbeing. Stop focusing on things and experiences that won't matter in the long run. Find what does align with your true nature and focus on that, even if it looks unconventional to others.

Reflect:

- What are you treating as a big deal that's actually just noise or someone else's expectation?

- How could you break down the things stressing you out to see if they really matter?

- Are you willing to erase old judgments and write a new story for yourself?

- What would life look like if you focused on what truly aligns with your nature, not what the world says is important?

Your life is yours to shape. Adjust your perception, and make it count.

May 23

Keep working, but don't make it a performance for sympathy or applause. Do what needs to be done because it's right, not because you want attention.

This wisdom powerfully calls you to adjust your perception of work and effort, shifting your focus from chasing fleeting external rewards or wallowing in emotional states to embracing the inherent purpose and virtue of your actions.

In a world obsessed with guilt marketing and constant validation, true strength lies in working not for an audience, but for a deeper, internal reward. Your effort is a direct expression of your character, not a performance.

The core guidance here is to align your actions with your inner moral compass that guides you to act decisively when needed or to wisely refrain from action. By focusing on this principle, your perception shifts from the *outcome* of your labor – like success or wealth – to the integrity of your effort, meaning you work because it's simply the right thing to do, because it aligns with your values, and because it genuinely contributes positively, even in the quietest of ways.

You're not here to be the hero of a struggle story. You're here to move the needle in your corner of the world, quietly, steadily, and with integrity. Let your satisfaction come from knowing you showed up, not from how many people clap or commiserate.

Your Takeaway

Adjust your perception so that you see effort as purpose, as a way to contribute and to do the right thing. You'll become less concerned with the perceptions of others and more focused on serving your highest purpose and the common good.

Reflect:

- Where in your life are you looking for sympathy or applause instead of just taking pride in your own effort?

- How would your energy shift if you worked for the sake of the work and not the recognition?

- What's one area where you can quietly focus on the good you're doing, without seeking attention?

- Are you willing to adjust your perception and find meaning in purpose, not pity?

Work with heart, not for a spotlight. Your perception makes all the difference.

Concept 13: Focus on What You Can Control (*Dichotomy of Control*)

Most of life isn't up to you. But how you show up is all you.

May 24

You're more than just a body dragging itself through the day. Don't waste your energy worrying about what you can't control and focus on keeping your spirit alive and present.

True strength, freedom, and dignity come from recognizing your consciousness as separate from and superior to the mere physical form it inhabits. Your essential being isn't defined or limited by the body's fleeting condition.

By focusing on cultivating the strength, wisdom, and virtue of your soul and mind, you choose to be the master of your own internal experience, rather than a slave to the temporary vessel you occupy. This liberation allows you to act with intentionality and maintain peace, and brings you to understand that you *cannot* control the physical body's eventual decay, its susceptibility to illness, and its finite existence.

What you *can* control is your soul, consciousness, and your inner self. You control its judgments, its values, its responses, its resilience, and its purpose. You decide whether it's pathetic; enslaved by the body's whims, or powerful; directing the body with wisdom.

That's how you live contented and truly free.

Your Takeaway

You can't control aging, what other people do, or what tomorrow brings. But you *can* choose whether you let your energy get swallowed up by things you can't change, or whether you bring your full, awake, and present self to whatever's in front of you. If you focus only on survival, routine, or the stuff outside your control, you'll miss out on what actually makes you alive. Your real power is in waking up, right here, right now, and deciding to live with intention, no matter what life throws at you.

Reflect:

- Where are you just going through the motions, instead of choosing to be fully present?

- How much energy are you spending on things you can't influence?

- What would change if you put your focus back on what you *can* control and your attitude, your effort, your presence?

- Are you ready to wake up and live, instead of just 'getting by'?

Remember: Your body's along for the ride, but your spirit is driving. Make the most of your journey.

May 25

You're made of the same stuff and causes as everything else: changing, shifting, but never lost. You don't control where you came from or where you'll end up, but you can always choose what you do with your piece of the story.

You're not separate from the universe. You're built from the same matter and energy that's been cycling through everything: stars, trees, your ancestors, all of it, for who knows how long. Nothing is ever really lost, it just changes shape and moves on to the next chapter.

You don't get to pick how or when you arrived on this planet. You won't get to script every moment of your legacy after you're gone, either. But you *do* get to choose how you show up, how you use your energy, and what meaning you make out of your time here.

Worrying about things outside your reach – where you came from, what happens after, the big cycles of life and death – doesn't move you forward. What's fully in your control is how you respond, how you live, and what kind of impact you make while you're here.

Change is a given. Your power is in how you handle it, not in trying to escape it.

Your Takeaway

You can't control your physical impermanence or the universe's constant transformations, but you can control your response to this reality. You choose to resist with anxiety or embrace with acceptance. Free yourself from clinging to what won't last, and redirect your energy to acting with purpose, integrity, and joy.

Reflect:

● Where are you losing sleep over things you'll never control, like your origins or what happens after you're gone?

- How does it feel to know you're part of a bigger story, always changing and shifting?

- What's one thing you can control about how you show up, right now?

- Are you willing to let go of what's out of your hands, and focus on making the most of your moment?

You're just one chapter in the universe's story, own your part, and let the rest unfold.

May 26

What hurts you isn't what's happening around you or what other people do. It's what you decide to believe about it. Keep your mind steady, and you stay unshaken.

True harm originates not from external events or other people, but from our internal interpretation of those events.

First, *external factors are neutral.* External factors – be it someone else's behavior or a change in your environment – are not inherently detrimental to you. They are simply events occurring in the world. Imagine them as neutral data inputs. Your peace is not contingent on the inner guidance system of others or on flawless operating conditions.

Second, *the power of your internal labeling system.* Your vulnerability lies squarely in your internal labeling system: the part of your mind that assigns 'good' or 'bad' to these neutral inputs. If you choose not to apply the 'bad' label, then the perceived harm dissolves. This is where your absolute control resides.

Third, *even physical discomfort is neutral.* Your body might signal distress, but your mind has the capacity to refuse to judge that physical experience as inherently bad, even with the most visceral experiences, like pain or illness. You can quiet that judgmental part of your mind.

Fourth, *universal neutrality.* The concept that anything that can happen to anyone – regardless of their moral standing or how in tune they are with life – is morally neutral itself. Both good and bad people can get sick. Both good and bad people can face financial loss. These events are not moral judgments from the universe, they are simply part of the universal process.

By embracing these four points, you shift your focus entirely from trying to control or eliminate external events – which are largely beyond your power – to mastering your internal response to them. Your true strength comes from your ability to choose your judgment, to reframe your perceptions, and to maintain an unshakable inner calm, regardless of what's unfolding around you. This is the ultimate act of self-empowerment.

Your Takeaway

Nothing has the power to wreck you unless you give it permission. You can't control other people's choices, or how the world changes, but you *can* control how you interpret it. What happens to you isn't personal. It happens to everyone, good or bad, ready or not. What you get to choose is your response. The world doesn't get to write your story, your beliefs do.

Reflect:

- Where are you letting outside circumstances define your mood or self-worth?

- What would happen if you stopped labeling every challenge as 'bad' or 'unfair'?

- How could you practice holding steady, even when life's messy?

- Are you willing to reclaim your power from your circumstances, and put it back in your beliefs?

You can't control everything that happens, but you always control the story you tell yourself about it. That's real freedom. Use it.

May 27

You might not be perfect, but you control how you act. Excuses won't cover up choices you're making right now.

You might not have all the talents you wish you had, and maybe you'll never be the sharpest mind in the room, but the powerful qualities you *can* offer are those entirely within your control. Kindness. Integrity. Endurance. Acceptance. Generosity. Self-control. You don't need a special gift for these, just a willingness to step up, every day.

Stop hiding behind the story that "I just wasn't made that way." Grumbling, bragging, blaming, or changing your mind every five minutes aren't hardwired. They're habits, and habits can be changed. Maybe you're not perfect, maybe you move a little slower or miss things sometimes. That's perfectly fine. But you're always free to act better.

Focus on what you can actually offer: showing up real, steady, and true, no matter what the world thinks of your 'talent'. Your legacy isn't about what you can't do, it's built on all the good you *can* do, just by choosing it.

Your Takeaway

The best traits you can have only requires deciding to have them. If you're slow to change, you can work on it. The key is to not ignore your faults or get comfortable with them. You're responsible for the quality of your own character. Own it, and start showing up as your best self today.

Reflect:

- What qualities are already yours to offer, no special talent needed?

- Where have you been making excuses instead of making choices?

- What's one small habit you can drop today that's not serving you?

- How would your life look if you leaned into what's fully in your control?

Don't wait to be admired for gifts you never had. Own the ones you can grow, right now. That's your real power.

May 28

Either there's a bigger order to life, or things just happen. Either way, stressing out about what you can't control is pointless. Trust what you can steer, and let the rest be.

In both scenarios, your control lies in acceptance. The wisdom isn't in definitively proving which option is correct, but in realizing the implications for your inner state.

If the universe is controlled by a grand design, you can find peace by surrendering to the flow. Focus your energy on your own actions and responses within this system, rather than trying to micromanage or complain about the universe's code. Your control lies in aligning with it.

If the universe is led by random chaos, you can find peace by letting go of expectations for perfect order or fairness. Outcomes are unpredictable, and therefore, getting emotionally agitated by them is pointless. Your control lies in your non-attachment to external results and maintaining internal stability amidst the chaos.

When you remember that you can't control the grand design, or lack of one, you give yourself permission to breathe. You can stay calm in the chaos, trust your role, and let the universe do its thing. All that's left is to focus on your choices, your character, and your actions. That's your real power, and it's more than enough.

Your Takeaway

Life is messy, unpredictable, and sometimes makes zero sense, but your serenity is independent of external events. Choose your response to the universe's unfolding, rather than letting its processes dictate your peace of mind.

Reflect:

- Where are you losing sleep over questions you can't possibly answer or control?

- How would your life feel if you focused only on what's yours to shape?

- What might you release today if you trusted the process, even when it's mysterious?

- Are you ready to let go of what's outside your circle, and put your energy into your next right step?

You don't need all the answers. Just own your part, show up fully, and let the rest unfold.

May 29

Life will present you with challenges and obstacles. Some of them will certainly be upsetting, but you get to decide if you let them ruin your day. Your real power is in choosing not to label an experience as 'bad'. That keeps you untouchable.

All of the things outside of you – pain, insults, setbacks – can hit the parts of you that are built to feel them. Your physical body or your immediate circumstances might register these impacts, and it's natural for them to complain or react.

The outside world has a mind of its own. People will say things. Plans will fall apart. Your body might get tired or even hurt sometimes. All of that can happen without your permission. But those things only go as deep as you let them.

You can't always control what comes at you, but you *always* control the story you tell yourself about it. You're not obligated to label every inconvenience, setback, or criticism as a catastrophe. The pain, frustration, or discomfort might hit your outer layers, but your inner guide? That's your territory. If you don't buy into the story that "this is bad, this is ruining me", you keep your power.

Choosing your response is like emotional judo: let the blow land, but don't let it knock you over. You get to say, "Yeah, that was hard, but I'm still here, still choosing how I see it, still in charge of my next move."

You don't have to be a victim to what life throws at you. You get to keep control by choosing not to let outside forces shake your inner calm. That's how resilience is born.

Your Takeaway

You have the power of choice. You have the agency to decide how you label these experiences. This is where your control lies. By exercising this choice, you become the gatekeeper of your own mind, ensuring that your serenity remains uncompromised by anything outside your control.

Reflect:

- What external event or opinion has been dragging you down lately?

- How can you reframe it, so it doesn't have the power to define your day?

- What story do you want to tell about yourself in the face of challenges?

- Are you willing to let go of judgment and reclaim your peace, even when life gets messy?

What happens outside is one thing. What you decide about it? That's where your freedom, and your power live.

May 30

Other people's choices and moods aren't yours to control or carry. You're here to help and connect, but your mindset, your peace, and your power are yours alone.

You can't live other people's lives for them. You might care, you might want the best for them, but at the end of the day, everyone has their own inner guidance system. Their decisions, drama, or even their personal growth is not your responsibility. You're here to show up with kindness, but you don't have to be the emotional sponge for everyone around you.

Focusing on what you can control means drawing a clear line: "I'm responsible for my choices, my reactions, my emotions." Someone else's negativity, bad decisions, or even success doesn't get to dictate your mood or your self-worth. That's freedom, and it's not selfish, it's healthy.

This isn't about checking out or not caring. It's about understanding that your misfortune or your happiness shouldn't depend on what anyone else is doing. You can support, uplift, and cheer on, but you don't have to let their chaos become your crisis.

Next time you catch yourself caught up in someone else's spiral, pause. Step back. Remember whose mind and heart you actually get to control. That's where your power lives, right inside your own inner guide.

Your Takeaway

The Universe didn't design your peace to be controlled by someone else's bad behavior.

You hold the reins of your own mind. Protect your space. Own your power. That's how you keep your life steady, no matter what others do.

Reflect:

- Where are you carrying responsibility for someone else's choices or mood?

- How can you stay supportive without letting their energy disrupt your peace?

- What would change if you put your focus back on your own mindset and actions?

- Are you willing to let go of what's not yours, and take full ownership of your own well-being?

You can't steer someone else's ship, but you can always captain your own.

May 31

You can let go of a lot of your stress just by changing the way you think about things. Step back, zoom out, and see how small today's worries are in the big picture.

Half the stuff weighing you down isn't reality, it's just the stories you're telling yourself. Most of your worries and hang-ups that live rent-free in your head were created and fueled by your beliefs, not the facts. The good news is that you can clear out that mental clutter any time you choose.

When you catch yourself spiraling, pause and pull back. How big is that problem compared to the universe, or even just to your whole life? Our time here is a blink. Before you were born, there was eternity. After you're gone, eternity keeps rolling. Suddenly, that text you didn't get or that meeting that went sideways doesn't seem so important.

You don't control the universe, but you can control your perspective. When you make space in your mind by letting go of what doesn't matter, you get your power back, more peace, more clarity, more room for what's real.

Your Takeaway

A lot of the stress you carry is due to your beliefs and your judgments, but you can choose to change and control them. Free yourself from the chaos you've been *choosing* to carry. That's how you claim peace. That's how you own your power.

Reflect:

- What worries are you holding onto that are just beliefs, not facts?

- How does your problem look when you zoom out and see the bigger picture?

- What mental clutter could you clear out today to give yourself more peace and space?

- Are you ready to stop letting small stuff run your life and focus on what you *can* control?

Let go of what's not yours to carry. Focus on your mindset, your perspective, and the way you respond, that's where your real control lives.

June 01

No one gets to decide your character but you. If someone criticizes your character, that's on them, just make sure it isn't true. You control your integrity, no matter what anyone says.

People will judge, assume, or gossip no matter what you do. But the part they don't control is *who you choose to be.* You get to decide if you're honest, genuine, and kind. Their opinions are just noise.

Your integrity is yours to own, every single day. If someone calls you out for being underhanded and it's not true, their words don't stick. What matters is what's real, not what's rumored. And if you ever feel yourself slipping, that's your cue to check back in with your values, not to impress anyone else, but because you refuse to live any other way.

Don't let other people's narratives steer your choices. Stay focused on what you can control: your actions, your character, your standards. That's real power, and no one can take it away, unless you hand it over.

Step up. Own your goodness. Don't just talk about it, live it every single day. That's how you keep yourself real.

Your Takeaway

Being good and straightforward is all on you. No one else can force you to lose those qualities unless you give up on them yourself. If you can't hold on to that integrity, that simple, honest self, it's time to rethink everything. Because reason – your true guide – doesn't waste time on anything less.

Reflect:

- Are you letting someone else's opinion shake your sense of who you are?

- How would your life change if you stopped defending yourself and just kept living true?

- Where can you double down on your own integrity, no matter what others think?

- What qualities do you want to embody, regardless of who's watching or what they say?

You can't control the crowd, but you can always control your own story. Make it a good one.

June 02

Don't be shocked when life presents you with surprises, it's just what life does. You can't control what shows up, but you can always control how you handle it.

Why are we always so surprised when things go sideways? Social trouble and personal setbacks are just part of the human experience.

What you *can't* control is the fundamental code of the universe: natural cycles, the behavior of others, and unforeseen challenges. A fig tree *will* bear figs, the universe *will* produce its outcomes, a patient *will* get fevers, and the wind *will* be contrary. These are givens, part of the system's design.

What you *can* control is your response to these natural occurrences: your preparation, your mindset, and your actions. Focusing on what you can control means letting go of outrage or disappointment every time something unpredictable happens. Your real strength is in your response, not in trying to micromanage reality. The universe is going to do what it does, so instead of getting caught off guard, expect the unexpected, and put your energy into how you'll show up when it happens.

Every challenge, every twist, every surprise? That's just life being life. You don't have to like it, but you do get to decide your next move. This is where your true agency lies.

Your Takeaway

You should expect life to unfold with its full spectrum of experiences, both easy and difficult. Your power lies not in wishing for a different reality, but in mastering your reaction to the one you're given. Don't be surprised by the predictable, instead focusing your energy on how you skillfully navigate it.

Reflect:

- What's one thing life has thrown at you lately that caught you off guard?

- Are you spending more energy fighting reality or figuring out your response?

- How would your mindset shift if you stopped expecting smooth sailing and started focusing on your own navigation?

- Where can you let go of surprise and lean into choice instead?

You can't control the storm, but you can always steer your ship. That's your power, own it.

June 03

Even the most powerful families and their legacies fade away. No matter how hard people try to control the future, everything changes and passes. So focus on what you can shape: your choices, your actions, your today.

Consider the fate of even the most powerful dynasties, like past tech giants or social media empires. Their entire inner circles, from founders to rising stars, eventually face the end of their run. This applies to entire corporate cultures and family legacies too. Just like those last active account notifications, people strive to build their brand or secure generational wealth, but someone is always the last to log off. It's the digital demise of every lineage.

You can't control how long your influence lasts, how people remember you, or who comes after you. You can't control the legacy others leave behind. You can't control the fact that families, empires, or even entire communities eventually fade away. What you *can* control is how you show up now, how you treat people, the values you live by, and the energy you bring to the day you have.

Focus on what you can control: how you treat people, how you respond to setbacks, and how you live your values today. Let go of the rest. Don't waste energy trying to hold onto what's slipping through your fingers like sand. That's where freedom begins.

Your Takeaway

In the end, nothing lasts forever. You don't get to guarantee the future, no matter how hard you try. Let go of the anxiety over legacy and outcomes you'll never see. Invest in what's actually yours: your actions, your mindset, your present moment.

Reflect:

- Where are you spending energy trying to control the uncontrollable, like your legacy or how you'll be remembered?

- How would your focus shift if you poured it into your actions today, instead of trying to script tomorrow?

- What do you actually have power over, right now?

- How can you bring more presence and purpose to your everyday life?

You don't have to chase forever. Show up for now, and let the rest unfold.

June 04

Everybody has their own version of happiness. Mine is keeping my mind healthy, meeting everyone with kindness, and taking life as it comes, one moment at a time.

You can't control what lights someone else up or what makes them spiral. Chasing other people's definitions of happiness is a losing game. Your real power is in how you show up, how you treat others, and the attitude you bring to each experience.

Happiness isn't about everything going your way, it's about having your internal guide – your mindset, your heart, your perspective – tuned in and steady. Can you look at people – every single one, even the ones who push your buttons – with understanding instead of judgment? Can you face every situation with an open mind, not running or hiding, but working with whatever comes your way?

You don't get to choose every circumstance. You do get to choose your response. And real freedom lives in accepting what you can't change, and putting your energy into what you can. When your inner world is solid, outside drama can't shake you. That's the kind of happiness no one can take away.

A healthy mind is one that practices radical acceptance and universal empathy.

Your Takeaway

While external circumstances or fleeting pleasures might bring temporary joy, lasting happiness is an inside job. It's not about what you acquire or what happens *to* you, but about the health and function of your own mind.

Reflect:

- Are you measuring happiness by what you can control, or by things out of your hands?

- How can you practice kindness and acceptance even with difficult people or moments?

- What would change if you focused less on circumstances and more on your mindset?

- Today, where can you let go and where can you show up more fully?

You don't need perfect conditions to find peace. Focus on your own inner wisdom and let that be enough.

Concept 14: Choose Your Response

You can't always prevent the blow. But you can decide what you do next.

June 05

Free yourself from mental notifications. Reclaim your bandwidth for learning, and stop aimlessly wandering. The true distraction isn't just external noise, but people meandering with no purpose. You choose your response, and you direct your own course.

Life throws distractions at you all day. It's easy to get sidetracked, to get lost in other people's drama or mindless doomscrolling.

But you have a choice: you can either drift aimlessly or steer toward something meaningful. Choose to lean into curiosity. Choose to learn, to grow, and to focus on what truly matters. Every moment that you direct your energy counts. Ask yourself, "Am I wandering or working toward something real?" Choose wisely. Your life deserves it.

Your Takeaway

Your attention can be so easily hijacked by external distractions. Learn to turn inward and focus your energy on what really matters – yourself.

June 06

A clear mind stays clean, without leftover bitterness or regrets. It finishes its part fully, with honesty and calm. Realize this, and you'll find strength.

In the mind of someone who has consistently chosen to process and purify their thoughts – someone who's truly refined their inner values and beliefs – you won't find any toxic residue, no festering grudges, or corrupted morals. You won't carry baggage around, leave things half finished, or cling to things that no longer serve you.

There's power in choosing your internal responses carefully and processing your experiences in a way that leaves no room for bitterness or regret. It's about living a life so fully realized in each moment that when the final curtain falls, there are no loose ends or unplayed scenes.

That's the power of choosing how you respond, letting go of what poisons you, and showing up with integrity. When you live like that, you're ready for whatever comes with peace and pride.

Your Takeaway

When you've worked through your baggage, your mind will be honest and steady. No hidden agendas, no harmful attachments. You're fully present, fully responsible for your story.

June 07

Happiness comes from having your mind in the driver's seat. When a negative thought pops up, you don't have to wrestle with it, just notice it, and let it go. No drama, no anger, just a choice.

You can't always control what shows up in your mind, whether it's old habits, anxious thoughts, or the seeping negativity from those around you, but you get to choose how you respond.

The secret is that happiness is about who's running your mental show. If your inner guide – your inner wisdom, your truest self – is at the wheel, you can meet those old patterns with calm. This isn't about punishing yourself for old thoughts, it's about gentle but firm boundaries. When that familiar voice of worry, insecurity, or irritation pipes up, you don't have to fight it. Just notice it, acknowledge where it came from, and let it pass.

The more you practice this, the less those unhelpful impressions run the show. You're not a slave to your first reaction. You get to choose, every time.

Your Takeaway

Emotional reactions are frequently just echoes of past habits. By choosing your response, you assert direct control over your internal environment, effectively disarming and removing unhelpful thoughts and emotions before they can take root.

Reflect:

- What thought patterns or old habits keep showing up for you?

- How can you practice noticing them without reacting or judging yourself?

- What would change if you simply let them go, no drama, no struggle?

- Who do you want in charge of your mind: old habits or your true self?

Happiness isn't about having perfect thoughts and it's about choosing your response, again and again.

June 08

Don't let yourself get swept up in other people's emotional storms. Be kind, help where you can, but don't lose your perspective or start taking on their stress as your own.

Just because someone else is caught up in turmoil doesn't mean you have to join them. Your job isn't to dismiss their feelings, but to offer support *without* losing your own center.

This is about empathy with boundaries. Be there for your people. Help, listen, and care. But don't trick yourself into thinking every little setback is a world-ending tragedy. Remember what's truly important. You don't have to mimic their anxiety or outrage to prove you care.

When you're surrounded by drama, pause and ask yourself, "Am I helping, or am I absorbing stress that isn't mine? Am I remembering what's actually worth getting worked up over?" You can be present and compassionate without letting yourself spiral into chaos.

Choosing your response is about holding your ground, offering what you can, and keeping your sense of proportion, no matter how loud the noise gets. Keep your cool. Choose your response wisely. That's how you stay sane and in control.

Your Takeaway

You can show empathy for others without being swept up by their emotions. Show kindness, compassion, and understanding simply by showing up for those you love.

Reflect:

- Where in your life do you get swept up in other people's drama or urgency?

- How can you offer real support without taking on emotions that aren't yours to carry?

- What would it look like to stay steady and kind, instead of reactive or overwhelmed?

- Are you clear on the difference between empathy and enabling?

Empathy doesn't mean losing yourself. Choose your response, show up with care, but keep your center.

June 09

When life shakes your calm, learn to bounce back fast. Don't let the disruption steal your rhythm.

Life's going to present you with challenges in the form of stress, setbacks, and disruptions. When that happens, you'll feel shaken, off balance, and lost. The longer you let that disruption linger, the harder it is to stay steady.

What matters is how quickly you find your footing again. The more you practice getting back to your center, the stronger you become at holding your peace. Mastering this rhythm is your real power. When life rattles you, don't stay rattled. Choose to reset. Choose your response. Keep moving forward with steady calm.

Your Takeaway

Life will throw curveballs at you, but it's important to find your balance again. Each time you do, you'll become stronger, more resilient, and more in control.

June 10

You don't have to let every situation mess with your head. Things don't have power over your mind unless you give it to them. You can always choose silence and peace.

Not everything happening around you needs your opinion or your stress. You don't have to jump in and form a snap judgment or let your mind spin into overdrive. Things, events, people, and situations don't hold the power to shape your opinions on their own. You decide how to see things.

Choose your response. Decide what deserves your attention and what doesn't. Keep your mind clear and your focus sharp. That's how you stay in charge.

Your Takeaway

Your mind gives experiences meaning, whether good or bad. Keep your mind clear and don't let the world's noise pull you off balance.

June 11

Whenever something triggers you, pause and ask, "What is this really, and how long will it even matter?" Don't let temporary situations control your lasting peace.

Most of what rattles us in the moment won't matter a week from now, but in the heat of the moment, everything can feel like the end of the world.

Choosing your response starts with zooming out. Separate the facts from your feelings, and examine the situation. "What's really going on here? Is this actually a big deal, or is it just stressing me out right now? Does this have any real, lasting impact or is it just another blip in the day?"

By seeing things clearly, you get to decide how much energy to give them. You can acknowledge the feeling, but you don't have to hand over your peace. When you put things in perspective, you can respond thoughtfully instead of reacting impulsively. You're in control of how much power any moment has over your mood.

Your Takeaway

When faced with any situation or object, choose your response by not just reacting to the surface, but by understanding the root cause. Analyze what something truly *is* and how long it can genuinely impact you, rather than letting its immediate presence overwhelm your perception.

Reflect:

- What's one thing bothering you right now that probably won't matter tomorrow?

- How can you pause and break down the facts before you react?

- Where are you giving away too much energy to things that aren't built to last?

- What would shift if you chose your response based on what really matters, not just what's loudest?

You get to decide what's worth your energy. Pause, get perspective, and respond with intention.

June 12

Pain happens, physically or mentally, but your mind gets the final say on how much it takes over. You can choose to keep your head clear, no matter what's going on outside."

Pain is a part of life. Your body becomes tender, your heart aches, or your head pounds. Your body can sound the alarm, but your mind decides what to do with it. You get to choose how you relate to that pain.

When adversity hits, your first reaction might be that you can't handle it. Take a moment to pause and breathe deeply. The pain itself is real, but the story you build around it is up to you. You can let it become your whole world, or you can see it as just one part of your experience.

Choosing your response means refusing to let pain define you or your day. You don't have to label every discomfort as a disaster. Your thoughts, your desires, and your reactions are all under your control. The outside world can bring struggle, but nothing truly bad can get inside unless you open the door and invite it to stay.

Your mind is your sanctuary. Guard it. No matter what's happening out there, you get to choose peace, clarity, and how you move forward.

Your Takeaway

Pain is a negative input, but your mind has the power to preserve its own clarity and tranquility by refusing to play into it. You can choose your response by deciding not to assign pain ultimate power over your mental state.

Reflect:

- Where in your life are you letting pain write the whole story?

- What would change if you saw pain as an experience, not a definition?

- How can you practice keeping your mind steady when discomfort shows up?

- What's one response you can choose today that puts you back in the driver's seat?

You can't always control what happens, but you always choose how to meet it. That's your real superpower.

June 13

If someone wronged you, that's their issue, not yours. And maybe they didn't even mean it. So let your first thought be: "What virtue can I practice here?"

When someone hurts or offends you, it's on them, not you. But sometimes people mess up out of ignorance or confusion, not because they're trying to wrong you. Sometimes what feels like a personal attack is just someone fumbling, lost in their own mess.

Don't rush to assume the worst or carry the weight of their mistakes. Instead, keep your mind clear and your judgment fair. You can choose how you respond by not letting their actions steal your peace or your power. Let go of the need to fix what's out of your hands.

Focus on what *you* can own and change. That's real power. That's choosing your response.

Your Takeaway

Someone hurting you says more about them than it does about you. You can't control others, you can only control your reaction.

June 14

Carry yourself with intention, whether you're moving or still. Just like you check your appearance before a meeting, take care with how you show up in your whole body. Be authentic and do it naturally, not for show.

The way you hold yourself matters. Confidence isn't just about your words or mindset – your body language is broadcasting long before you open your mouth. Are you slouched and closed off, or are you present, grounded, and steady even when no one's watching?

Stand up straight. Move with purpose. Let your face and posture reflect the intelligence, calm, and self-respect present in your mind. Show up with presence, not just out of habit, but out of self-leadership.

Don't overthink it or make it a big production. This isn't about striking a power pose, it's about making sure your outer self matches your inner clarity. Let it be a matter of fact, a natural result of owning who you are and how you want to walk through the world.

Your Takeaway

Your physical presence should be stable and purposeful, serving as a non-verbal indicator of your focused mental state and reflecting your inner calm and intentionality.

Reflect:

- How are you showing up in your body when things get tough? Are you shrinking or standing tall?

- What small shift in your posture or presence could help you respond to stress more intentionally?

- Are you acting for approval, or for your own self-respect?

- What would it look like to let your actions, big and small, match the calm, focused energy you want to bring?

Remember: Choosing your response isn't just about your thoughts, it's how you carry yourself through every moment. Keep it intentional. Keep it authentic.

June 15

We're all connected, born to support each other, each playing a role in the bigger picture.

Ten Pillars of Inner Strength:

1. Understand Our *Interconnectedness*: We're all part of the same human network, designed to support each other. Don't let perceived slights break this fundamental connection.

2. Recognize Others' Programming: Observe how people behave, from their casual interactions to their core beliefs. Understand that their principles often constrain their choices, even when they seem proud of actions you might deem flawed.

3. Acknowledge Ignorance, Not Malice: Don't complain if someone acts correctly. If they do something wrong, it might be due to an error in their understanding due to ignorance. No one willingly chooses to be fundamentally unjust or unkind.

4. Check Your Own Code: You're not perfect. Even if you avoid certain transgressions, you still have the potential for them. Sometimes, it's just fear of consequences or reputational harm – not true virtue – that keeps you from making the same mistakes as others.

5. Avoid Snap Judgments: You can't be entirely sure of others' true intentions. Many actions serve a larger, unseen purpose.

6. Embrace Life's Brevity: When anger or impatience starts to take over, hit pause. Don't waste precious time on fleeting irritation.

7. Own Your Perceptions: It's not the actions of others that corrupt your inner peace, it's your interpretation of their actions. Anger

dissipates when you realize that external events can't shame or diminish you.

8. <u>Recognize the Cost of Anger:</u> The emotional toll of getting angry or upset often outweighs the initial event that triggered it. Your reaction causes more internal damage than the external stimulus.

9. <u>Deploy Authentic Kindness:</u> Genuine kindness is your most powerful defense against both those who are misguided and actual wrongdoers.

10. <u>A Reality Check:</u> It's illogical to expect 'bad actors' not to do wrong. To accept that they harm others, while expecting them not to harm you, is both self-centered and unrealistic. You choose your response to their inherent nature, not their behavior.

Your Takeaway

The way people act is often out of your hands, but how you respond is all you. We're wired to live and work together, to support and uplift, even if the world doesn't always play along. Life is short. Your peace of mind depends on *your* thoughts, not their behavior. At the end of the day, you can't expect everyone to behave correctly. That's just reality. But you can expect yourself to keep choosing your best response: calm, clear, and true to your values.

Reflect:

- Where do you find yourself losing your cool because of someone else's behavior?

- What could shift if you focused on responding with kindness and clarity, instead of frustration or flattery?

- Are you holding onto anger or resentment that isn't yours to carry?

- What's one way you can show up as your best self, even when others aren't?

Choosing your response is about owning your impact. Be steady, be kind, and let your presence change the room, not your reactions.

June 16

If it's not the right move, don't execute. If it's not the truth, don't broadcast it. Your impulses should be on your leash.

Just because you feel like doing something doesn't mean you should. You always have a choice. When you're tempted to cut corners, lash out, or say something just to win an argument, that's your moment to pause and check yourself. Doing the right thing isn't about being perfect, it's about having the courage to stop when your gut questions, "Is this true? Is this right?"

The truth is that your impulses will try to run the show. They'll tell you to act fast, clap back, or go along just to avoid awkwardness. But real power is hitting pause, even for a split second, and asking, "Is this the kind of person I want to be right now?" That's how you start choosing your response instead of being ruled by knee-jerk reactions.

You get to control the story you tell with your actions and words. You get to show up honestly, even when it's uncomfortable. That kind of control is your power. It keeps your life real, your relationships solid, and your mind clear. That's how trust gets built, within yourself and with everyone around you.

Your Takeaway

Just because you have the impulse to do something, doesn't mean you need to. You can turn away from reckless paths, and turn towards decisions that feel right. Pause and choose your response with intention.

Reflect:

- When was the last time you caught yourself before saying or doing something you'd regret?

- How can you practice hitting pause before acting on impulse?

- Are you letting your mood steer your choices, or are you in the driver's seat?

- What would it look like if you made integrity your baseline, not just your ideal?

Remember: You're not your first impulse, you're the one who gets to decide what happens next.

Concept 15: Take Responsibility for Your Life

This is your story. Own the pen.

June 17

You've been putting life off for too long, time's running out, and this moment won't come back.

How many chances have you let slip by? How often have you ignored the signals life's been sending?

The universe isn't waiting around forever, and neither is your time. You're part of something vast and powerful, but that doesn't mean you get unlimited do-overs. A deadline's set and your life's a ticking clock.

Stop waiting for some perfect moment. Stop delaying, take responsibility, and own your life. The only way forward is through action, starting today.

Your Takeaway

Stop procrastinating your life and use the time you have for something worthwhile.

June 18

Most people don't really get what it means to take action or make choices. It's not about what's on the surface, but about seeing the deeper meaning and owning it.

Just going through the motions – clocking in, running errands, keeping up appearances – doesn't mean you're actually living with intention. Real responsibility is about seeing past the surface and asking yourself, "What does this *really* mean for me, for others, and for the kind of life I want to create?

Own your role in the big picture. When you *steal*, are you taking from others' opportunities or your own integrity? When you *sow*, are you planting habits, ideas, or actions that will grow into something meaningful? When you *buy* or *keep peace*, are you investing in your values or just chasing convenience? When you *see what needs to be done*, are you stepping up or looking away?

Taking responsibility for your life isn't just about not messing up, it's about tuning into a deeper vision, the kind that asks, "Why am I making this choice? How does it line up with my values? What's the ripple effect here?" The real significance of your actions won't show up on your to-do list, it's in the meaning you give them and the ownership you take.

It's not about external validation or quick wins. It's about truly understanding your impact, owning your choices, and doing the work that aligns with who you want to be.

Your Takeaway

Taking responsibility means sharpening that deeper vision. Start paying attention to the impact behind the act. Whether you're building something, having a hard conversation, or just showing up, don't settle for surface-level living.

Reflect:

- Where are you just going through the motions instead of choosing with purpose?

- What's the real meaning behind the actions you take every day?

- How can you tune in to the deeper 'why' and step up your ownership?

- Are you ready to see your life with more honest, courageous vision?

Your choices have weight, if you're willing to see it and claim it. Step up and take the reins. This is your life, so own every move.

June 19

Think how much lighter life feels when you stop obsessing over what everyone else says or does, and just focus on your own choices: making them honest, good, and true.

Most of your stress doesn't come from your own actions, it comes from wasting mental energy on what everyone else is doing, saying, or plotting. You scroll, you gossip, you replay conversations in your head, and suddenly you're carrying around baggage that was never yours to begin with.

Taking real responsibility means redirecting all that attention back to your lane. Ask yourself, "Are my actions lining up with who I actually want to be?" When you keep your eyes on your own work, making your moves with integrity, clarity, and kindness, you get a taste of real freedom. You're not trapped by other people's drama or darkness. You don't have to rush yourself trying to please, react, or compete.

Don't let other people throw you off. You have your own race to run. The more you stay on your track, with purpose and steady steps, the more power and peace you'll find.

Your Takeaway

Don't let your attention get hijacked by the negative actions of others. This isn't about ignoring others entirely, but about reclaiming your mental space and directing your energy toward what you can truly control: your own integrity and impact.

Reflect:

- Where are you giving away your attention to things you can't control?

- How would your life feel if you focused only on your actions, not everyone else's?

- What's one way you can bring more honesty and intention to your choices today?

- Are you running your race, or letting others set your pace?

Step up, take the wheel, and let go of the noise. Responsibility starts with you, and that's where your freedom is found.

June 20

Trust the process, accept what life brings, and take ownership of how you respond to whatever appears on your path.

Consciously release your rigid expectations and allow the grand narrative of life to unfold as it will. This perspective means taking responsibility for engaging with your own story as it's written, rather than fighting against plot twists. Life hands out surprises, setbacks, and curveballs on its own timeline. You can fight it, complain, or wish it were different, but that just drains your energy and keeps you stuck. You're the main character, but you don't control the entire script. Your power lies in how you play your part.

This isn't about passive surrender. It's about radical acceptance: meeting life where it is and choosing your attitude, your words, and your actions in response. That's real responsibility. It's saying, "Whatever comes, I'll work with it. I'll make something out of it. I'm not a victim, I'm the author of my next move."

Your Takeaway

You don't get to choose everything that happens to you. Your power is in how you show up, adapt, and write your own response in every new moment.

Reflect:

- Where are you resisting reality instead of embracing what is and making your best move?

- What could shift if you stopped blaming circumstances and started owning your response?

- How would your life change if you trusted the process and focused on your power to choose?

- What's one thing you can accept and then take action on today?

You can't control the hand you're dealt, but you always control how you play it. That's your superpower. Use it.

June 21

Everything unfolds according to the laws of this universe. There's no alternate reality, no escape hatch. This is it, so own your part in it.

Every win, loss, progression, setback is part of the grand system we call universal nature. It's all connected and unfolding exactly as it's meant to.

You don't get to opt out and you don't get a redo. Responsibility starts with facing that truth. Instead of daydreaming about a perfect world for you, show up in *this one* and take charge of what's actually yours to shape: your mindset, your actions, and your impact.

When you stop imagining how things 'should' be and start engaging with how things *are*, you step into real power. You become a participant, not a bystander or a critic. Don't waste energy wishing for a different universe, take ownership of your role in this one. Own your part in that flow. That's real power.

Your Takeaway

This is your life, right here, right now, in the only reality that exists for you. You can't control every situation nor every outcome, but you can show up in your life in a way that matters.

Reflect:

- Are you waiting for life to be 'just right' before you take responsibility?

- What could you change if you fully accepted this moment as your starting point?

- How would you show up differently if you knew this was the only reality you'd ever get?

- What's one thing you can do today to own your part in your world?

No more 'someday' or 'somewhere else'. This is your universe, and it's time to own your place in it.

June 22

Wake up. Most of what's stressing you out is just a bad dream, don't let it control your reality. Get clear, take charge, and respond to life as it is, not as your fears make it out to be.

How many times have you lost sleep replaying some worst-case scenarios, only to realize it was all in your head? Most of our stress and anxiety are just stories we tell ourselves that aren't actually happening right now.

Responsibility starts with waking up to that. Sober up, snap out of autopilot, and get honest about what's really happening in your life. Escape from the mental fog of made up problems. You have the power to shake them off and choose a different story.

Every time you find yourself spiraling or getting lost in your worries, hit the mental reset. Ask, "Is this actually happening, or is it just fear dressed up as reality?" Reclaim your focus. Step back into your life, wide awake, and respond with intention instead of reactivity.

Your Takeaway

The anxieties that feel so real are just a projection. Wake up, and realize the problem you're facing is no more substantial than the one that haunted you in your sleep.

Reflect:

- What dreams or fears have been running the show in your life lately?

- How can you tell the difference between what's real and what's just mental noise?

- What would change if you showed up fully awake, right now, and owned your next move?

- Are you willing to let go of the old story and respond to what's actually in front of you?

You don't have to be ruled by yesterday's worries or tomorrow's fears. Wake up, take responsibility, and write your life: consciously, courageously, and in the present.

June 23

Don't get discouraged when you slip up. Keep coming back to what's right for you, not as a punishment, but as real self-care. Growth isn't about being perfect. It's about choosing again, because living with integrity actually feels good.

Sometimes sticking to your principles feels like trying to build muscle: you start strong, fall off, then pick it back up again. If you mess up or lose momentum, don't throw your hands up in frustration. That's just life and no one's perfect.

Responsibility means returning, again and again, to the practices and choices that bring out your best. Think of it like reaching for your favorite comfort after a rough day, not as punishment, but as relief, like putting on your favorite sweater after a storm.

Don't see self-discipline or growth as a chore. See it as coming home. Be genuinely content if the majority of your actions are aligned with your best self. You're allowed to fall down, but you're responsible for getting back up. Keep showing up for your life, because that's how habits are built and character is formed.

When you live with purpose and integrity, it doesn't just look good on paper: it feels good, deep down. Wisdom and wholeness aren't burdens, they're your natural state, and coming back to them is the ultimate self-respect.

Your Takeaway

Stop beating yourself up for mistakes. Take the time to reset and reconnect with your authentic self. If most of your moves are in the right direction, celebrate that.

Reflect:

- Where are you beating yourself up for not being perfect instead of starting again?

- What if every 'reset' was an act of self-care, not self-criticism?

- How does it feel to come back to your core values after drifting off course?

- Can you find joy in the process of returning, not just in getting it right?

Progress isn't a straight line. Take responsibility, keep coming back, and let the practice become your peace.

June 24

Respect the bigger picture, and respect the power inside of you. The same energy that drives the universe is running through you, so own it and act like it matters.

You're not just a bystander in life's big story. There's a force, a wisdom, a creative current behind everything. Everything out there moves to its rhythm, and so do you.

Your mind, your choices, and your inner drive aren't random. They're the instruments of that same universal power. When you ignore your own ability to choose, create, and respond, you're not just letting yourself down, you're missing your piece of the cosmic puzzle.

Taking responsibility means honoring your inner power. Treat your decisions, energy, and self-control with the same respect you'd give the most important job in the world. Your life isn't something happening to you, it's something you're helping shape, every single day.

When you do that, you can step fully into your role as the driver of your own journey. That's real responsibility and it's where your true power lies.

Your Takeaway

Respect the universal power that harnesses all of life, including you. Stop blaming outside forces. You're in charge of how you play your part.

Reflect:

- Where are you giving your power away in blaming, waiting, or playing small?

- How would your choices shift if you believed the same energy in the universe is in you?

- What's one area of your life where you can take back the wheel, starting now?

- Are you respecting your own mind and decisions, or treating them like they don't matter?

You are not powerless. You're a co-creator. Take responsibility for your piece of the universe and show up like it counts — because it does.

June 25

Some people won't show love or respect to those around them now, but crave validation from strangers in the future. This makes as much sense as being angry that people from past centuries didn't write you a thank-you card.

Why are we so concerned with being remembered by people we'll never meet, when we can't even give credit or kindness to the people right in front of us? Chasing approval from the future or wishing you had it from the past is just another way to dodge responsibility for your life *now*.

You can't control your legacy or rewrite history. All you really own is your presence, your choices, and how you treat the people sharing this moment with you. Want to live a life you're proud of? Focus on being real, respectful, and responsible *today*. That's where your actual power lives: not in someone's future speech or a history book, but in the impact you make, face-to-face, right here and now.

Stop giving away your energy to imagined fans and critics. Take responsibility for your actions and relationships in this life with these people. That's what matters. That's where real meaning lives.

Your Takeaway

The only approval that truly matters is the respect and integrity you show to the people around you today. Focus on living your life now, with honesty and purpose.

Reflect:

- Where are you chasing validation from people who aren't even in your life?

- Are you showing up for the people around you, or just dreaming about future recognition?

- How would your choices shift if you took full responsibility for your actions at this moment?

- What respect or appreciation can you give today, instead of waiting for someone else to hand it to you?

The past is over. The future is a mystery. Responsibility is lived in the present so don't waste it chasing shadows.

June 26

Struggling to get out of bed? Remember, showing up, contributing, and doing good is what you were made for. Hitting snooze is easy, but living with purpose is where your real energy comes from.

We all have mornings when staying in bed feels like being in the safest, warmest place on earth. Every muscle in your body says, "Just five more minutes." But rest is simply part of your survival. Every creature does it. What makes you *human* is the drive to get up and contribute, to bring something positive into the world, even when you don't feel like it.

Taking responsibility for your life means remembering you're here for more than just comfort. The fulfillment and pride you're craving comes from showing up and making a difference, not from hiding under the covers.

Next time you're tempted to drift back into dreamland, remind yourself that you weren't made to just exist, you were made to engage. Get up, do something meaningful, and watch your energy come back online. Responsibility isn't a burden, it's how you tap into your real power and your deepest joy.

Your Takeaway

Drag yourself out of bed not because you *have* to, but because it's who you are, and doing work that moves the world forward recharges you better than any extra hour under the covers ever could.

Reflect:

- What's your real reason for wanting to stay in bed: comfort, or fear of facing the day?

- When have you felt most alive: hiding from life or stepping into it?

- How could reminding yourself of your purpose help you take responsibility for your choices?

- What's one small action you can take today that aligns with your higher self, even if it's hard?

Don't sleep on your life. Wake up, step up, and give yourself the chance to feel proud of what you do, starting right now.

June 27

Either life has meaning and a bigger plan or it's all just random. Either way, blaming your circumstances or playing the victim gets you nowhere. Ask yourself: Are you living on autopilot, hiding out, or actually showing up as the real you?

You can't control every event, but you're 100% responsible for how you show up in response.

Responsibility means facing yourself, no excuses. When life gets messy or things feel unfair, ask yourself, "Am I acting with integrity? Am I living awake, or just drifting through my days? Am I blaming or stepping up? Am I letting myself slide into old habits, or am I choosing to stand up and do better?"

Your power is always in how you respond to the hand you're dealt. Instead of getting stuck in worry, regret, or finger-pointing, reclaim your agency, hold yourself to your own standard, and make the next right move.

Your Takeaway

Taking responsibility means actively engaging with your choices and ensuring that you're in alignment with your inner guide.

Reflect:

- Are you searching for someone or something to blame, or are you taking ownership of your choices?
- How would your life look if you stopped worrying about the big "why" and focused on who you're being, right now?
- What questions do you need to ask yourself to cut through your own excuses?
- What's one way you can show up more honestly, more awake, and more in charge today?

Life doesn't owe you answers. It invites you to step up, own your story, and be someone you're proud of, no matter what's happening around you.

June 28

Look beneath the surface to understand what really drives actions: pain, pleasure, death, and distraction. Everything means what you choose to make it mean.

Things aren't always what they seem at first glance. Take a moment to peel back the layers and see what's really going on. Investigate the true purpose behind your actions and the actions of others. Think deeply on the meaning of pain or pleasure, and the nature of death or fame.

When your mind feels scattered, remember: you're the only one behind your distractions. No one else is truly holding you back.

Everything is exactly as you choose to see it. Take responsibility for your choices, your triggers, your actions, and your attitude. By taking ownership of how you interpret your world, you change your view and your experience. That's what taking responsibility really means, that's the only way you turn things around.

Stop waiting for the perfect moment. Start here and now. Your life is yours to shape.

Your Takeaway

Everything in life is filtered through your perspective. Taking responsibility means owning your perspective, your reactions, your life. Face reality head-on. Own your power to choose how you take it.

Concept 16: Don't Procrastinate, Take Action Now

The moment is already here. What are you waiting for?

June 29

No matter how long you live, you only ever lose the present moment — and that moment is slipping away right now.

In the end, a long life and a short life come down to the same thing: the present moment slipping away. Every moment, no matter how many you have, passes the same way for everyone.

You can't lose the past, it's already behind you. You can't lose the future, it still awaits you. You can only lose the present moment, and it's disappearing with every second.

Why put off what matters? Stop waiting for some perfect time that doesn't exist. Take action *now*, because this moment is all you have, and it's all that counts. Start where you are, with what you have. That's how you win the life you want.

Your Takeaway

The only time you truly have is right now. Later isn't promised. Living fully means showing up for this moment, right now.

June 30

Life is ticking away, and your sharpness won't last forever, so act now, while your mind is clear.

Aging doesn't just wear down your body, it dulls your mind, your judgment, your clarity. That mental edge is your most valuable tool, and this means your chance to make good decisions, learn, and grow is limited.

There won't always be time to get your act together or figure things out. The clock's ticking on both your life and your ability to live it fully.

Don't procrastinate. Start now. Use your mind fully, make smart moves, and live consciously *today*. This moment is your power. Don't waste it.

Your Takeaway

The first thing that fades away isn't your body's functions. It's your ability to think clearly, to judge yourself honestly, to read the world as it truly is. You can't afford to wait for the perfect moment or delay what matters.

July 01

Be ready to act with purpose and for the greater good. Be ready to pivot if someone gives you a better, wiser path. Don't get stuck.

Procrastination is the silent killer of potential, and action beats overthinking every single time. When you see what needs to be done — especially if it helps someone, solves a problem, or pushes your community forward – do it.

First, act with a clear purpose. Your decisions should serve something bigger than your ego or convenience – they should genuinely benefit the people around you and contribute to the greater good.

Second, stay open. If someone calls you out or offers a better way, don't get defensive or cling to your pride. Be ready to pivot, but only if the new direction is truly fair and moves the collective forward.

This isn't about chasing likes or applause. It's about doing the right thing, at the right time, because you're committed to results that matter. The clock is ticking, and the only way forward is one move at a time, starting now.

Your Takeaway

Real action is about being bold *and* humble, moving with purpose, but being willing to shift gears if someone shows you a better way. If new information comes in or someone points out your blind spot, be mature enough to change direction. Pride is not your friend, progress is. Get moving now, with reason and humility as your guide.

Reflect:

- Where are you overthinking when you could just take the next right step?

- Who could you listen to, not just to defend yourself, but to genuinely get better?

- Are you willing to adjust your course if it means a more just or positive outcome?

- What action have you been putting off out of fear or need for approval?

Get moving. Adjust as you go. The world needs your action, not your hesitation.

July 02

Break big tasks into small actions, and don't let other people's stress or attitude knock you off track.

You'll never get things done by pushing through with brute force or stressing yourself out by overthinking. It's about showing up, breaking the job down into doable steps, and just starting.

The secret to taking action is to tackle things one piece at a time. Don't let overwhelm or other people's moods throw you off. It all gets easier when you stop looking at the mountain and just take the next step up the path.

Mastering the art of moving forward means staying cool, methodical, and steady, even if the people around you aren't. Keep your eye on the goal, take it step by step, and don't let anyone else's drama derail your progress. That's how you win, one calm, intentional move at a time.

And when someone around you becomes impatient, frustrated, or even angry? Don't let it infect your pace or your peace. Stay methodical. Handle what's in front of you. The only way to actually get anywhere is to do what you can, right now, with a clear head. That's how you build momentum, and that's how things change

Your Takeaway

Taking action isn't about rushing or reacting in panic. It's about breaking down what you need to do into manageable steps and handling each one with calm focus. When others lose their cool or throw shade, you don't mirror that energy, you rise above it.

Reflect:

- What's the 'mountain' you've been staring at instead of just taking the step on the path?

- How can you break your next action down into bite-sized steps?

- Are you letting other people's stress or impatience get in the way of your own progress?

- What would happen if you just started, calmly, step by step, right now?

Stop overthinking. Take action. Let momentum do the rest.

July 03

Complete whatever is your responsibility, without letting pointless distractions, social media, or other people's chaos interfere with your goals.

Every minute you spend getting sidetracked by things that don't matter – doomscrolling, chasing someone else's approval, worrying about what people are saying or doing – is a minute you lose from actually building the life you want. Most distractions are either mindless or senseless. You don't need to let their confusion become your confusion.

If you want to beat procrastination, you need to decide what's truly yours to do today, and put your energy there. When someone else gets lost in their own mess or starts spinning out, remember that you're not required to follow them.

Taking action is about discipline and clarity. You don't need permission, and you don't need to fix every mess around you. Keep your focus locked on your own mission and priorities.

Your Takeaway

You can't control the chaos around you, so why waste your energy on it? Stay locked in, act with purpose, and don't let anything that's off-course pull you away from your path. That's how you move fast and get real results: no wasted time, no procrastination.

Reflect:

- What's your #1 priority today and what's just background noise?

- Where are you letting other people's confusion or drama distract you from your real work?

- What would shift if you focused only on what's truly yours to do?

- How can you redirect your energy from distractions to action, starting now?

Don't waste your drive chasing every shiny object or fixing every storm. Handle your business, stay in your lane, and watch your momentum build.

July 04

You have everything you need to handle your life, right now, right where you are. You don't need anyone else's applause or a perfect resume to take action and live fully.

The world wants you to think you're always missing something: a new skill, more credentials, another follower, or a stamp of approval. But you're already wired with everything you need to start. You don't need to be famous or have everything figured out to make a real impact.

Nature made you whole. You have the ability to focus, act, and do good, without waiting for permission or perfection. Living well isn't about being on display or mastering every subject, it's about showing up, being true to yourself, and doing what matters.

Taking action means trusting you have enough right now to do the next right thing. You don't need every box checked before you begin. Fulfillment doesn't require flash, it takes intention, humility, and consistency. If you can be kind, self-sufficient, and committed to a purpose bigger than your ego, you're already winning.

Stop putting off what you know is yours to do because you think you're 'not ready'. Start now, with what you have, and let that be enough.

Your Takeaway

What really matters is being self-reliant, staying humble, keeping your focus on what benefits everyone, and living in tune with the deeper flow of things. Stop waiting for permission and start owning your space.

Reflect:

- Where are you holding back, waiting for someone to notice or approve before you act?

- What if living well was about your daily choices, not your highlight reel?

- How would your day change if you believed you already had enough to begin?

- What's one action you can take right now to serve your purpose, no matter who's watching?

Don't wait for perfect conditions or the perfect version of yourself. Your power is in what you choose to do *today*.

July 05

Focus on what matters right now, because wanting to be better tomorrow means you're delaying the good you could do today.

When you put your responsibility and growth off until 'tomorrow', you become stuck in a loop of postponing growth. You feel frustrated because deep down, you know you *should* be acting now, not waiting for some future version of yourself.

But tomorrow doesn't owe you anything. The only time you truly have is right now. Stop waiting for the perfect moment or the right mood. Get your hands dirty today, imperfect as it may be. Action beats intention every single time.

Don't delay becoming the person you want to be. Show up now.

Your Takeaway

Your future self depends on the choices you make in this moment. Stop procrastinating what's good for you.

July 06

Keep your mind clear and your actions sharp. Don't let busyness or the negativity of others dull you.

When you do things, do them with purpose. When you speak, be clear. When you think, focus. Keep your inner self stable and don't let it get scattered or shrink away from challenges. Don't confuse just being busy with actually being productive or truly living.

People will bring negativity or chaos into your life, like someone contaminating a clear spring, but that spring just keeps flowing, washing away the dirt without a trace. You can be that spring too – steady, pure, and strong – if you guard your self-reliance, kindness, simplicity, and integrity every hour of every day. That's how you remain unbreakable.

Keep your mind flowing clean and your heart open. That's how you keep moving forward, no matter what.

Your Takeaway

Get moving with intention, speak with clarity, and think with purpose. Own your power now.

July 07

Don't get sidetracked by things that don't actually matter for who you're meant to be. What makes you a good human isn't found in chasing the wrong things, it's in letting them go and focusing on what really counts.

Let go of what doesn't build your character, light you up, or help you serve. Too often, we waste time on things that have zero to do with what actually makes life meaningful.

The real goal is to live a good life.Let go of what doesn't build your character, light you up, or help you serve. Too often, we waste time on things that have zero to do with what actually makes life meaningful.

You don't diminish yourself by missing out on distractions, you actually become more yourself. If something isn't core to what it means to be human, courage, kindness, integrity, purpose, don't give it your energy.

The stronger, better version of you is the one who can let go of all that noise, who doesn't cling to the unnecessary or panic when it's taken away. Focus on what matters to your core – your growth, your values, your purpose – and take action there.

Your Takeaway

Don't procrastinate what's real by focusing on what's irrelevant. Every day you spend hustling for things that don't matter is a day you're not building the life that *does* matter. Sometimes being a better person is about what you walk away from, not what you add.

Reflect:

- What are you spending time on that doesn't actually grow you or anyone else?

- Are you chasing things just because others are or because they truly matter to you?

- What could you accomplish if you put your energy into what really matters for your growth, purpose, or well-being?

- Where can you let go of something unnecessary, so you can act now on what's important?

Focus on your essentials. Leave the rest. That's how you move forward and that's how you live fully, right now.

July 08

Stop searching for a list or definitions about what a good person should be, and just get out there and be one.

You don't need to read another think piece or listen to another podcast about what it means to be a good human. You already know the answer. The clock's ticking, and the people who actually make a difference are the ones who *act*.

Quit stalling. Enough with the hypotheticals and overanalyzing and get in the game. Show up with honesty, integrity, kindness, and courage. Hold a door open. Tell the truth when it's difficult. Listen with your full attention. Help someone, even if it's inconvenient. Being a good person isn't about theory, it's about doing the next right thing, right now.

Don't let your fear of imperfection or need for approval keep you from taking action. No more 'someday'. No more waiting for the perfect moment. You become the person you want to be by acting like it, today.

Your Takeaway

Talk doesn't build character, but actions do. Be the good person you claim to admire *right now*. The world doesn't need more takers, it needs doers.

Reflect:

- Where are you overthinking what it means to be good instead of just living it?

- What's one small action you can take *right now* that lines up with your values?

- How would your life change if you let your actions speak louder than your intentions?

- What are you waiting for?

Don't wait to talk yourself into being a good person. Just start. Be it. The world needs less theory and more good, starting right now.

July 09

Are you positively contributing to your society, your community, your network, your world? That's a win: don't forget it, and definitely don't stop doing it.

If you want to stop procrastinating and start living on purpose, shift your scoreboard. Don't measure your day by how many emails you cleared or how many boxes you checked, measure it by whether you left the world a little better than you found it.

Did you help, support, or uplift someone today? Did you take one action that added value beyond just yourself? Every time you contribute, you grow. You get stronger. You build the habit of taking action *now* instead of waiting for the perfect moment.

Taking real, meaningful action, especially when it serves the common good, isn't just a gift to others. It's of benefit to you, too. You're shaping your character, your reputation, and your impact, one choice at a time.

Don't overthink it. Don't put it off. Make "how can I help right now?" your daily starting point, and never stop checking in with that question.

Your Takeaway

Helping others contributes to your wellbeing as well. Keep moving, keep giving, and keep making a difference, because that's how you grow, thrive, and win.

Reflect:

- What did you do today that made someone else's load lighter or their day brighter?

- Are you measuring your success by action, or by overthinking and planning?

- How could focusing on service help you beat procrastination and move into action?

- What's one thing you can do *today*, no matter how small, that contributes to the common good?

Action for others is action for yourself. Keep moving. Keep serving. That's how you build a life that matters, one day at a time.

July 10

You don't have to wait for the future. You can live the life you want by focusing on what's right in front of you.

If you stop getting in your own way, you can actually live the way you want. Focus on what matters: living with honesty, fairness, and acceptance. Accept your life as it is because nature brought you here for a reason. Speak the truth. Act justly. Don't let other people's bad behavior, opinions, or your body's distractions stop you.

When you honor the wisdom inside you, you stop feeling like a stranger in your own life. You stop being surprised by what happens and start steering your own ship. So stop waiting. Start living your values today. That's how you become the person the universe expects you to be.

Your Takeaway

Stop putting off the progress you could be making today. Start living with integrity and purpose.

Concept 17: Live in the Present Moment

You can't breathe yesterday. You can't touch tomorrow. You only ever have now.

July 11

Let go of the mental clutter and focus on the now. Your lifespan is a micro-moment, your world a tiny blip. Prioritize the present, it's all you truly control.

Your mind loves to wander, replaying regrets or stressing over the future, but none of that lives in this moment. Life is happening now. Not yesterday, not tomorrow. Your real power is in the present, the only place where change and choice exist.

Ask yourself, "What can I do right now? How can I bring my full self to this moment?" Showing up fully builds the life you want. When you live in the present, you stop fighting what *is* and start moving with what *can be*.

Your Takeaway

The past and future slip away. You're only ever real in the present. Take time to center yourself where you are, and recognize what you can do to change your life.

July 12

When life gets heavy, remember this: everything happens according to nature, the wrongs of others aren't your burden, and this moment, right now, is all there is.

Key Principles for Resilience:

1. Universal Alignment: Recognize that everything that happens is part of a larger, natural order. Fighting it is futile, accepting it is liberation.

2. External vs. Internal: Understand that the 'wrong' done to you originates from someone else's internal state. Their actions cannot corrupt your character or inner peace unless you allow them to.

3. Timeless Patterns: Acknowledge that suffering and challenges are not unique to you or your time. They are universal, ever-present human experiences.

4. *Interconnectedness:* Remember our shared humanity. Despite our differences, we are all connected by a common intelligence, making empathy and understanding vital.

5. Inner Power: Affirm that your mind possesses a strong capacity for reason and choice, which is stronger than any external force or fleeting emotion.

6. Detachment from Possessions: Realize that nothing is truly 'yours' permanently. Possessions, relationships, and even your physical body are temporary. Detachment reduces the grip of loss.

7. Perception is Reality: Embrace the profound truth that your experience of reality is shaped by your interpretation. You have the power to choose how you perceive any event.

8. Live in the Now: Understand that the present moment is the only reality you ever truly possess or experience. The past is gone, the

future uncertain. Focus your energy and attention on what is directly in front of you.

In essence, this is a mental toolkit for navigating adversity by shifting focus from external events to internal resilience, ultimately fostering a sense of peace and purposeful living.

Breathe into now. Ground yourself in this moment. This is where your power lives, right here, right now.

Your Takeaway

You are more resilient than you think, and your peace is within your control, even when external circumstances are not. By understanding your place in the universe, your connection to humanity, and the power of your own perception, you can transform suffering into a path for inner strength and acceptance.

July 13

At this very moment, no matter where you are, you can choose to be content, to act with kindness, and to control your thoughts and what you let into your mind.

You have the power at this very moment to find deep contentment with your reality.

You can choose to act with integrity, treating everyone with fairness and respect without letting distractions or assumptions cloud your judgment.

You can train your mind to fully process information, ensuring nothing triggers or unsettles you before you've truly understood its context. Your mind is your gatekeeper. You get to decide what thoughts and feelings enter.

Living in the present means owning your thoughts, your actions, and your emotional state. Make this your daily default setting. That's how you unlock inner peace and resilience, regardless of the chaos around you.

Your Takeaway

You can decide to be present and find contentment in what's around you. Be kind in your actions. Stay curious and clear in your mind. Be fully present, because this moment is where your power lives.

July 14

Life is too short to stay stuck in the past or the future. Use your time wisely, stay clear-headed, and simply be in the here and now.

You've probably caught yourself spiraling over how someone treated you, or stressing out over what just happened. Freedom awaits when you stop making it personal. If someone's acting out, that reflects badly on them, not you.

Life's short, so why waste your time feeling frustrated? Instead, show up fully in the moment. Use your reason to steer you straight, act with fairness and clarity.

When you get a break, don't check out or act on autopilot: stay sober-minded, present, and intentional. That's how you squeeze the most out of this one and only life you have.

Your Takeaway

You need to maximize the present moment with clear thinking and action. Even in your downtime, stay grounded and don't let yourself get carried away by fleeting thoughts or distractions.

July 15

Everything flows and changes. Nothing lasts. Getting upset is just wasting energy on something that's already passed.

Life is like a river: always moving, never the same. What's happening right now is already slipping away, and no one knows for sure what's next.

Why bother spending your energy feeling angry, stressed, or upset? Remind yourself that this moment is all you have. Wouldn't you rather focus on what's in your control?

Breathe into it. Let go of what's gone and what's not here yet. When you live like this, the noise quiets, and peace steps in. That's how you stop wasting your life and chasing what can't be caught.

Your Takeaway

We are all on limited time. Let go of what bothers you and focus on what you can change.

July 16

Your body feels everything but can't judge. Your mind only truly cares about what it's doing right now, not the past or the future.

Think of your body like a sponge. It soaks up everything without any filtering and can't tell what matters or what doesn't.

Your mind, on the other hand, concentrates best on one thing at a time: whatever thought or task you're doing right now.

Worrying about the past or future is just distraction, what really counts is what you're doing at this very moment. Instead of scattering your energy across what's gone or what might be, bring your focus back to right now.

Living fully means giving your mind to what's in front of you, not being pulled by regrets or worries. This focus keeps you grounded, free from distraction, and able to act with clarity. Embrace the power of the present: this is where life happens, and where your true strength lies.

Your Takeaway

While your body can only react instinctually, your mind only truly cares about the activity it's focused on right now. Past actions and future plans are outside its immediate concern. Live fully and free by embracing the current moment.

July 17

Clear your mental cache. Stop letting external forces pull your strings.

Your mind can be distracted, yanked around by every passing thought or emotion, but you get to choose where your attention goes.

Shrink your focus to this very moment. Keep your focus on what's real and immediate. Recognize what's unfolding, whether it's your experience or someone else's. Deconstruct every situation into its root cause and core components. And finally, let go of past wrongs.

Master your mind by mastering the moment.

Your Takeaway

Living fully in the present means decluttering your mental space and keeping your attention locked on what genuinely counts.

July 18

Don't get overwhelmed by your whole life story. Focus on the task right in front of you; it's never unbearable when taken one moment at a time.

It's easy to get caught in an infinite scroll of worry when you start mentally reviewing your entire timeline: the past failures, future mistakes, and missed opportunities.

But none of that is relevant in this live moment. Focus on the task in your immediate view. Is there anything about this exact second that's truly unbearable? Probably not.

Remember, only this current snapshot of your life can really impact you. The past is offline, the future hasn't loaded yet.

Staying grounded in the present isn't always easy, but it's the only way to level up with courage and inner peace.

Your Takeaway

Disregard what's behind you or what hasn't happened yet. Take the present moment as it comes. If your mind starts to wander, challenge yourself to remain where you are.

July 19

Death is natural and comes for us all. In the big picture, no one's timeline is as important as we make it out to be.

The past is a black hole behind you, the future is a fog ahead, and you, right now, are just a blip in the middle.

Stressing yourself out about making every second count or struggling to leave a legacy behind can actually pull you out of the present. Don't get caught thinking you have to make your mark to matter. What makes life meaningful isn't about what everyone remembers. It's how you *show up* for the moment you're in, right now. Laugh, connect, be kind, and don't take yourself so seriously.

The bottom line is to stop overvaluing the length of your timeline. Focus on the quality, on living fully right here and now.

Your Takeaway

Live your life. We're all here for a blip and that's what makes *now* matter.

Reflect:

- Are you letting fear of 'not doing enough' keep you from enjoying what you have right now?

- Who are you comparing your life to and what does that really get you?

- If you knew your timeline didn't define your worth, how would you show up today?

- How can you let go of the pressure to 'make your life important' and just be present?

In the end, it's not about how much time you get. It's about how real you are with the time you have.

July 20

If you've truly paid attention to what's happening right now, you've already seen what the past held and what the future will bring, because it's all the same patterns in a new design.

The present moment holds the same raw ingredients as every moment that's ever happened, and every moment that will ever come. Everything meaningful that could possibly happen – human nature, struggle, loss, joy, growth, heartbreak, connection, healing, laughter – is right here, right now. The characters change, but the storylines are rewinding on a loop.

The real skill is staying present and centered, knowing the show's been on forever and will keep rolling long after we're done binge-watching.

Embrace that, and you'll start living in the moment that truly matters.

Next time you catch yourself getting lost in 'what was' or 'what could be', remind yourself that you already have everything you need to experience the fullness of life, right here, right now.

Your Takeaway

If you're searching for something new to finally make you whole or happy, you'll be waiting forever. Learn to 'wake up' to the patterns, lessons, and gifts already in front of you.

July 21

If you don't know where you are or what it all means, you can't know yourself or your purpose. Why chase the approval of people who are just as clueless?

Real power is about knowing where you are, why you're here, and living that truth, right here, right now. Everything else is just a distraction trying to steal your focus.

If you want real peace, be present. Don't just chase moments, *live* in them. Stop outsourcing your value to the crowd and start checking in with yourself. Ask yourself, "What's my purpose here? How can I tune into my true potential? What really matters to me in this moment?"

When you are present, you stop being a puppet for other people's expectations and start being the author of your own life.

Your Takeaway

Let go of who the crowd wants to see. Concentrate on who you're here to become.

July 22

Your life's a limited edition. Don't waste it wishing for a reprint.

Your lifespan isn't something you should resent or wish away. The time you've been given is enough if you live it fully and with intention.

Stop counting the years and start counting the moments you truly show up. Gratitude for your time frees you from fear and regret. Focus on this day, this hour, and this breath.

When you embrace your time, you unlock the power to live well, right now. Your power lies in how you cultivate your current season.

Your Takeaway

Accept that your life is fleeting and finite. Learn to delight with curiosity and wonder at whatever arises. Be present, savor every moment, act in alignment and live with intention.

Concept 18: Prepare for Adversity

You can't control what's coming, but you can train for it.

July 23

Every morning, mentally prepare for the digital noise and 'energy vampires' you'll encounter.

Start each day by reminding yourself that you'll encounter people who are pushy, ungrateful, harsh, deceptive, or selfish. They're often operating from a place of ignorance, not truly grasping what's beneficial or detrimental. They're lost in confusion, not evil by nature.

While they might test your patience, none of their words or actions can truly hurt you, because they can't corrupt your own inner integrity. Mentally prepping for the chaos in this way keeps your mind stable and your heart receptive, no matter what curveballs life throws.

Today, when the world feels harsh and people feel cruel, try to breathe in the connection. Hold space for their confusion, but don't lose your peace. Peace isn't about perfect people, it's about your choice to stay grounded when chaos tries to pull you under.

When you reflect tonight, ask yourself, "Did I remember the bigger picture? Did I keep my calm, even when it wasn't easy? Did I treat the hard moments as chances to practice kindness not anger?"

Your Takeaway

Life will test you by putting frustrating and rude people in your way. When someone pushes your buttons, remember that they can't poison your heart unless you let them. You're not just surviving the day, you're shaping how you show up in every challenge.

July 24

Pause and name what you're really facing: see it clearly, call it what it is, and break it down to the fundamentals. That's how you keep it real and stay objective.

Adversity loves to show up dressed in drama and confusion. It's overwhelming, uncontrollable, and almost irresistible. But don't let yourself get swept up in the story, stop and strip it down. Give it a name, describe it, and break it into its parts.

The more you can label what's actually happening, the less power stress or a setback has over you. Are you experiencing fear or disappointment during a difficult conversation? Or is it just your ego taking a hit?

Take action with an honest self-inventory. Naming your emotions and challenges helps you process them, moving you from reactivity to clarity and sharpening your objectivity. It helps you see things as they really are, not as your emotions or biases might color them. Ask yourself, "What's the real significance of this moment in the bigger picture? Will it matter in five years? Is this just one tiny scene in my much bigger story?"

Preparing for adversity means training your mind to stay clear and steady, no matter what comes your way. This honest, methodical approach is your best defense against being swept away by chaos or false impressions.

Your Takeaway

Whenever something catches your attention — an event, a feeling, a thought — take a moment to break it down. Strip it to its core, name it clearly, understand its parts and how they fit together.

July 25

Don't just have a mind, use it to own your life.

When you experience adversity in your life, what's your default response? Do you panic, freeze, or distract yourself for hours? Or do you pause, breathe, and let your mind do what it was built to do: solve, adapt, and get you through?

Your most powerful tool is your reason and ability to think, problem-solve, and step back from the chaos, yet it's so easy to disregard when you're in a stressful situation.

We spend so much time wishing for a different situation, a shortcut, or someone else to swoop in and save us. But if your reason is the edge you need when life throws a curveball. It'll give you the clarity to handle it, respond instead of react, and find your way through.

Next time adversity knocks on your door, check in with yourself. Are you using your head, or are you letting fear and frustration run wild? You have everything you need, you just need to use it.

Your Takeaway

You have an incredible ability to think clearly, anticipate challenges, and plan your moves, and yet sometimes it's easier to let distractions or emotions take the wheel. When you let your reason run the show, it'll be so much simpler to handle whatever life throws at you.

July 26

People will sometimes block your path, but your mind can turn those obstacles into new opportunities.

Being human means you're wired to do good and put up with people, even the difficult ones. Some days, people get in your way. They push back, complicate your plans, or test your patience. It feels like a roadblock, and it's tempting to get stuck in frustration or anger, but your mind is built to adapt. You don't have to smash through every barrier head-on.

Sometimes the smartest move is to pause, shift, and find a different path. You have the power to keep moving forward even when the way isn't clear, and it's a good chance to test your resilience, creativity, and calm under pressure.

This is the mindset that turns setbacks into stepping stones.

Your Takeaway

Your mind can bend, adapt, and turn any roadblock into fuel for your journey. That obstacle isn't a stop sign, it's a stepping stone. It can become part of your momentum, not a dead end.

July 27

The best way to light up your own day is to notice the shine in others, their hustle, their integrity, their kindness. Notice those qualities, and let them lift you up.

When adversity hits and life's weight feels heavy, it's all too easy to get tunnel vision. Everything is hard, you're all alone, and you'll never stop feeling this way, but this is just a story you tell yourself.

Instead of focusing on what's wrong, flip the script and examine the people around you. Who do you know that gets things done, no matter what? Who keeps it real, always stands for what's right, or steps up with kindness when no one else will?

This is about reminding yourself that you're not the only one fighting the good fight. When you see the good in others, you tap into real, living proof that resilience, integrity, and generosity *exist* and are contagious. It gives your brain something solid to hold onto when everything else feels shaky.

So when you need a boost, make a mental list of the people in your life who show up with strength. Maybe it's your friend who always listens, your coworker who never quits, or the neighbor who brings a smile even on demanding days. Let their strengths fuel you. Use their light to find your own.

Your Takeaway

Focusing on the positive qualities of the people around you can help take your mind off difficult experiences. Preparing for adversity isn't just about building your internal resilience, it's also about tapping into the collective strength and positive energy you see in others. Carry that inspiration with you.

Reflect:

- Who do you know that models resilience or kindness, especially under pressure?

- How can focusing on the strengths of others shift your own mindset during hard times?

- What quality do you admire most in your inner circle and how can you lean into it yourself?

- Are you letting the positive examples around you inspire you, or are you brushing them off?

You're not in this alone. Surround yourself both mentally and emotionally with real-life reminders that strength, goodness, and hope are closer than you think.

July 28

Pain comes in waves: some unbearable, some lasting. The mind stays calm by stepping back, keeping its center steady even when the body protests.

Pain can strike like a sudden attack: overwhelming and hard to counter. Sometimes it's so sharp that it knocks you down, while others are chronic, lingering but manageable.

The mind's true power is in stepping back, pulling away just enough to keep calm when the body's hurting. Your muscles might burn, your nerves might sting, and your head might ache, but that inner guide of yours doesn't have to break, even when the body protests loudly. You can learn to keep your mind and core steady.

Withdraw your focus. Find the calm within that can't be taken away. The hardest battles aren't just physical, they're the ones you win by holding steady inside.

Your Takeaway

When pain visits, whether fierce or persistent, remember that while you can't always control the body's shout, you *can* protect your peace and inner calm.

July 29

Chasing after what's never going to happen will make you miserable. Don't waste your energy trying to make people be something they aren't.

Beating your head against the wall hoping someone else is going to have a magical change of heart is a fast track to exhaustion and disappointment. There are some things in life that are just not in your control.

Preparing for adversity means learning to spot what's actually in your lane, and what's just a black hole for your energy. Wishing the world were different won't change reality. There will always be people who act out, cut corners, or stir the pot. Expecting them to do otherwise, without some serious personal transformation, is a setup for frustration.

So instead of chasing what's impossible, double down on what you *can* shift: your mindset, your boundaries, and your responses. Don't waste your power trying to fix people or situations that aren't ready or willing to change. Protect your peace, keep your standards, and invest your energy where it actually makes a difference.

Your Takeaway

If you want to stay grounded, focus on what's real and within your control. That's how you prepare for adversity, by mastering what's right in front of you.

Reflect:

- Where are you pouring energy into fixing the unfixable?

- What could happen if you focused on what you can control?

- How would it feel to stop expecting others to act outside their nature?

- How can you respond differently when someone's behavior lets you down, again?

You can't steer someone else's ship, but you're the captain of your own. Let the impossible go, and put your strength where it counts.

July 30

Your peace is found not in what you keep, but in what you can release.

Welcome challenges with grace. Don't stiffen up. Don't cling rigidly. Holding on tight only weighs you down. Letting go isn't a weakness. It's wisdom in action.

Acceptance isn't surrender, it's strength. It's knowing when to stand firm and when to let go, freeing your mind and heart from unnecessary struggle.

Prepare for adversity by practicing this balance every day. Gracious acceptance and easy release build resilience that carries you through whatever life brings.

Try this practice: Take what comes, make your peace with it, and then release it without drama.

Your Takeaway

Holding on to what you can't change only drags you down. Give in with acceptance of your situation. That's how you keep moving forward, even when the road is rough.

July 31

When the universe closes a door, it's not a punishment, it's a path forward that you just can't see yet.

Sometimes it feels like the universe just ghosts you. You show up, you put in the work, you try to do right by everyone, and you're still left hanging. Doors slam in your face, or you don't catch the break you were hoping for. It's easy to start spiraling: "Why me? Why now?"

But what if the challenge isn't a punishment, but an assignment? What if the silence is space to grow grit, resilience, or a new kind of wisdom? It's not about being chosen or forgotten. It's about learning to keep showing up with heart.

Adversity doesn't mean you're being neglected. Sometimes it's the universe's way of shaping you and sculpting a level of strength and clarity you can't develop when life is too easy. You don't have to like it, but you do have to own it.

The next time you feel overlooked, remind yourself: "Maybe this is happening *for* me, not *to* me." Remember, you're not out here by accident. Trust there's meaning in the mess, even if you can't see it yet. And keep moving forward, with or without the applause.

Your Takeaway

See adversity as an opportunity to examine your path. Maybe it's time to pivot or try something new, or maybe this difficult situation is a chance to build something stronger inside yourself before the next wave hits.

August 01

The choice isn't between what happens and what doesn't. The only choice is how you meet it.

In your life, you will face a variety of hard, inconvenient, and unavoidable situations. Everyone on this earth encounters frustrating moments that infuriate, anger, and sadden them.

But you don't have to be a doormat or just *take* what happens. You get to choose *how* you respond – that moment between event and reaction is your power zone.

Voluntary acceptance isn't about giving up or being passive. It's about owning your peace, even when the world demands otherwise. You can face whatever life throws your way with calm and dignity, rather than resistance and constant noise. That choice, this voluntary compliance, is your most powerful tool to meet adversity head-on and keep your internal peace undisturbed.

Next time adversity hits, remember that you don't have to be swept along. Steer your own ship.

Your Takeaway

Preparing for adversity means choosing acceptance. Not from a place of defeat, but from a position of inner power.

August 02

True peace is not the absence of external trouble, but the presence of a mind that is unassailable by it.

Life can throw you curveballs that come out of nowhere: layoffs, a breakup, illness, or interpersonal drama that you never saw coming. It can feel like the universe just picked you up and tossed you into chaos. But no matter the situation, you still have the power to protect your inner calm.

Whatever situation you find yourself in, ask yourself, "Is my soul in crisis because of what's really happening, or because of the story I'm telling myself? What's actually threatening my well-being, and what's just fear or frustration in disguise?"

No storm gets to decide your mood. The world can be overwhelming, but your real job is to keep your center steady and to choose not to become bitter, desperate, or self-pitying.

Wherever you are, whatever gets thrown your way, your challenge is the same: Can you meet this moment without losing yourself?

That's the real mark of resilience. That's how you prepare for adversity, by knowing your calm is yours to keep, no matter what chaos you're dropped in.

Your Takeaway

No matter what situation you find yourself in, you can still align with your center and maintain your inner calm. Own your reaction and stay steady no matter what life brings.

August 03

Don't waste energy on who's at fault. The universe isn't against you, and people aren't your enemies, they're just misguided.

People make mistakes, but it's rarely out of pure malice. People stumble because they don't know better or are caught up in their own struggles.

Preparing for adversity means letting go of blame altogether. Trying to find someone to blame only wastes your energy and steals your peace. When you stop pointing fingers, you free yourself from bitterness and frustration.

Shift your focus to what you *can* control, your response. Focus on understanding, patience, and finding your own steady ground amidst life's challenges. That's how you stay strong and clear-headed, no matter what unfolds.

Your Takeaway

When life throws adversity your way, don't get stuck in anger or blame. Accept that people are flawed and often act from ignorance, not intent to harm. Keep your mind clear and your heart open.

Concept 19: Reflect Daily on Your Actions

You can't grow what you don't examine.

August 04

Focus on your effort, not the outcome; speak your truth, not their expectations; and you'll find your happiness in the work itself.

Every single day, show up fully for the tasks right in front of you with clear thinking, steady focus, and kindness. Stay anchored in your values without getting pulled off-course by distractions, and be genuine through your words and actions.

Engage with what's happening without expectation or avoidance. Find satisfaction in knowing you're doing what's right, in line with your nature, and speak your truth with honesty and integrity.

Tonight, when you look back at your day, ask yourself:

● Did I act with intention?

● Was I kind and honest?

● Did I keep my spirit steady, no matter what came up?

If you can say yes to even one of those, you're on the right track. The good life isn't out there waiting, it's right here in how you show up for yourself, one choice at a time. No one can take that away from you.

Your Takeaway

If you can handle each moment with integrity without getting sidetracked, you're already living well. Your daily choices build your character.

August 05

The way you handle small obstacles is the blueprint for how you'll handle big ones. Live every detail with your highest purpose in mind.

Your core principles should always be equipped, refined, and ready for any challenge. You never know when you'll need to act, speak up, or make a choice that really counts. Are you operating from your best, or just reacting?

No matter how minor or low-stakes a task seems, bring your full focus to it. Every small moment is a chance to practice what you preach; every move you make connects your individual self with something expansive.

You can't truly excel without being fully engaged and prepared, understanding that your small actions are integral to a much larger game.

Your Takeaway

Keep your principles easily accessible in every moment, ready to guide how you move through the world, connect with others, and honor something bigger than just yourself.

Reflect:

- Am I showing up as the person I want to be, even in the chaos?

- Did I tap into something higher and not just hustle for myself?

- Are my actions making me proud, both on the human level and in the bigger scheme of things?

Success isn't just about what you do, it's about how you show up, again and again, with your best self at the ready.

August 06

The actions of others and the resulting outcomes are often predictable. Wishing for a different outcome is pointless.

People show you who they are, not who you wish they'd be. Expecting them to act outside their nature is a waste of time and energy. When someone acts *exactly* as they always have, exactly as you should've predicted, don't spiral or take it personally. Their actions reflect back on them, not on you.

Focus on showing up every day, on the actions you take to engage with life, and on the choices you make in every interaction.

Your Takeaway

Your actions and mindset are the only things truly within your control.

Reflect:

- Did I waste energy wishing reality was different?

- Did I accept what *is* and respond with clarity and peace?

Let people be who they are. You focus on being the kind of person *you* respect, one choice, one reaction at a time.

August 07

The mark of a life well-lived isn't about what you acquired, but how you behaved when no one was watching and how you treated people when they were at their worst.

Before you dive into the next item on your to-do list, pause. Ask yourself, "How have I shown up lately?" Have you honored the people who raised you? Spoken to your partner with patience? Showed up for your kids, your friends, your coworkers, and *yourself*, with presence and respect? Have your words built bridges or burned them? Have your actions made situations better or more difficult?

Reflect on all you've faced, the hardships you've endured, the challenges you've overcome. Recall the moments of grace: the times you chose kindness over anger, held steady through pleasure and pain, looked beyond status or insult, and responded with courtesy even to the discourteous.

Make this reflection a daily habit. It keeps you honest, humble, and focused on living a life worthy of the legacy you want to leave. That's how you honor your journey and grow wiser with every step.

Your Takeaway

Look back on how you've treated those around you. Show up today like the person you promised yourself you'd become, with a clear heart, a steady mind, and the courage to live aligned.

August 08

The first wave of emotion is not your fault, but the second one, which you build with your judgment, is entirely your responsibility.

Your rational mind shouldn't be swayed by every mood swing, stress flare-up, or random ache and pain. Feelings come and go like waves. Your body sends signals, flares that demand your attention. You can't control that, but your mind doesn't have to *judge* those feelings as good or bad. Next time your body or mind acts up, notice it, breathe, and let it pass through.

Keep that mindset sharp every day, and watch how your actions become clearer, steadier, and more intentional.

Your Takeaway

You get to choose what internal messages you answer and which ones you let fade out. You don't have to let temporary feelings control your actions.

Reflect:

- Did I let my mood drive the show today?

- Did I keep my hands on the wheel, noticing the weather but steering my own course?

Simple doesn't mean easy, but it *is* powerful. Keep practicing. The world, and your body, will always give you signals. Your job is to stay at the helm.

August 09

Do the right thing and push for it. If you hit a wall, your job isn't to break through but to find the next right thing to do.

Push to persuade others when the situation demands it, but don't wait for their approval to make your move. When you know what's right, don't hold back from speaking up or taking action even if others hesitate or push back. Justice isn't about waiting for permission.

This isn't giving up. It's mastering control over your reaction. Use the setback as your stage to show patience, humility, or wisdom. Remember, you approached with intention but also with flexibility. You never planned to force what's impossible.

Reflect daily on this balance between resolve and acceptance. It's the operating system for wise action.

Your Takeaway

Don't waste your energy fighting or grieving the roadblock. Shift gears with grace and acceptance.

Reflect:

- Did you do what was right, even when it was tough?

- Did you know when to push and when to let go without regret?

This balance is real success. You're growing not just in action but in character. And that's the win.

August 10

Your peace isn't an external reward, it's the internal echo of a life lived with integrity.

Sometimes, the world outside gets loud, messy, and exhausting. Step back and turn your focus inward. Your rational mind naturally finds peace when it knows it has acted justly. That calm, quiet satisfaction isn't something to chase outside yourself, it comes from within, from knowing you've done what's right.

Make it a daily habit to check in with yourself. Are your actions aligned with justice? Does your mind feel at ease because of them?

When you cultivate this inner harmony, external chaos loses its grip. Reflecting daily like this builds a steady foundation of peace that no circumstance can shake.

Your Takeaway

When you act justly, there's a natural peace that follows, not from others' approval, but from your own integrity.

Reflect:

- Did you act with integrity today?

- Are you at peace with the choices you made?

When your inner self is aligned and content, nothing outside can shake your calm. That's your sanctuary and your strength.

August 11

Don't confuse the difficulty of a journey with the impossibility of the destination. If the path exists for anyone, it can be paved by you.

If someone else has done it, it's not off-limits to you.

The goal might feel insurmountable. Maybe it's getting up earlier, speaking up at work, healing old wounds, or making it through a rough week. But before you tell yourself "that's just not for people like me," pause. Consider that others in the past have done it, and that means you can too.

Just because it's hard doesn't mean it's impossible. Don't let your brain trick you into thinking that you're an exception to the rule. When you hit those roadblocks, remember that your limits aren't fixed. They're just invitations to lean in, learn, and push through.

Every big win, every quiet act of courage, every tiny victory over resistance is proof it can be done.

Your Takeaway

Reflect on your actions every day. See where you can stretch yourself just a little bit more.

Reflect:

- Where did you talk yourself out of trying?

- Where did you forget you're built from the same raw material as anyone you admire?

Next time, instead of "I can't," try "How can I?" You're wired for growth. You're made for more. If it's humanly possible, it's humanly possible for you.

August 12

A million things have to go right inside you just for you to read this. The same is true for every moment in the world.

Think about your average day: your brain is juggling memories, to-do lists, and worries, while your body's digesting a meal, breathing, healing, and tapping its foot to a beat. That's just you, in one moment.

That same kind of nonstop, complex activity is happening across the entire universe, all in motion, all connected.

When you understand how much is going on inside *and* out in the world all at once, you realize just how small your daily struggles really are. It's a powerful reminder to stay grounded, to keep your focus on what you can control, and to reflect honestly on how your actions fit into this huge, moving whole.

You're part of a massive, unfolding story. Own your role, keep showing up, and check in with yourself every day, because every moment counts.

Your Takeaway

The complexities of your body and mind play out on a bigger scale in the universe around you. Recognize what's in your control and what you need to let go.

Reflect:

- What's moving inside you right now?

- What's moving outside, in the bigger world?

The universe is constantly in motion and so are you. Lean into that complexity. Instead of being shocked by how much there is to hold, see it as proof that you're part of something huge, alive, and always unfolding.

August 13

You are not an island, and trying to be one is an act of self-harm. Your true strength is found in the connections you make, not the ones you cut.

You were born as part of a bigger whole, connected, wired into society and life itself. When you disconnect by rejecting your role in the world and your community, you become out of sync, struggling, and incomplete.

You don't have to be alone. You have the power to choose to repair what's broken and reconnect yourself to the flow of life and community. No matter how many times you've drifted, you can come home to yourself and your people, whenever you decide.

Ask yourself, "Am I cutting myself off? Or am I actively choosing to be part of something bigger, showing up with humility and connection?"

That's where real strength and purpose live.

Your Takeaway

We're designed for connection, not isolation. Even when you burn bridges, you always have the option to rebuild new ones.

Reflect:

- When was the last time you reached out, even a little?

- What simple action could help you reconnect, with yourself, with others, or with the bigger world?

It's never too late. You're built for belonging. That's the daily challenge: reflect, reach out, and give yourself permission to come back to the circle.

August 14

Before you can teach the world, you must be a student of it.

Real leadership starts with humility. You can't step up as a leader until you've learned how to follow, listen, absorb, and respect what comes before you.

Life works the same way. Before you can guide others, you need to be humble enough to walk behind, to absorb lessons, and to build your foundation. Each role, leader or follower, is part of growth.

Reflect daily on where you stand. Are you open to learning, even if it means stepping back? Are you ready to lead when your time comes?

This awareness keeps you grounded, patient, and prepared. Leadership isn't a title, it's a journey. Every day offers a chance to move forward on that path.

Your Takeaway

Being open to guidance is the foundation of growing into someone others want to follow. Choose to follow before you decide to lead.

Reflect:

- Where have you been a good follower?

- Have you taken the time to learn from those who came before?

- Are you ready to lead with humility in your heart?

Leadership isn't about authority, it's about service, example, and the willingness to keep learning. That mindset is real power.

August 15

Your internal locus of control can be far more powerful than the emotions and impulses that usually disturb you. What's running in your head right now? Is it self-doubt, fear, mistrust, or desire? Tune into your core strength to override that autopilot.

Inside you lies a force stronger than the fleeting passions that yank you like a puppet on strings. Whether it's fear, whispering doubts, mistrust clouding your vision, or desire pulling you toward something fleeting, you can overcome them all by developing an internal locus of control.

Start by being honest with yourself and naming what has the strongest hold on you at this moment. This reflection helps you take back control instead of being swept away. Each day, check in with your mind. Notice what's driving your actions. This simple practice keeps you grounded, free, and aligned with your highest self. Reflect daily, it's how you grow stronger and wiser with every choice.

Your Takeaway

Give your inner core the overruling control in every situation. Stay steady, clear, and strong.

Reflect:

● What's really running the show in your mind?

● Is it fear making you hesitate? Mistrust closing you off? Desire pulling you off course?

Naming these feelings gives you a chance to step back and say, "Hey, I see you. But you don't have to control me."

That awareness is your freedom. Your ability to be the boss of your own mind, not a puppet to fleeting emotions.

Today, practice catching those strings and gently choosing which ones you let guide you.

Concept 20: Maintain an Attitude of Gratitude

Gratitude isn't about ignoring struggle, it's how you survive it with grace.

August 16

The world doesn't happen to you, it happens with you. Find your peace in being a willing participant.

Everything around you – the ups, the downs, the twists and turns – are woven together by a grand design, a fate that guides even fortune itself.

You're not separate from this vast, interconnected whole, you're part of it. What's good for the whole universe is good for you, even if it comes through change, loss, or challenges.

Make peace with this truth. Let it guide you every day. Stop chasing endless knowledge or distractions that leave you restless. Be content not because life is easy but because you see the big picture. Be grateful not only for the sweet moments but for the difficult ones that make you grow.

When you do, you won't end life grumbling or wishing for more. You'll finish with calm, with true serenity, and with a heart full of thanks to the world that carried you.

Your Takeaway

Drop the endless need for answers in books or other people. Cultivate gratitude for the life you have and the chance to be part of something greater.

August 17

Your best life isn't a collection of things you've won, but the unshakable contentment that comes from knowing you've lived with integrity.

The true measure of a well-lived life is not found in the accumulation of external victories, nor in wealth, fame, or power, but in the enduring peace of a well-formed character. Nothing outside of you can match the quiet power of a soul that's aligned.

A person's greatest achievement is a rational mind that has found its self-sufficiency, that remains tranquil and steady not because of fortunate circumstances, but because it is anchored in virtue.

This peace is the natural result of acting with justice, honesty, moderation, and courage, and of accepting with grace what is beyond your control.

Nothing material can rival the satisfaction of an upright conscience. The only rational choice is to commit yourself fully to this inner path, making room for nothing else.

Live a life where your happiness is not a fragile thing dependent on the world's approval, but an unshakable contentment built on the solid ground of your own integrity.

Your Takeaway

There is nothing better in this world than showing up with integrity, staying grounded in reason, and facing life with courage. That's gratitude in action, honoring what's already been given to you.

August 18

The clock in your head is a human invention. The only real timing is the universe's, and it's always right on schedule.

How often do we fight what *is* simply because it's not what we *wanted?*

Your personal pains and successes are not random occurrences, but rather a simple part of nature's rhythm. The path to true peace lies in ceasing to fight against reality and instead aligning yourself with it completely. It means trusting that every event, no matter how chaotic it seems, is unfolding in its own perfect and necessary time.

Don't waste your energy trying to control the world or by complaining about the hand you're dealt. Instead, find your sense of belonging, not in a team, country, or title, but in the grand, rational whole of the universe itself.

Embrace this cosmic citizenship, and you will find a serene acceptance that makes you feel at home wherever you are and with whatever is.

Your Takeaway

Whatever shows up in your life isn't random. Find gratitude in the sense of belonging to the world.

August 19

The highest form of giving is when you forget you ever gave.

Some people approach good deeds like a transaction, tallying up favors and expecting a return on investment. Others might not explicitly ask for payment, but they still hold onto a mental scoreboard, subtly feeling entitled to recognition or reciprocation.

But the people who perform acts of kindness without seeking validation or keeping a digital or mental log simply flow onto the next opportunity to help. That's the ultimate aspiration: to be someone whose giving is as natural as breathing, not fueled by likes, shares, or applause.

While our culture often celebrates those who publicize their good deeds and crave external validation, missing this deeper truth traps you in a transactional mindset that ultimately caps your capacity for true generosity. Embracing this doesn't mean you stop making a positive impact or disengage from your community. It means you contribute with an unburdened heart, free from hidden agendas or expectations.

Genuine fulfillment blossoms when your actions are an authentic expression of who you are, rather than a strategy to gain something in return.

Your Takeaway

Real gratitude means you do good and you let it go. When gratitude is your posture, goodness becomes your rhythm.

Reflect:

- Would you still show up with kindness if no one noticed?

- Would you still give if there was no "thank you"?

That's the kind of quiet, steady integrity that changes the world, one unrecorded act at a time.

August 20

When everything external is temporary and out of your hands, the only real work is building a character you can be proud of until the end.

In our modern world of endless stimulation and digital legacies, it's easy to get lost in the pursuit of what is fleeting. But the things we chase — money, pleasure, status – captivate our attention for a moment, then fade into irrelevance. It can feel like integrity and kindness have been replaced by a culture of constant outrage and self-promotion.

When every external measure of success feels hollow and our own perceptions are unreliable, the answer is not to despair, but to calmly accept that your life is finite and your control is limited.

Your purpose is simple and powerful: live in harmony with the natural order, contribute positively to your community, and practice the discipline of enduring what you must and abstaining from what you should.

The only things that truly matter are the things you can control: your own actions, judgments, and character. Bearing and forbearing with grace is the real legacy.

Your Takeaway

What matters is how you *show up* in the time you've been given. Be grateful for the life you have and be just, honest, and kind.

August 21

Your gratitude for others is a light you shine on them that also brightens your own path.

When life feels heavy, don't spiral. Turn your attention to the good in the people around you. Who do you know that shows up with integrity? Who's quietly generous? Who keeps going, keeps caring, keeps *trying*, even when no one's paying attention?

There's nothing more uplifting than seeing these virtues shining in those you care about, especially when they come together like a chorus of goodness.

Keep these qualities front and center in your mind. Let their strength remind you of your own. Let their virtues pull you back into hope. Let them remind you that goodness isn't just possible, it's alive and well in the world you're part of.

If you keep your heart tuned to what's right in the people around you, you'll always find a reason to smile. Even in the dark, someone's light is shining. Notice it. Name it. Give thanks for it. Gratitude doesn't have to be grand. Sometimes it's just recognizing the effort.

Your Takeaway

Gratitude grows when you celebrate the light in others, and it's one of the surest ways to brighten your own heart.

August 22

Appreciate your life, but don't cling to it. Your happiness is an open hand, not a clenched fist. Treasure your blessings enough to enjoy them, but not so much that their absence would break you.

Instead of chasing what you don't have, look closely at what's already in your life, those things and people you're truly lucky to have. Remember how much you'd long for them if they were gone. That kind of gratitude grounds you in what's real and precious right now. But don't let your appreciation turn into attachment that leaves you vulnerable to pain. Be grateful, but don't get too attached. Enjoy what you have, love it fully, but keep your heart steady so that if they slip away someday, you won't be crushed.

Gratitude isn't about clinging on, it's about celebrating with calm, knowing everything changes. That balance, that steady thankfulness, is a cornerstone of lasting peace.

Your Takeaway

It's easy to look where the grass is greener and to miss what's right in front of you. Gratitude is about seeing things clearly and appreciating what you have.

August 23

When someone disappoints you, ask yourself what they value, not what you expected. Their actions are just the sum of their beliefs.

To achieve true peace in your interactions with others, the first question you must ask yourself is not about what you expected, but about what they truly value.

If you understand that someone operates from a worldview where their self-worth is tied to praise or their primary motivation is money or comfort, then their actions become entirely predictable.

You won't be surprised or personally offended when they chase validation or prioritize a paycheck over integrity, because you'll recognize their behavior is simply the inevitable outcome of their deeply held beliefs. By viewing their actions not as a malicious attack but as the logical sum of their beliefs, you can respond with compassion or a calm indifference, rather than with anger or resentment.

Be grateful that life's taught you to value integrity, not applause. Peace, not chaos. Truth, not ego.

Your Takeaway

Choose perspective over offense and understanding over judgement. Be thankful you see it differently.

August 24

Peace isn't a place you arrive at, it's the posture you hold in this moment, with a clear mind, a kind heart, and open hands.

The blueprint for a truly good life is a simple, repeatable practice that you can engage in every single moment.

First, it begins with the discipline of thinking clearly, checking your assumptions and ensuring your judgments about the world are based on reality, not on the knee-jerk emotional reactions that cause so much stress.

Second, this clarity then informs your actions, which should be aimed at making a positive impact on your community and serving a purpose beyond yourself.

Third and finally, you find your deepest peace by practicing a willing acceptance of everything that happens, not as passive resignation, but as an active choice to let go of what you cannot control.

By focusing on these three internal choices in the present moment, you stop chasing happiness in external outcomes and discover a powerful and unshakable tranquility that is always within your reach.

Your Takeaway

Gratitude is learning to work with what you have, regardless of the situation. The good life is already in your hands when you choose truth, service, and radical acceptance.

August 25

Expecting everyone to be a good person is like being mad at a rainstorm for being wet. The flaw is in your expectation, not in the event.

To find peace in an unpredictable world, you must first stop being surprised by human flaws.

In a global community of billions, the existence of selfish, dishonest, or thoughtless people is an undeniable certainty. It's unrealistic to hold onto the expectation that they don't exist.

The greatest harm in any negative interaction is not what these people can do to you, but the anger and stress that you choose to inflict upon yourself in response. Your job is to hold yourself accountable for your own judgment.

True good is its own reward. When you act with kindness, you are fulfilling your own nature. The tranquility you seek comes from a commitment to doing what is right for its own sake, managing your expectations of others, and finding your ultimate fulfillment in the integrity of your own actions.

Your Takeaway

A mind that's cultivated gratitude sees clearly. Recognize that you have the inner tools of kindness, patience, and forgiveness. You can handle what shows up and still choose to do good even when others don't.

August 26

Stop worrying about what lasts, and start living like everything you have is fuel for the fire you're building.

The key to finding peace in a chaotic world is to first gain perspective on our own fleeting existence. Once a moment is gone, it is gone forever, and all the things we worry about will become just as insignificant. So why waste your limited time being consumed by anxiety? View every setback, challenge, and opportunity not as a burden, but as raw material.

Everything you experience – this breath, this interaction, this opportunity – is all a gift, and gratitude is how you turn fleeting seconds into something sacred.

Cultivate a mindset like a strong furnace that can take in everything that's thrown into it, good or bad, and use it to create more light and heat. Your job is to stay grounded, process every experience with reason, and use it all to fuel your personal growth and purpose until the end. Take today and burn bright.

Your Takeaway

Be like a fire that turns everything it's given into light. Be thankful not just for what's going *right*, but for the chance to keep becoming the person you're proud to be, right here, right now.

August 27

Live with a purpose, trust the process, and remember that from a high enough altitude, all the things you're worried about look like a speck.

To live a good life, you must constantly keep three points in mind.

First, live with an unwavering sense of purpose and integrity, knowing that your actions are the only thing you truly control. When it comes to the world's events, whether you believe they are random chance or part of a grand design, your role remains the same: to accept them without complaint.

Second, regularly remind yourself of your own temporary nature. You began as a single cell and will end with a final breath. This awareness strips away vanity and helps you focus on what truly matters.

Third, take a mental step back and gain perspective. Imagine looking down from a satellite at the endless cycle of human life, from interpersonal dramas to workplace worries. From that vantage point, all our worries and ambitions appear singularly unimpressive.

By focusing on your character, accepting what you can't change, and consistently zooming out on life's trivialities, you can live with both purpose and tranquility.

Your Takeaway

Align your actions with your values, show up with purpose and accept what's outside your control. Walk with intention, let go of the noise, and give thanks.

Concept 21: Contemplate Impermanence Regularly

Everything changes. Remember that and you'll suffer less, love deeper, and live freer.

August 28

Stop chasing trends that expire and praise that fades. The only thing you need to understand is that everything is temporary, and your peace is the only prize that isn't.

When you stop idolizing what fades, you start grounding yourself in what lasts. Your character, your choices, your connection to something deeper.

Our rational mind is the only reliable tool we have to cut through this noise and see things for what they truly are. It's the faculty that can fact-check the value of online validation, realizing that it comes from a crowd whose opinions are as temporary as their attention spans. It's the tool that allows us to see death not as a terrifying end but as a natural part of the cycle, akin to the change of seasons, of day becoming night, and the motion of breath, inhaling and exhaling.

Today, instead of just recognizing that life is short, feel it. Let that truth sharpen your priorities,soften your ego, and wake you up to what actually matters.

Your Takeaway

By cultivating a clear mental state, free of false beliefs and external anxiety, we can find a profound and peaceful connection to the rhythm of the universe and live a life of genuine purpose.

August 29

Your title doesn't exempt you from the finish line, and your fear won't change the outcome.

To find peace with your own mortality, you must first accept that death is the great equalizer. No title, no intellect, and no impact grants you immunity from impermanence. You're not here to outlive everyone, you're here to live well while you're here.

Your body is just a temporary vehicle, a collection of cells and systems, while your consciousness is the superior part of you. Death is a form of liberation, freeing your mind from the pains, pleasures, and anxieties of the mortal world. By understanding and accepting this, you can live your life free from the fear of its end.

Your Takeaway

Your accomplishments, status, or knowledge are ultimately irrelevant to the end of your life. Your job is not to cling, nor to fear, but to walk your path with clarity, integrity, and peace.

August 30

Stop fighting the tide. Be a wave that rides the current with purpose, and when you crash on the shore, be thankful for the journey.

No one escapes the turn of time. Your life is a fleeting chapter in a vast history, a rapid sequence of arrivals and departures among people you know and love. From a single cell to dust, our physical existence is a brief and fragile biological process.

You're not here to beat time, nor to waste it chasing legacies or stressing over things that won't last. You're here to *honor* it, to live fully in the moment you've been given with honor and integrity.

When your time comes, may you take your leave with a sense of peaceful completion, like the last light of a sunset, grateful for the day that was given and serene in its fading.

Your Takeaway

Real power isn't in outlasting death, it's in living the days you do have with honesty and kindness. This moment is all we truly have.

August 31

Don't let a bad moment become a bad hour. The irritant has already expired, but your reaction is still running.

Reality is a constant data stream, its activities ceaselessly changing and its causes too complex to count. It's almost impossible to find stability in this world of constant flux. The past is a vast, unsearchable archive, and the future is a yawning void where everything will eventually be consumed. Current events rise and fall, people come and go, and emotions pass through us all like the ever-changing weather.

In this context, it's pointless to get angry or stressed out over a bad email, a traffic jam, or a rude social media comment. The moment you were upset about has already been swept away.

By internalizing this truth, you can free yourself from the emotional churn of a world that is always changing and find a lasting sense of inner peace. Nothing stays the same, except for the way you choose to show up.

Your Takeaway

Life doesn't stand still, not for you, not for anyone. The moment you're in is already gone. Meet this moment not with resistance, but with grace.

September 01

Don't get attached to the scrolling feed. Your life is just as temporary as a passing post, and what you're chasing will be obsolete tomorrow.

Life is a blur. You're standing in a stream where nothing stays still, not even for a second. That new opportunity is already changing. That moment you wanted to hold on to is already gone. Everything is in flux, so why get attached like it's going to stay? Loving what's here is beautiful. Clinging to it is where the suffering starts.

Trying to own a moment is like trying to hold on to a sparrow mid-flight. It was never yours. It just passed through. Think about your breath. You borrowed it yesterday. You'll return it tomorrow. This whole life is a sacred inhale, and one day, a final exhale.

Live like you know nothing is permanent. Don't grasp. Don't cling. Let life move through you like wind through an open window.

What matters is not how long you hold something, but how fully you show up while it's here. That's the path to peace amid constant change.

Your Takeaway

Clinging to the impermanence of life will not bring you happiness. Learn to let go and move through life, fully present no matter what happens.

September 02

Don't be afraid to turn the page. The story can't get to the good parts if you keep rereading the same chapter.

Change is not a force to be feared, but the very engine that drives all of existence. Without it, nothing worthwhile could ever happen. You can't get a nourishing meal unless the ingredients change and are prepared. You can't grow a beautiful garden unless the seeds change and break open.

The personal transformations you face, whether they feel like a loss or a gain, are not isolated events. They are part of the same natural, necessary cycle that gives us the changing seasons and the growth of all living things.

Pause. Breathe. This too is nature doing what nature does. You're not being punished. You're being invited to evolve. Today, stop resisting the shift. Lean in. Let it carry you somewhere new.

Your Takeaway

Change isn't chaos, it's choreography. When life shifts under your feet, when something ends, falls apart, or shows up unexpectedly, don't panic.

September 03

The applause is a fleeting echo; the character you build is the only song that lasts.

To find tranquility, continually remind yourself that everything is temporary. Look past the surface of things and consider the inevitable decay and fragility of everyone and everything.

The most celebrated pop star will one day be a forgotten name, and the person who remembers them will also eventually be gone. This pursuit of fame and external validation is futile.

On this tiny planet, people don't even agree with each other, and often contradict themselves. The whole earth is no more than a speck in the universe, and all our striving, conflicts, and fleeting moments of glory are happening on an infinitesimally small stage.

By internalizing the impermanence of all things and viewing your life from a *cosmic perspective*, you can free yourself from the anxieties and ego-driven pursuits that dominate so much of your time.

Your Takeaway

Everything eventually disappears: the achievements we praise, the people who praise them, and the legacy you hope to leave behind. Live in the present, with the honest character of who you are.

September 04

Stop fighting the script. The universe is either a perfect design or a continuous improvisation, but from your vantage point, it's all the same. Your only job is to be the actor who doesn't forget their lines.

Every experience – joy, loss, victory, heartbreak – has been lived before. Different faces, different names, same old dance.

To find peace, you must first accept that the events of the universe are either part of a benevolent design or an unbreakable chain of cause and effect. Regardless of which you believe, the conclusion is the same: worrying is a useless endeavor. We will all one day return to the earth, and even the greatest mountains and oldest forests will eventually be swept away in the endless cycles of nature.

The only thing you can truly control is your internal response, your own composure and reason. When you put your fleeting anxieties, your grudges, and your pursuit of fame against this vast backdrop of time and change, you will see them for what they are: utterly unworthy of your attention. By embracing this truth, you can find a deep, unshakeable peace.

Your Takeaway

You're part of a universe that's always shifting. Instead of clinging to permanence, live *aware* of impermanence. Once you stop trying to make everything last forever, you'll finally start living fully in what's here, right now.

September 05

You can't hold on to a handful of water. The wisdom is in enjoying the flow, not in trying to possess it.

Nothing you see is frozen in time. Coffee cools, mountains crumble, bodies age, and careers come to a close. Everything is already in the process of breaking down, shifting, moving toward its end. Change and decay aren't exceptions, they're built into the very fabric of existence. Everything that comes into being is already on its way out.

This isn't cause for panic. It's your *invitation* to wake up. To love what's here now. To show up while it still matters. To loosen your grip and trust that this cycle of becoming and undoing is nature's rhythm, not a glitch. Next time something slips away, don't cling. Bow to the law of impermanence and then move forward, lighter and more alive.

Contemplating impermanence like this grounds you in reality and frees you to live fully right now.

Your Takeaway

Life doesn't wait. It doesn't ask for permission to change. This isn't a cause for despair, it's the natural rhythm of life. When you keep this truth in mind, you start to let go of clinging to things that won't last. You begin to live lighter and appreciate the moment without grasping.

September 06

Don't let the fear of a final chapter keep you from appreciating the story.

You don't get to keep anything forever. Not your loved ones. Not your moments. Not even your breath. When you hug your partner, your friend, your child, keep in mind how precious it is. When you sit at the dinner table, or hear laughter in the next room, or watch someone sleeping peacefully, don't disregard it. This moment isn't promised. That's why it's sacred.

Just as we accept that a beautiful flower must eventually wilt, we must accept that every human life has a natural end. By consciously preparing your mind for the possibility of loss, you are not loving less, you are building the resilience to face tragedy with grace.

The goal is to be fully present and loving in the moment, free from the anxiety of clinging to what cannot be held. This practice allows you to cherish your time with loved ones more deeply and find inner peace in the face of life's inevitable changes.

Your Takeaway

To find tranquility, you must first accept that everything is temporary, whether it's your life or that of a loved one. Don't run from impermanence. Let it open your heart wider. Let it remind you to show up *fully* before life quietly moves on.

September 07

The old must fade for the new to flourish. You're just a season in an eternal garden.

Soon enough, you won't be here. The same goes for everything around you: the places, the people, the things you know and hold dear. Everything changes, breaks down, and fades away, making space for the next wave, the next generation. It's just how nature works.

So why get so caught up in holding on or fearing loss? When you really accept impermanence, you free yourself from needless suffering and start living with a deeper appreciation for the now.

The question isn't, "How do I make this last forever?" The real question is, "How do I show up fully while it lasts?"

Let that awareness sharpen your focus, what you do today matters because it's all you really have. Don't waste your time chasing the illusion of forever. Love fiercely, give freely, and don't hold back the good in you.

Your Takeaway

Nature isn't cruel, it's just *efficient*. It changes. It lets go. It clears space for what's next. Embrace change, and you'll find peace in the flow.

September 08

Don't confuse a good performance with a good person. The applause always fades, but what's left when the spotlight fades is the only thing that's real.

So many people push themselves to the edge chasing fame, fortune, or power; always dissatisfied, always hungry for more, consumed by their relentless ambitions and overwhelming pride. Ultimately, their lives end like any of ours.

Ask yourself, "If none of this lasts, what do I want to stand for while I'm here?"

Use what life gives you to build a life of fairness, balance, and connection to something greater. True strength comes from quietly living your values, knowing that all the noise and ego will fade away anyway.

Focus on what lasts, your character, your integrity. That's how you rise above the ashes.

Your Takeaway

Instead of wasting your energy reaching for influence or control, be a good person. Whatever you build, let it be your character.

Concept 22: Develop True Resilience

Resilience doesn't mean you don't feel it. It means you choose what leads: your pain or your purpose.

September 09

Everyone's journey ends the same. Resilience isn't about avoiding the end, but how you walk through life.

Death doesn't play favorites. It takes superstars, small-town heroes, tech geniuses, world travelers, and quiet thinkers. Famous speakers, legendary philosophers, fearless generals, and the loudest cynics who scoffed at life's fleeting nature all end up in the same place.

What really matters is how you treated the people around you: the liars, the cheats, the honest, and the friends. Treat them with kindness, honesty, and justice, even when the world around you isn't always fair or kind, and that will become your real legacy.

That's resilience: standing tall in a world that's always changing and knowing you did right, no matter what. Everyone ends up at the same finish line. What counts is the journey and how you walk it.

Your Takeaway

What's the point of fearing death if there's no way out? How you treat the people around you is the real measure of a successful life. That's true resilience. That's how you show up strong, no matter what comes your way.

September 10

We're all riding the same unstoppable current. Resilience means flowing with it, not fighting the tide.

Every one of us is moving with the flow of the universe, like leaves caught in a strong river current. We're not separate from it, we're part of it. Just like your limbs work together without resistance, your life is woven into the whole fabric of existence.

Remember all the giants: financial, technology, science, entertainment and more. They were great, wise, legendary, and yet time swallowed them whole. Maybe their names still echo, but even they became part of the eternal flow.

This isn't meant to bring you down, it's a call to build real resilience. Life moves fast, changes nonstop, and nothing stays the same. The smart move is to cooperate with that flow instead of fighting it. Align your mind and actions with the rhythm of life.

That's how you stay steady when everything else feels like it's rushing past. That's how you develop true resilience, not by resisting the current, but by learning to ride it.

Your Takeaway

Every body, person, and thing is carried along by the universe's vast current, and resisting the flow only wears you down. True resilience is about riding the wave with grace, finding your place in the current, and keeping your balance no matter how wild the water gets.

September 11

Your wiring is designed to handle this. Don't be calm out of ignorance or for a performance, be calm because you've done the work.

We're innately capable of handling any difficulty that comes our way. Our rational minds and natural capacity for endurance are sufficient for any external event.

Some people can handle difficult situations with composure for flawed reasons. They might remain calm out of obliviousness, simply not grasping the severity of a situation, while others achieve a similar effect by feigning composure for an audience.

If people can get through hardship with such weak coping mechanisms, a person who bases their calm on wisdom and a deep, rational understanding should be infinitely more resilient. You have the ability to build genuine inner strength, a peace that's earned, not just performed or based on ignorance.

Today, walk forward not because it's easy, but because resilience is already wired into you. Trust that, and show yourself what you're really made of.

Your Takeaway

Your strength doesn't come from escaping challenges, but from meeting them with clarity and character. Whatever you're encountering, you have the inner resilience to manage it. You wouldn't be facing this if you weren't uniquely prepared for it.

September 12

Life will always present challenges that are inherently part of your journey and there's no point in resisting them. Instead of dwelling on what's difficult, focus your energy on moving through it.

What happens to you is exactly what's meant to happen. Your circumstances are perfectly aligned with your unique nature as a human being.

Why waste energy complaining or resisting? The universe doesn't present you with anything you can't handle. Trust that whatever life serves up, it's within your capacity to endure it.

Stop fighting what's natural and start accepting it. When you realize that life's challenges are just part of your human nature, you unlock the power to stay steady, calm, and strong no matter what.

You were built for this. The struggle is part of your path, not a detour from it. Embrace it, learn from it, and keep moving forward.

Your Takeaway

Accept that some experiences are just part of your path, and no amount of grumbling will alter that. Save your energy for responding effectively rather than lamenting the inevitable. Resilience means accepting what comes, trusting that you're built to endure, and showing up ready to face whatever is next.

September 13

Pain is the alarm. Suffering is your decision to panic.

This is a practical strategy for managing pain and suffering. It's a way of thinking that strips away the fear of pain by logically categorizing it.

The central argument is simple: all pain falls into one of two categories. It's either so intense that it's a critical failure that will shut you down quickly, or it's chronic and manageable. You can live with a pain that doesn't kill you.

The key to enduring chronic pain is to separate your mind from the physical sensation. Think of your mind as the pilot in a cockpit. The body is the rattling fuselage, feeling the turbulence. Pain is the vibration and noise, but suffering is the pilot's decision to panic. By refusing to let your mind be impaired, you can maintain your tranquility and rationality, leaving the body to experience the pain on its own.

The lesson is clear: don't fear pain because it's either brief and fatal, or long-lasting but manageable. The key to enduring it is to recognize that your mind is a separate faculty that can remain calm and in control, no matter what your body is experiencing.

The next time you feel overwhelmed by pain, stress, or heartache, ask yourself, "Can I step back? Can I make room inside myself for this without collapsing?" That's resilience. Not avoiding the hard, but staying rooted while the hard passes through.

Your Takeaway

The body may ache, but the mind – your inner core – can stay calm, clear, and untouched. This isn't about pretending it doesn't hurt. It's about remembering you don't have to *identify* with the hurt. The pain might visit, but it doesn't get to run the place.

September 14

Even if the world falls apart around you, stay rooted. Stay joyful. Not because it's easy, but because nothing outside you controls your peace.

Stand firm, no matter what's happening around you. Even if the whole world seems to be against you, even if chaos tears at your body and spirit, your mind can still find calm. You don't need the world to be quiet for you to be steady. You don't need approval to stay grounded. You don't need perfect circumstances to grow stronger.

Your judgment is like a calm voice telling the chaos, "This is what you really are", stripping away the noise of opinion and fear. Your resilience says, "I've been waiting for a challenge like this, this moment is my chance to act with wisdom, compassion, and strength."

Every circumstance, no matter how wild or harsh, is just raw material for your mind and spirit to shape into something meaningful. Nothing is truly new or beyond your capacity to handle, it's all familiar ground for a resilient mind.

That's how you turn turmoil into triumph.

Your Takeaway

Nothing happening outside can make it impossible for your mind to stay steady, to see clearly, or to use the situation wisely. That's the essence of resilience. Not avoiding the fire, but learning to forge your character in it.

September 15

The detour isn't a failure, it's just a different way to get there. The point of the journey is the journey, not the road you were expecting.

If you want to build a meaningful life, you have to focus on what's in front of you. It's not a single, grand achievement, but a sum of individual, intentional choices.

The key to contentment is to focus on doing each small thing as well as you can, right now. No one can stop you from being successful in this way because true success is defined by your internal efforts and character, acting with integrity, wisdom, and self-control, not by external outcomes.

External obstacles are inevitable, but they can't prevent you from being a person of virtue. When a project hits a roadblock, or a plan falls apart, the wise response is twofold: first, calmly accept the obstacle as a fact of reality, and second, pivot with a creative spirit to what is still feasible.

This new path is just as vital and contributes just as much to the person you are building as the original one would have. True success is internal, and obstacles are not reasons to give up, but opportunities to pivot and build resilience.

Today, don't wait for perfect conditions, focus on what's in front of you, and bring your full integrity and trust to it.

Your Takeaway

Life is built in the *now,* with this next choice, this next conversation, this next breath. You don't control the outcome. You don't control what hits you. But you do control how you show up: with justice, with calm, with wisdom. That's resilience: not doing everything you planned, but doing what you *can* with strength and grace, especially when the plan falls apart.

September 16

The captain doesn't control the waves, but they do control the ship. Your resilience is found in the helm, not in the ocean.

To build resilience, you must first confront and accept life's most challenging realities, starting with our own mortality. A truly resilient person doesn't fear death, instead seeing it as a natural part of life, no different from the changing seasons or the inevitable aging of a living thing.

Just as we accept the final, brilliant colors of autumn as a natural stage before winter, we should see death not as a tragedy, but as a necessary and awaited conclusion. This perspective allows us to remove death's terrifying status.

The true strength of resilience comes from embracing the full cycle of life and finding peace in the understanding that an ending is not a flaw, but a fundamental part of the journey.

Your Takeaway

When you've trained your mind to trust life's design, you stop fighting reality and stop clinging. With that surrender comes unshakeable strength. Face endings not with fear, but with clarity, grace, and a heart at peace.

September 17

Don't pray for an easier road, pray for a stronger spirit. The road is the road, but your spirit is the journey.

Every difficulty you face is either within your innate resilience to handle or it isn't. If it's a manageable challenge, complaining is a waste of energy – your job is to simply put up with it and get through it. If a difficulty is truly unbearable, it will eventually end, which means your suffering will soon be over. In either scenario, panic, resistance, and anxiety are useless and only drain your strength.

The real source of your strength lies in your mindset. We are far more capable of enduring things than we think, and the key is to mentally reframe any hardship. That one mental shift turns chaos into challenge. It turns pressure into training. It turns survival into strength.

Our resilience isn't about the absence of hardship, but about our ability to change our perspective on it. The ultimate source of our strength comes from our ability to accept what we cannot change and to find purpose in the process of facing it.

Your Takeaway

Learn to choose your mindset. By choosing to see a difficult event as a challenge to grow stronger or as a necessary part of your purpose, you can render it tolerable. You're not here to escape life's weight. You're here to rise under it.

September 18

The mountain doesn't care how you feel. It simply presents a path. Your resilience is found in choosing your next step, not in wishing the climb were easier.

True resilience isn't about avoiding hardship, it's about building an inner fortress that external events can't breach. It begins with the understanding that our actions and intentions are the only things we truly control. Ask yourself, "What's the wisest move I can make with this situation, this challenge, this mess?" Blaming outside circumstances for our unhappiness is a surrender of this power.

Lasting contentment isn't found in comfort or luxury, but in a life of purpose, integrity, and sound judgment. A truly resilient mind is a force of nature and it can navigate any obstacle, seeing it not as a roadblock, but as a chance to grow stronger.

Challenges don't break a person of character, they forge one. When you step back and view your personal troubles in the context of the greater community and the natural order, they shrink in importance. By mastering your inner world, you become an unshakeable force, ready to meet any challenge with a quiet, confident resolve.

Your Takeaway

Stop waiting to feel inspired. Resilience isn't about wishing the moment were different, but by moving with strength in the imperfect one.

September 19

We are all connected by a common thread. If you snip it to hurt someone else, the fabric unravels around you too.

Human beings are fundamentally social creatures, interconnected like threads in a tapestry. When a person intentionally isolates themselves from another, they are effectively snipping a thread and weakening the entire fabric of society. This separation is a self-inflicted wound, often born from disdain or anger.

However, we have an innate capacity to rebuild those connections. This restoration is a conscious choice to mend relationships and rejoin our community, but while reconciliation is possible, it's not the same as a bond that was never broken. Each emotional separation makes it harder to fully reintegrate and leaves a scar on the relationship.

The ideal is to be a part of the same community, living side by side, even if we don't share every single belief. Ultimately, our well-being is tied to the well-being of the whole. Isolating ourselves harms us as much as it harms others, and a continuous effort to stay connected is the ideal.

Your Takeaway

Authentic resilience isn't about enduring alone, it's about belonging, even when it's hard. It isn't about breaking away, it's about mending. It comes from the understanding that true strength often comes from connection, from standing together, not apart.

September 20

When the world is a storm, your mind is the lighthouse. It can't stop the waves, but it will always show you where to go.

You can spend your life trying to figure out if the world is on a fixed track, run by some divine master plan, or if it's all just random, chaotic noise. But your peace of mind doesn't actually depend on which one of those is true.

If everything is pre-decided, what's the point of fighting it? The only rational move is to accept what you can't change. If the universe has a plan and you think there's a higher power involved, don't just sit around and wait for a miracle. The challenge is to live with integrity and purpose so you make yourself ready for a hand-up. And if it's all just chaos, be thankful you have a mind that can create its own order in the mess.

A crisis can come through and take your body, your job, or your peace of mind, but it cannot take your actual mind. It's the one thing that can't be harmed unless you give it permission. Your mind is an unconquerable fortress, and by choosing to focus on your own thoughts and character and accepting the external world for what it is, you can find a tranquility that nothing can shake.

Your Takeaway

Whatever this life is, your power stays the same. You choose how to respond. Your judgment, your courage, and your will stay within your control unless you hand them over.

Concept 23: Value Integrity and Authenticity

You don't need to impress anyone. You just need to be real and rooted in what's right.

September 21

Don't save your best performance for the final scene. Play every scene as if it's the final one, and the whole story will be a masterpiece.

We all get caught up in distractions, ego, and annoyance with our circumstances. Start looking at every single thing you do as if it were the last time you'd ever get to do it. It works because it makes you stop worrying about things you can't control and start focusing all your energy on your own actions and character. It helps you act from a place of reason and principle, not from some emotional impulse you'll regret later.

The challenge is to bring your full self, honest, present, grounded, to everything. Not with perfection, but with integrity. No half-hearted effort, no emotional spin-outs, and no dragging old resentment into today's decisions.

Living a good, content life isn't an impossible spiritual quest. It's just a handful of truths you live by, done consistently, with unwavering integrity. That's how you live with purpose, not by accident, but by a series of choices you're proud of.

Your Takeaway

Act like your time is sacred, because it is. Keep it simple, respond with kindness, lead with principle, and be faithful to your values. That's what makes a life clean, aligned, and worthy.

September 22

Don't look for someone to hold you up. The only thing that can straighten you out is the spine you build yourself.

Stop dragging your feet, acting selfishly, and being a hypocrite. Don't overcomplicate things with fancy words or waste everyone's time with endless chatter.

Move with clean energy. Not from ego, not from fear, not with a dozen conflicting motives clouding your clarity. Stay in alignment. Say what you mean. Do what you know is right. Let your actions speak without needing extra influence or applause. Let your inner compass be in charge of who you are and what you do, regardless of the job you have or the titles you hold.

You have to live like you're ready to walk away at any time, without needing a witness or a pat on the back. Find your own joy, find your own peace, and don't outsource your happiness to other people or circumstances. Don't be the kind of person who needs someone else to tell you how to act or who you should be. You must stand straight on your own, not wait for someone else to come and straighten you out.

Your Takeaway

You don't need outside validation to find peace. You don't need to contort yourself to earn your worth. You are already built to walk upright, so live in a way that doesn't need explanation, with presence, honesty, and a quiet kind of strength.

September 23

Time's running out and you still haven't centered your peace or learned to stay true no matter what's happening around you. So what are you waiting for?

Life isn't going to wait for you to finally 'have it all together'. Your timeline is uncertain, and the only guarantee you have is this moment. So why keep putting off the work of becoming your real, unshakable self?

Authenticity means stripping away the need to impress, and integrity means refusing to let outside chaos pull you off your values. If you're letting what others say or do make you bitter, fake, or reactive, it's time for a reset. Your only job is to show up honestly, show up calmly, and put your energy into the right action, every single day.

There's no bonus round for finally getting it perfect. The real win is living so true that even stress, criticism, or loss can't break your stride. Make simplicity, inner peace, and a clear conscience your baseline, not just your goal for 'someday'.

Your Takeaway

The challenge isn't to be perfect, but to stop putting off the crucial work of becoming the person you know you're supposed to be. Your time here is finite, so what are you waiting for?

Reflect:

- Where are you letting outside noise shake your character or distract you from your path?

- How can you simplify your actions and stay rooted in what really matters today?

- What would shift if you decided to let go of everything that isn't honest, calm, and purposeful?

- Are you willing to make every day count, not by being perfect, but by being real?

You don't get more time. Choose integrity now. Let authenticity be your legacy.

September 24

There's a difference between what you do and who you are. The gap between them is your work.

What are you doing with your mind right now? At this very moment, what's occupying the part of you that makes all the decisions?

Look inward with honesty. Is your inner world steady or scattered? Are you acting like a petulant kid throwing a tantrum? A moody, defiant teenager? A mindless drone just following the herd? Or are you being the rational, intentional adult in the room?

This isn't judgment, it's awareness. If you don't stop to notice the pattern of your behavior, you'll constantly be running on autopilot. Ask yourself, "What kind of person am I bringing to this moment? Am I thoughtful? Courageous? Anchored in truth? If not, you can take the time to shift your behavior.

Your Takeaway

Your being, your core, is always in motion. Living with integrity isn't a one-time decision, it's a moment-by-moment recalibration. Keep coming back. That's authenticity.

September 25

Don't let power or status turn you into someone you're not. Stay humble, stay kind, stay real, no matter how high you climb.

It's easy to let a little power, recognition, or status make you fake, guarded, or disconnected from who you really are. It happens to everyone, and you're not immune.

The gentle challenge is to resist letting the title go to your head. Your job, status, and reputation are all temporary. What you can truly control is your character. Lead with justice and kindness; be the kind of person you'd admire if you lost it all tomorrow: honest, down-to-earth, consistent, and generous.

Your time here is limited, and when it's all said and done, no one will remember the size of your office. The only thing that truly matters is the person you were and the good you did in the world. Stop chasing the temporary and start focusing on the permanent. Your value isn't in your title, but in your character and your commitment to humble service.

Your Takeaway

Power corrupts. Stay grounded, kind, and fair, no matter how high you climb. Your legacy is built on the moments you chose to be yourself, even when you could have played the game.

Reflect:

- Where are you letting titles, likes, or other people's opinions shape your actions?

- How can you show up more authentically, no matter what room you walk into?

- What would it look like to lead from values, not ego, today?

- Are you willing to measure success by how real and kind you were, not just by your wins?

Let the world chase the hype. Keep yourself honest and live for the simple things.

September 26

Don't let what someone else says about you become your inner monologue. Your reputation is their opinion, your integrity is your own business.

Is your character for rent?

People will test you. They'll gossip, lash out, manipulate, or disappoint you, but what other people say or do is their business. Your reaction, your attitude, and your integrity is all yours. The goal is to let that unshakeable core depend on your inner control, not outside approval.

Your worth is not up for negotiation, and your character doesn't shift with the mood of others. You have the power to make your goodness a permanent, unchanging part of who you are, like a foundation that holds a building steady.

Work to build that foundation so strong that external drama can't compromise it. Choose every day to be the kind of person who stands firm, no matter what.

Today, repeat it like a mantra: "Whatever they do, I remain me."

Your Takeaway

You're not here to match other people's energy, you're here to stay rooted in your values: honesty, calm, and kindness. Hold your integrity, amidst the din. That's what it means to walk in authenticity, with steady feet and a clear heart.

September 27

You're part of something bigger. Your choices don't just reflect you, they affect the whole. Every action that ignores the good of the collective tears a hole in your integrity. And deep down, you feel it.

You're not living in a bubble. Every decision you make, every word you say, every line you cross or hold sends ripples out into your community.

If your actions don't serve the bigger picture, you're not just stalling your own growth, you're tearing a hole in the social fabric.

Integrity and authenticity mean more than 'being yourself'. It's about being the kind of self that adds value, that cares enough to show up for the world around you. When you live a life that's entirely for yourself, focused only on your own gain and pleasure, it creates a real rupture in your sense of purpose.

Before you act, ask yourself, "Is this building something better, or just serving my ego?" The strongest kind of integrity is the kind that lifts everyone up. If you want your life to have real integrity and feel whole, you have to find your purpose in contribution, not just consumption.

Your Takeaway

Selfish moves might feel easy at the moment, but they disconnect you from what actually makes life meaningful, like connection, contribution, and legacy. You're a part of the whole, and every single thing you do should serve the purpose of making the world a little bit better in some way.

Reflect:

- Where are you making choices that serve only you, not the bigger community?

- What would shift if you measured success by impact, not just personal wins?

- How can you realign today with the kind of integrity that makes a difference beyond your own bubble?

- Are you ready to show up as the most authentic, community-minded version of yourself?

Integrity is about what you bring to the table, not just what you take away. Authenticity isn't selfish. It's honest, grounded, and deeply connected to the world you're here to help shape.

September 28

Your ego is heavy, but the weight of ignorance is far heavier. Learn to set the first down so you can carry less of the second.

Integrity isn't about always being right, it's about being open to what's real, even when it means admitting you missed the mark. If someone calls you out and they're right, celebrate it. Growth comes from owning your mistakes and shifting course, not from doubling down on your own ego.

Truth isn't your enemy, it's an upgrade. The only real damage comes from clinging to old stories, defending bad habits, or refusing to see what's in front of you. Authenticity is about being teachable, not unbreakable. It's about building your life on reality, not on pride or pretending.

If your aim is to be your best self, keep the door open for new information, better ideas, and honest feedback. Nothing honest can harm you, but denial always does. Don't get stuck in your own echo chamber. Be bold enough to pivot, and wise enough to let truth set you free.

Your Takeaway

If someone can show you that something you thought or did was mistaken, you should gladly change. The real harm is what you do to yourself when you persist in your own self-deception and stubbornness. Stop protecting your ego and start pursuing what's real. Changing your mind isn't a sign of weakness, it's the best evidence of growth.

Reflect:

- Where are you resisting change just to protect your ego?

- How can you get more comfortable with being wrong, so you can keep moving forward?

- What would your relationships and work look like if you valued truth over being right?

- Are you ready to make growth, not pride, your top priority?

Stay teachable. Let truth shape you. Authenticity isn't about being flawless, it's about being honest enough to course-correct when it matters.

September 29

If you ever earn the right to call yourself authentic, conscientious, amenable, and dignified, don't trade it for applause, influence, or convenience. If you lose your way, don't spiral: regroup and return to who you said you wanted to be.

It's easy to call yourself honest, kind, and good, but labels don't mean much unless you actually live them out. Your real power comes from holding tight to the ones that matter most: integrity, self-awareness, resilience, and genuine acceptance of your life as it unfolds.

You'll slip sometimes – everyone does. The move isn't to beat yourself up or pretend it didn't happen, but to just pause, reset, and come back to your true north. Let those values comfort and guide you without worrying whether others will see it. This is about the relationship you have with yourself, and how you show up when no one's watching.

Life is short, and faking it for approval is a waste of your limited time. The best you can do is stay grounded in who you really are and keep realigning, even after setbacks. If you can pull that off, you'll find a sense of peace and belonging nothing external can give you.

Ask yourself, "Am I living as the true me, or am I just playing a role?" Let these qualities be your anchor and compass, guiding you through any storm. If you slip, retreat not in shame but to gather your strength and recover your center.

Your Takeaway

Choose authenticity and integrity. Holding onto these qualities isn't about chasing praise or labels from others, it's about living a life that changes you from the inside out.

Reflect:

- What core values do you want to be known for, and are you actually living them?

- When you lose your way, how quickly do you come back to yourself, and what helps?

- How can you make your values your 'vessel', not just your decoration?

- Are you ready to stop clinging to old patterns and live a life that actually fits the real you?

Don't let the world name you, let your actions and integrity do the talking. Your real net worth is the character you've built. The rest is just a borrowed number.

September 30

Train yourself to see the flow of change. Everything shifts. Everything moves. When you really get that, you stop chasing control, and start anchoring yourself in what matters: living with integrity, and letting the rest unfold.

Make it a daily habit to notice how everything around you is in constant motion, changing, evolving, shifting. This isn't just observation, it's training yourself to see life clearly and objectively.

When you do that, you start to detach from the fleeting, your body, others' opinions, the noise of judgment. Deep down, you know you'll leave all this behind someday. Why waste energy on distractions? Instead, commit fully to integrity: to doing what's right, just, and authentic no matter what.

Let go of trying to control outcomes or people's reactions. That's out of your hands. Train your focus on the things you can control. Own your actions with honesty and embrace your life's path. All of it, the smooth and the rough.

This is authenticity in action: living true to yourself, grounded in justice, and trusting the natural flow of things. Ask yourself today, "Am I chasing approval or am I walking my path with integrity?"

Choose integrity. Be real. And watch how freedom follows.

Your Takeaway

Integrity means you commit to justice and right action, not to chasing status or approval. When you see how temporary everything is, it frees you up from the drama and distraction. You can step back from the rat race and put your energy into what's actually yours: your next honest move, your next kind word, your next brave decision. Stay steady, follow your own true code, and let change do its thing while you keep it real.

Reflect:

- How much energy are you wasting trying to control what's out of your hands?

- Where could you be more present, letting go of distraction and anchoring in your values?

- What would shift if you stopped worrying about people's opinions and focused on the next right step?

- Are you willing to accept change as a constant and let your integrity be the anchor?

Change is inevitable. Authenticity is your move. It isn't about being liked, it's about being true.

Use integrity as your compass through the chaos.

October 01

Integrity doesn't need a spotlight. It shows up in your tone, your presence, your choices. Real sincerity is quiet, fake sincerity is a mask with a hidden agenda.

When someone says, "I'm going to be honest with you," your guard goes up because true authenticity doesn't need a preamble. It's immediately obvious in your voice, your eyes, and your actions.

Stop trying to manage other people's perceptions and just *be* an honest person. Integrity isn't a performance you put on for a specific moment, it's a fundamental quality you build over time. It should be as undeniable as your presence in a room. Trying to fake it is exhausting, and it creates what you could call 'strategic relationships' – connections that are hollow and untrustworthy. The world's full of people selling an image. Be the one living your truth so clearly that no one can mistake you for anything but real. When you do, your character becomes its own evidence, and you'll find you don't have to try so hard to convince anyone of anything. Living with integrity not only earns respect but also builds trust and deep connection.

Ask yourself, "Am I showing up as my true self? Am I surrounding myself with people who do the same?" That's what real friendship and real life are built on.

Your Takeaway

True integrity is the energy you carry, the way your words and actions line up, and how easy it is for people to feel what's real around you. Be the kind of person who doesn't have to say a word for others to know what you're about.

Reflect:

- Where are you 'talking a good game', but not living it out in your actions or presence?

- How can you show up with open-book energy with no disclaimers, just realness?

- What would change if your integrity was something people could *feel*, not just hear about?

- Are you ready to ditch calculated sincerity for the kind of honesty that needs no introduction?

People who are 'being real' never need to announce it. Let your life do the talking. Be real, especially when no one's watching.

October 02

See things clearly. Strip away the drama, get to the root and then do the next right thing. That's it. One honest word, one kind action at a time. No need to rush, just keep showing up with truth and patience.

Happiness – that deep sense of peace and purpose – comes from seeing life clearly, exactly as it is. That means not getting caught up in stories or illusions, but recognizing the true matter and cause behind what happens. It also means committing, with your whole heart, to doing what's right and speaking the truth. No shortcuts, no excuses.

When you live this way, life becomes a seamless chain of good actions, one flowing naturally into the next. No gaps where doubt, regret, or hesitation sneak in. Patience and acceptance aren't passive here, they're active choices to stay truthful and steady, even when things get messy. This steady, honest rhythm creates a foundation for real joy and freedom.

Ask yourself, "How can I link today's good deed to the next? How can I stay present, clear, and committed to the truth in every moment?"

That's where happiness and fulfillment live, in patient acceptance and purposeful action. Ready to live that chain reaction today?

Your Takeaway

Happiness is the quiet work of living with clarity and purpose.See things as they are, not as your emotions paint them to be. Name the moment. Understand its cause. And then do what's right. Patience is in that rhythm. Acceptance is in that trust. You don't need to fix everything, just move with integrity, moment by moment.

Concept 24: Exercise Patience and Acceptance

You can resist reality, or rise within it.

October 03

People will be rude, selfish, careless, even cruel. Don't be shocked, be ready. They're not the enemy. They're human, just like you.

Some people today are going to test you. They'll cut you off, speak without thinking, forget the favor you did yesterday. Don't take it personally. Their pain and ignorance drive those behaviors.

You've seen clearly what's good and bad, what's right and wrong, and now you can understand that these people aren't truly your enemies. You share something deeper, a part of the same human intelligence, the same spark of something bigger.

Don't let their nonsense infect you. You don't have to get angry or hate them. We're designed to work together, like parts of the same body. When you resist or reject others, you're fighting your own nature.

Instead, accept what comes with patience. See the difficult people for what they are, misguided, not malevolent, and keep your peace. Because that's how you stay true to yourself and keep moving forward.

Your Takeaway

The only thing that can truly harm you is *you,* by letting the behavior of others change your character. Don't give your peace away. Don't mirror their mess. Be the one who stays grounded. We were made to work together, not fight with each other. Patience is your strength. Acceptance is your freedom, and compassion is your secret weapon. Use it.

October 04

When something triggers you, pause and name it. Strip it down to what it really is, and don't dramatize it. Define it. That's how you stay grounded. That's how you stay free.

When something happens, your first instinct is usually to react: quickly, emotionally, and often inaccurately. Slow down and strip it down to its core. Take a second to define what the thing actually is, not what you *feel* about it. Get past your emotions and see the raw facts.

Ask yourself two simple questions: "What is this thing, really? And where does it actually fit in the grand scheme of things for the world, not just for you?"

The more clearly you see something, the less power it has over you. It's about gaining a level of clarity that nothing else can give you. The more you practice this, the more you'll be in control of your reactions and the less you'll be overwhelmed by daily life.

Your Takeaway

Patience isn't just about waiting calmly. It's about *seeing clearly,* naming the moment, understanding its shape, and refusing to get swept up in your first impression. Acceptance is meeting reality with your eyes open and your mind steady.

October 05

Peace lives not in the past but the present. Focus instead on what truly lasts: a steady mind, honest words, and a calm acceptance of whatever life brings.

There is no such thing as forever. Immortality isn't about being remembered on plaques or in books. That's just vanity, a distraction from what truly matters.

What's worth your focus? A just mind, meaning fairness and integrity in how you think and act; actions that genuinely help others and build community; speaking the truth with no angle; and the ability to embrace life's twists and turns, seeing them as necessary and part of a greater rational design.

This isn't some passive resignation. It's an active, powerful acceptance, recognizing that everything changes, everything fades, but your inner compass, your reason, your kindness, those are what give life meaning.

So next time you find yourself chasing legacy or approval, ask yourself, "Am I building my character, or just chasing shadows?"

Exercise patience with the fleeting nature of fame, acceptance of life's flow, and focus your energy on what really counts. That's how you find peace that lasts longer than any name or story.

Your Takeaway

Your power lies in living with intention now. Patience means letting go of the illusion of control over how you're seen. Acceptance means meeting the moment as it is, not as you wish it would be. Wisdom is choosing to care less about your name, and more about your nature.

October 06

The universe gives you what you need, not always what you like. Sickness, loss, and detours aren't punishments. They're prescriptions meant to shape you.

Just like a doctor prescribes treatments, like exercise, cold baths, or walking barefoot despite pain, sometimes life hands you experiences like illness, loss, and hardship.

Both kinds of prescriptions – the doctor's and life's – are part of a bigger plan that's meant to bring healing or growth, even if it doesn't feel that way right now. The universe's prescriptions aren't random. They're connected, like bricks forming a wall or stones in a pyramid, all part of the larger structure of your life and the world.

No one likes going through something difficult, but imagine welcoming challenges like you would a doctor's strong medicine, knowing it's aiming to fortify you. When you resist what life hands you, you're basically pulling apart the bricks of your own well-being.

Patience means accepting what's prescribed for you, even the harsh parts, because each experience is woven into your unique story for a reason. Your struggles are part of a larger whole, contributing to something bigger than just you.

Next time life feels unfair or brutal, try shifting your view. This is part of your healing, your growth, the unfolding of your story. Acceptance isn't about liking what happens, but choosing peace with it so you can keep building.

Your Takeaway

Sometimes life hands you something heavy not as a punishment, but as part of your growth, unfolding, and deeper healing. Every challenge and every twist in your path is part of a bigger structure, one you can't always see from where you're standing. Patience isn't pretending it doesn't hurt. It's knowing the pain has a place. And acceptance is trusting that nothing is wasted, not even this.

October 07

Let doing the next good thing with presence and purpose be enough. That's where peace lives: not in results, not in praise, but in quietly showing up for what's needed.

Real joy and rest aren't found in chasing endless distractions or in solo pursuits. They come from moving steadily from one meaningful, helpful action to the next, being useful to others, showing up in your community, your work, your relationships. Do this while staying mindful of something bigger: your higher purpose, your values, or simply the spirit that guides you.

It's not about rushing or doing everything at once, it's about mindful presence in each act, knowing you're part of a larger flow. When you focus on this rhythm, serving others with intention and staying connected to your inner compass, you find a calm joy that patience alone can't buy. This way, life's ups and downs don't throw you off balance because you're anchored in meaningful movement, not in outcomes or external approval.

When you feel restless or impatient, remind yourself: the work is the joy, the service is the rest. Keep your eyes on the next step, keep your heart steady, and trust that moving forward with purpose is where peace lives.

Your Takeaway

When life feels heavy or uncertain, we usually want to escape, fix everything, or get ahead. But peace isn't *out there*. It's right here, in the next helpful, honest action. You just need to keep moving gently, usefully, one choice at a time. Patience isn't waiting for ease, it's choosing to walk with intention, even when things feel uncertain.

October 08

The real tragedy isn't your body slowing down, it's your mind giving up before it has to. True strength is revealed not by avoiding hardship, but by enduring it.

Sometimes your body keeps ticking, but your mind checks out early. You're physically present, but mentally, you're done. This happens because life throws us curveballs: stress, disappointment, exhaustion. And without patience and acceptance, our minds can collapse under the weight.

But what if you flipped the script? What if, instead of letting your mind give up, you trained it to stay curious, to breathe through discomfort, to accept what is without resistance?

Resilience is the ability to bounce back by leaning into patience and mindfulness rather than pushing against reality. When we practice acceptance, our brains release less stress hormones, helping us build mental stamina.

The real strength isn't in muscles or endurance, but in how long your mind stays present, engaged, and hopeful, no matter what the body is doing. Next time you feel like mentally giving up, remember that your mind's power to hold steady is your secret weapon.

It's not about ignoring pain or struggle, it's about accepting them with grace and moving forward anyway.

Your Takeaway

It's time to take a break when your mind checks out or when you stop caring or stop hoping. Rest if you need to, but don't retreat from your own mind. Recommit, not to perfection, but to presence.

October 09

No one chooses to be wrong, cruel, or unfair, not if they really understand the truth. So remind yourself of that. It'll soften your heart and stretch your patience.

It's easy to get frustrated with people who just don't seem to get it: who act unjustly, selfishly, or with zero self-awareness. But no one willingly chooses to be wrong or unfair. No one wakes up wanting to be unjust, unkind, or excessive. People act out of ignorance, pain, or fear, not because they don't want to do what's right deep down.

When you remember that, it softens your heart. You stop getting so frustrated or impatient with others when they mess up. It doesn't mean you ignore bad behavior, but you meet it with patience and understanding, knowing everyone's on their own journey.

This perspective helps you stay grounded, avoid unnecessary conflict, and keep your own kindness intact. Next time someone disappoints or hurts you, try stepping back and thinking, "They don't want to be this way, they just haven't found a better path yet." That's how you exercise real patience and acceptance, by recognizing the humanity in everyone.

Your Takeaway

Understand that most people haven't found their clarity yet. Instead of getting angry or upset at others, breathe into compassion. You don't have to agree to stay gentle. You just have to remember we're all still learning.

October 10

The biggest obstacle on your path isn't the rock in the road, it's the conversation you're having with yourself about how the rock shouldn't be there.

Life has bitter moments, sharp edges, and dead ends, but you don't have to moralize them. The gentle challenge is to stop asking "Why is this happening to me?" and just deal with it.

This is emotional efficiency. Not coldness, but awareness and *clarity*. Some things will hurt. Some people won't play fair. Some situations will rub you raw. But can you accept it *without* turning it into a narrative? Can you simply say, "That's not for me" and move on?

Nature isn't messy, it's masterful. Even the parts you want to throw out will be recycled into something new. So today, when you hit discomfort, don't dramatize. Just observe. Accept. Adjust. Pivot. Patience means letting life be life, without needing it to apologize first.

Your Takeaway

Stop fighting against the way things are and start using your energy to deal with the way they are.

October 11

If you can help someone grow, do it. If you can't, be kind anyway. That's why you have patience; not just for the 'easy' people, but especially for the ones who don't get it yet.

Stop fighting against the way things are and start using your energy to deal with the way they are. You won't be able to fix everyone. Some people won't listen. Some won't change. And some will keep doing the same thing that frustrates you. And quite frankly, some don't need fixing. Remember, you weren't built to control. You were built to *respond with grace.*

Regardless if they're not ready or willing to change, lean into your own kindness anyway, because kindness isn't just for people who 'deserve' it. It's a strength you carry inside you, a choice you make, no matter what others do. Even the universe shows kindness to those who stumble, helping them find small wins in health, luck, and moments of peace.

Ask yourself, "What's stopping me from doing the same?" Your patience and kindness don't depend on their readiness. They depend on your willingness. This isn't weakness, it's power wrapped in acceptance.

You're building resilience not by controlling others, but by mastering your response, and that is true freedom. So today, show up as someone who remembers their power. Not in fixing others, but in not letting their behavior change who you are.

Your Takeaway

Let people stumble while still offering blessings. Don't withhold compassion when someone's struggling. Kindness isn't weakness, it's a gift of awareness.

October 12

A mind that only wants the good parts of life is like a muscle that only wants to lift air. You can't get strong without resistance.

How often do we want life to serve us only good and pleasurable experiences? We crave bright lights, smooth praise, and successful outcomes, but life isn't curated just for your gratification.

A healthy mind is ready to face all that life throws at it: the good, the bad, the messy, the unexpected. A resilient mind doesn't ask the world to be softer. It gets stronger. It learns to say, "Whatever shows up, I can face it."

Acceptance isn't about giving up or settling for less. It's about embracing the full spectrum, the full experience, without shutting out reality. So today, when life delivers something loud, sharp, or uncomfortable, don't clench. Just notice, "This is the kind of mind I'm building."

Patience grows when you train your mind to be as ready, to be open, curious, resilient. When you stop resisting, you start living fully.

Your Takeaway

Acceptance isn't passive. It's a form of inner training. Be open to the possibilities of what can happen and what will happen. Patience isn't waiting, it's strength without resistance.

October 13

Your greatest act of defiance isn't a rebellion against the world, but the quiet choice to be your authentic self in a world that wants a performance.

Perfection isn't about being flawless or never messing up. It's about showing up for your life every single day, as if today might be your last. It's about living without turmoil, without internal chaos dragging you down.

Without listlessness or meaning, without going through the motions, without waiting for something better to come along, and without pretense or pretending to be someone you're not just to fit in or impress.

True character is calm. It's real. It's present. When you accept that each day is precious and uncertain, you stop wasting time on drama or fake versions of yourself. You bring patience to your challenges, acceptance to your limitations, and honesty to your actions. That's where real strength and peace come from.

Today, pause before responding. Breathe before assuming. Reflect before reacting. This is how we break the cycle. This is how we practice presence.

Your Takeaway

You get to choose what happens next. Let your wiser self speak before your reactive one does.

October 14

Hit the pause button on your emotions. See the facts of the situation, not the story you're telling yourself about it.

Most people react to what's on the surface level, but wisdom starts when you slow down and ask, "What's really going on underneath?" Peel back the wrapping on pain, pleasure, success, and failure, and you'll see it's rarely what you first assumed.

Pain isn't just suffering, it's a signal. Pleasure isn't just fun, it's a momentary experience. Death isn't a monster waiting to get you, it's just part of the natural cycle. Fame is fleeting, just a shadow.

No one else controls your inner peace or your reactions. Your distractions come from within. You have the power to decide how you take it all in. Everything is based on the meaning you give it.

Patience is about giving yourself the space to see things clearly, not just snapping to judgment or chasing instant fixes. Acceptance is realizing you can't control what other people do, or what life throws at you, but you *can* control how you see it. Life isn't about fighting every inconvenience or demanding that every moment feel good. It's about taking things as they are, and responding from a place of grounded clarity, not reactivity.

So when life feels overwhelming or unfair, pause and ask yourself, "Am I seeing this clearly, or through the fog of frustration and impatience?" This is your call to lean into acceptance, not as a defeat, but as a way to clear the way for real strength and calm.

Your Takeaway

Patience isn't about passivity. It's about accepting reality without surrendering your power. You don't have to love every twist, but you can accept that your perspective changes everything.

Reflect:

- Where are you reacting to the surface of things instead of getting curious about the real cause?

- How could patience help you see past discomfort or drama, to what's really needed?

- What would shift if you practiced accepting, not resisting, what you can't change today?

- Are you willing to slow down, get curious, and let your perspective be your superpower?

Let go, look deeper, and practice patience. That's how you move from chaos to clarity.

Concept 25: Understand True Friendship

Friendship isn't about convenience. It's about truth, trust, and mutual growth.

October 15

Real friendship is about truth, justice, and showing up exactly as you are.

Let's talk about what real friendship and leadership look like beyond just hanging out and sharing memes.

There are three big loves: family, truth, and justice. Those aren't just nice ideas, they're the foundation for how we connect and build trust.

Leadership is about valuing fairness and equality, where everyone plays by the same rules and that the best leaders prize the freedom of the people they serve.

Consistency is important. Think and consider deeply what is right and what is wrong. Be generous and ready to help others without keeping score. Be optimistic and confident in the love of your true friends. Never make your friends guess where you stand. No playing games, no hiding your likes or dislikes. Be clear, honest, and real.

That's what true friendship looks like. It's built on transparency, fairness, and a readiness to show up, flaws and all.

So next time you're with your friends, ask, "Am I being that kind of friend? Am I loving, truthful, and consistent, even when it's hard?"

Real friendship isn't about saying what's easy. Friendship in its purest form is real, consistent, and rooted in knowing and accepting each other without masks.

Your Takeaway

True friendship is built on shared values: justice, truth, generosity, and a deep confidence that you're loved, even when you mess up. It's about showing up with love that's honest, steady, and unmistakably *felt*.

October 16

If someone behaves badly toward you, that's their problem. Your responsibility is to remain who you're meant to be: a decent human being.

Friendship doesn't mean tolerating everything, but it *does* mean choosing who *you* want to be, even when someone else forgets who they are. You don't have to mirror someone's mess. Even when a friend lashes out, shuts down, or disappoints you, it's not your cue to stoop, react, or abandon your own values. Instead, hold steady. Be the example. Be the one who stays kind, clear, honest, and rooted.

True friendship isn't about perfect harmony, it's about choosing grace over ego, again and again. Not because they deserve it. But because *you* do.

Don't let someone else's behavior shape who you are. Lead with character. Stay the course. Be you. That's real strength. That's real friendship.

Your Takeaway

True friendship means maintaining honest communication and not sweeping issues under the rug. Instead of letting anger simmer, bring up your issue and talk it through regardless of the outcome.

October 17

The quickest way to disarm your own anger is to find the common humanity in someone else's mistake. You're both just people trying to figure it out. Before you react, run a three-step diagnosis. Check your own motives, check the bigger picture, and then check in with the other person's humanity.

Here's a powerful practice for dealing with people who rub you the wrong way or hurt you.

First, reconnect with your own beliefs, values, mindset and perspectives, and check to see if you are acting with justice and kindness right now. That's your baseline.

Second, zoom out and think about the mindset or flow of the universe. Remember, you're part of a bigger whole. It's easy to get caught up in our personal dramas, but this bigger picture reminds us to stay grounded.

Third, consider the other person's beliefs, values, mindset and perspectives. Ask yourself, 'Did they hurt me out of ignorance? Or was it something deliberate?" And even if they were wrong, recognize that their inner self is related to you at their core, like family.

This mindset shifts you from reacting in anger to responding with understanding. It's the foundation of true friendship: seeing others not as enemies, but as fellow travelers, sometimes stumbling but always connected.

Next time someone gets under your skin, try this three-step check-in. It won't fix everything overnight, but it's a game changer for your peace and your relationships.

Your Takeaway

Understanding true friendship means being able to zoom out, to see that we all have our own internal world, our own inner wisdom. Before you judge someone, try to understand them.

October 18

Your mind becomes what you feed it, so choose thoughts that strengthen your connection to others. You weren't made to go it alone. You were built to be in a community, and real friendship starts with the way you think.

Your mind becomes what you consistently feed it. Your thoughts are like a prism. They take the light of the world and refract it into a unique spectrum of understanding.

Why not choose thoughts that lift you up? Try telling yourself, "My ability to thrive is about *how* I show up, not *where* I show up." Living well isn't about where you are, it's about how you show up.

At the heart of it, we are wired for connection. It's baked into our very nature. Just like plants grow toward the light, people are drawn to community because that's where we thrive, where we become more fully ourselves.

The whole natural order is about service and support. Real friendship is about mutual care and mutual growth.

When you think about the people in your life, know that you weren't made to go it alone. Your mind will flourish when you lean into the community you're meant to be part of. True friendship isn't just a bonus, it's a core need. It's where we find our best selves.

Your Takeaway

Remember:

- I was made to be part of a community.

- I can live well right here, right now, with who I'm with.

- Serving others is part of serving my own purpose.

October 19

We're all part of the same team, even the ones who don't know it yet. Everyone's contributing to this life in their own way. The question is, are you doing your part with intention or resistance?

You don't have to like everyone. You don't have to agree with everyone. But you do have to recognize that we're all in this together. Some of us are consciously playing our roles, stepping up and contributing with intention. Others might resist the flow, fight what's happening, but even that resistance is part of the bigger picture. Whether you choose to be aligned or avoidant, you will be utilized by the universe either way.

The key point here is that you get to decide which side you want to be on. Will you choose to be part of the effort that moves things forward, that supports the common good? Or will you play a role that combats progress and fairness?

In true friendship and in life, it's about how you show up: your willingness to be part of something bigger, to support others, to bring your best self.

The universe is always calling on you to step into your role, make your contribution, and be a friend, not just to a few, but to the whole.

Your Takeaway

Understanding true friendship means realizing that *everyone* plays a role in this life; some with awareness, some in complete ignorance. If you want real connection, if you want to be someone people can trust and walk beside, choose the path that *builds,* not blocks.

October 20

Your forgiveness isn't about them deserving it. It's about you being free from the damage their ignorance could do to your peace.

It's human to still feel love or affection for people who mess up. At the end of the day, they're family in the broadest sense. Maybe they made bad choices or acted out of ignorance, but they're still part of your circle, your shared human experience.

None of us are perfect, and none of us will be here forever. You and they are on the same journey, headed to the same destination. And if someone hasn't made you worse than you already were inside, if they haven't broken your core, then hold space for that affection.

This isn't about excusing bad behavior or letting people off the hook, it's about recognizing shared humanity. Real friendship withstands mistakes because it knows people can grow, change, and that love isn't transactional.

So when you find yourself judging or wanting to pull away, pause. Ask yourself, "Am I protecting my heart, or am I shutting down a connection that's worth holding onto?"

True friends aren't perfect. They're real. And real is way better than perfect.

Your Takeaway

Unless someone has harmed your inner core, allow them a little grace. Everyone's time here is temporary, and with that short time it's not about keeping score. It's about staying soft in a hard world. That's what makes real friendship rare and worth the work.

October 21

The goal isn't to be less human, it's to be a better one. A better human understands that most cruelty is just a cry for help.

Most people act out of their own limited view of what's right and wrong. When you realize that their bad is often just a twisted or incomplete version of your own good, it gets easier to feel compassion for them instead of burning bridges.

It's not about excusing bad behavior, it's about recognizing they're stuck in a perspective that doesn't yet see the bigger picture. If you're still close to their way of thinking, forgiveness becomes a natural step. But if you've grown beyond that narrow definition of good and bad, then showing leniency isn't just kindness, it's wisdom.

True friendship and peace come from understanding where others are coming from, even when they hurt you.

So before you react, pause and reflect on these questions, "What's guiding their actions? How can I hold onto my values and still find space to forgive?"

Compassion doesn't make you a doormat. It makes you wise. And that wisdom is what true friendship is built on. That's how you protect your heart without losing your mind.

Your Takeaway

Not everyone sees the world the way you do. Decide to seek to understand instead of instantly reacting. When you can stay connected even through conflict, because you understand the *why* behind the behavior.

October 22

Stop complaining about your circumstances, especially to your friends. Real connection isn't built on constant critique. It's built on showing up with presence, not just problems.

It's way too easy to judge someone else's life from the outside, or to complain about your own situation just because it isn't always picture-perfect. Friendship, real friendship, is about meeting people where they are, not where you wish they were. It's refusing to gossip, criticize, or belittle another person's experience just to make yourself feel better.

The same goes for how you treat yourself. Don't become your own worst critic, always looking for what's wrong or missing, especially if you're living a life others might dream about. Gratitude is the soil where real friendships grow. When you stop comparing, stop judging, and start appreciating, both your world and your relationships get a whole lot richer.

A true friend supports, listens, and holds space, without jealousy, backhanded comments, or side-eye. And the best friendships start with the way you speak to yourself about your own journey.

Next time that you catch yourself complaining, pause. Ask yourself, "Is this building real friendships or just burning bridges?" Complaining is easy. Connection and understanding is where the real work and real joy is.

Your Takeaway

Friends are drawn to authenticity, not excuses. Keep your focus on building honest, humble relationships that aren't shaken by the trappings of life's highs or lows.

Reflect:

- Where are you judging someone else's journey instead of supporting them where they are?

- How can you practice gratitude for your own life, even if it's not perfect?

- What would your friendships look like if you swapped complaints for encouragement?

- Are you ready to be the kind of friend who values connection over criticism, to both yourself and others?

Real friendship means standing together, not standing above. Make your words build bridges, not walls.

October 23

If someone dislikes you, don't get lost in the reaction. Look deeper into their soul, their fears, and their story. You don't have to twist yourself into a knot to be liked. But you do have to treat them with kindness, because beneath it all, they're still your fellow human.

When someone disapproves of you or even resents you, it stings, but don't take it personally. Take a moment to look deeper and see who they really are beneath all that noise. Look past the attitude and into the *human*. Their pain. Their patterns. Their perspective. You don't have to get caught up in their words or judgments.

True friendship, and real maturity, isn't about being adored. It's about being able to see people clearly, even when they can't see you the same way. You don't need to lose your peace trying to make them like you or think well of you. That's exhausting and unnecessary. Your role is to stay benevolent, to offer kindness, even when it's hard.

The universe works in mysterious ways to guide them toward what they need, whether they realize it or not. Your job is to just keep showing up as your best self: steady, kind, and unbothered by their noise.

That's true friendship in action: seeing beyond the surface, holding space for others, and letting go of the need for approval.

Your Takeaway

Friendship isn't built on shared opinions. It's built on shared humanity. See them clearly, stay grounded in compassion, and don't let ego get in the way of your decency.

October 24

Even the best of us may die with people quietly relieved to see us go. That's not bitterness, it's reality. But don't let that harden you. Leave this life, and those around you, with grace. With no resentment. With love still in your hands.

Not everyone you love will love you back the way you hoped. Even when you've shown up with care and integrity, some people may still feel more at ease with your absence than your presence. Even those you labored for, prayed for, and quietly tried to support may misunderstand you or resent your silent standards.

But don't let that poison your heart. True friendship isn't proven in how people receive you. It's proven in how you keep showing up: with warmth, respect, and dignity, even when the connection is fading.

When your time finally comes, whether it's the end of a job, a relationship, or your final breath, let go without clinging, without resentment, without becoming cold.

You came into this life bound to others by nature. And when it's time to go, let nature release you just as gently.

Friendship doesn't always end with mutual applause. But it can end with peace if you choose grace over grievance.

Your Takeaway

Keep being a person who's friendly, kind, and calm. Don't leave with bitterness or resentment.

October 25

Hold your ground with clarity, but keep your heart open. People may push back, disagree, or even hurt you, but don't let that turn you cold. True strength is standing firm in your values and still choosing kindness.

It's easy to be kind when everyone's cheering you on. It's harder when people stand in your way, challenge your plans, or even cause you pain. But your job isn't to react, retaliate or give up on what you know is right. You have to be rock solid, unshakable in your decisions and your path. That's strength.

Strength isn't just about standing firm. It's also about *how* you stand firm. Keep your kindness intact. Don't let frustration make you harsh or bitter. Becoming harsh with people who block you is weakness dressed up as power. When someone opposes you, that's not your cue to fight them or cut them off. It's your cue to show them what integrity looks like in real time.

These people are part of your tribe, they're connected to you in one way or another. If you burn bridges or lose your cool you'll desert your own community, your own support system.

True strength is holding your ground *and* keeping your heart open. That's how you build trust and loyalty. Emotional intelligence is the ability to regulate your emotions and treat others well, even when they test you.

So ask yourself, "Can you stand firm without losing your kindness? Can you protect your boundaries without burning bridges?"

That balance is where true friendship lives.

Your Takeaway

Real friendship isn't about giving in or giving up. It's about holding your center *and* holding space for others to grow, even when they resist you. Stay steady. Stay kind.

October 26

The health of a friendship is measured not by how often you agree, but by how quickly you drop your pride to reconnect after you disagree.

When a friend criticizes you, even if it's harsh or maybe unfair, don't react by shutting down or pushing them away. Friendship isn't a courtroom. It's a connection. Lean in, try to heal the relationship, and restore the connection.

True friendship isn't just about the good times, but about weathering challenges with grace.

Give your teachers and mentors genuine, wholehearted praise, not just the polite kind, but the real, deep appreciation they deserve for shaping who we are.

When it comes to love for your kids, let it be unconditional, and real, not just a role or *duty*. Be genuine.

No matter who it is, the lesson is clear: show up authentically, embrace the bumps in the road, and build bonds out of love, respect, and real effort. If there's tension between you and someone you love, don't wait. Don't get stuck in pride or principle. Be the first to reach out.

Next time someone challenges you, pause and ask, "Am I holding the door open for this friendship to grow stronger?"

Your Takeaway

Real friends care enough to reach out, to repair, and to praise each other openly, not just when it's easy, but when it's humbling. True friendship isn't about being flawless. It's about being willing to go first when it matters most.

Concept 26: Cultivate Humility

Humility isn't thinking less of yourself. It's thinking of yourself less.

October 27

The sin of impulse is a wound, the sin of indulgence is a choice. One is a mistake of the moment, the other is a betrayal of the self.

When you make a mistake because you're angry, it's usually because something hurt you, triggered you, or made you lose your footing. But when you make a mistake because of desire, because you *chose* to give in to pleasure instead of doing what's right, that stings deeper. It wasn't a simple reaction, it was active indulgence.

That's what makes desire more dangerous and more blameworthy. Anger is often forced upon you, yet desire is chosen. You have the power to say no to temptation, but when you don't, you're giving in. Real strength isn't just about holding back anger. It's about mastering desire, being aware of it, owning it, and choosing what serves your highest self.

Next time you feel that pull, whether it's a craving, a temptation, or a lust for approval, ask yourself, "Am I acting out of reaction or choice? Am I serving my best self or just feeding a momentary itch?"

That's where true maturity lives. Not in giving in, but in choosing the better path, even when it's hard.

Your Takeaway

Own your impulses. Desire isn't the problem. Letting it lead us is. Real growth begins not in defending your mistakes, but in learning from them, one humbled choice at a time.

October 28

Life's a contact sport: stay humble, keep your balance, and be ready for anything.

Life isn't a perfectly choreographed dance. It's more like stepping into the ring, not knowing what the next round's going to throw at you. You can plan, you can prepare, but surprises will still emerge. Humility means remembering you don't have all the moves, and you're not in control of everything.

Stay grounded. Don't get cocky thinking you've mastered the routine, because one plot twist can floor you if you're not paying attention. Being humble doesn't mean playing small, it means staying open, alert, and adaptable, knowing you'll need help and resilience more than you'll need style points.

That means cultivating intelligent resilience to keep you balanced and aware. Imagine your mind and body like a wrestler's stance: grounded, steady, and alert. You don't freeze or panic. You don't get knocked over by surprises. You adapt and respond.

Our brain's flexibility – our ability to bounce back – is part of what protects us from being overwhelmed by stress. When you expect the unexpected, you build neural pathways that keep you steady instead of spiraling.

A calm, steady presence lets you flow with life's punches instead of breaking under them.

Real growth comes from getting up when you're knocked down, adjusting your stance, and admitting you don't have all the answers. It's about learning from each round, not pretending you're untouchable. Stay soft enough to adapt, strong enough to persist, and wise enough to know that everyone gets thrown sometimes.

Your Takeaway

You don't need to fight the waves. Instead, be the rock that they crash against but can't move. Stand ready for whatever's next, and don't let life's surprises throw you off balance. When you stay grounded, even the toughest moments can be handled with grace.

Reflect:

- Where are you acting like life should go according to your script, instead of staying open and adaptable?

- How can you bring more humility to your challenges? What about less ego or more curiosity?

- What would change if you saw setbacks as feedback, not failure?

- Are you willing to stay teachable, even when things don't go your way?

Humility keeps you on your feet, so you can keep wrestling, learning, and moving forward.

October 29

Don't look for meaning in the plot. The chaos is a given. Look for peace in the one thing you can edit: your reaction.

The modern world is a firehose of information, distractions, and drama. Your social media feed is full of things to desire and people to be upset with.

Challenge yourself to stop looking for meaning in all that noise. Stop chasing trends, getting angry at online arguments, and worrying about what other people think. It's all fleeting and has no real value.

The only lasting comfort comes from two core realizations. First, that everything happening around you is part of a bigger, messy, but ultimately functional system. Second, your integrity, values, and mind are completely your own. No one can ever take that from you unless you give it away.

Humility isn't about feeling small, it's about recognizing the wild, imperfect ride you're on and staying true to your own steady center. Find your peace there.

Your Takeaway

Our perceptions shift all the time because people change, but your inner compass and true self can't be forced off course. No one else controls your character.

October 30

Set your boundaries without building a wall of resentment. You can learn to protect yourself without deciding everyone is an enemy.

Think about the minor chaos of daily life. For example, imagine you're on a crowded subway. Someone bumps into you, maybe a little too hard. You don't assume they meant to hurt you or start fighting with them. You just stay cautious, keep your guard up, but you don't turn it into a personal attack.

Stop taking things personally. That person probably wasn't trying to hurt you, they were just trying to hold their own, and in the process, you got a little knocked around. The idea isn't to be a doormat, it's to be smart. You can learn to be more aware of your surroundings and protect yourself without turning a clumsy accident into a personal war.

Protect your peace, but don't turn every little thing into a battle. That's humility in action: knowing you're not the center of every conflict and that sometimes it's just life doing its thing.

Your Takeaway

People will sometimes hurt you, step on your toes, or test your patience, but it's not always because they want to hurt you. You can be cautious without turning into someone who's suspicious or hostile. Let things slide when you can and overlook those little scrapes with kindness.

October 31

The things you want most — peace, purpose, strength — aren't things you find. They're a resource you mine from inside yourself.

Beneath all the layers, the titles, the roles, and the achievements is a quiet reservoir of goodness, a deep reserve of strength, resilience, and purpose. It's a power source you access through consistent inner work only when you stop searching outside of yourself. Humility is recognizing that no matter how far you've come, you have more to learn and more to give.

Cultivating humility means continuously going inward, asking yourself challenging questions, staying curious, and realizing you're always a work in progress. Keep digging. When you do, your true strength surfaces, not with noise or ego, but as a steady flow of kindness, resilience, and wisdom that benefits everyone around you.

Your Takeaway

You can't fill the void inside yourself with social media or validation from other people. It takes effort, patience, and a willingness to go deeper.

Reflect:

- Are you spending too much time polishing the surface instead of exploring your deeper self?

- What area of your life could use a little less ego and a bit more humble curiosity?

- How might cultivating humility help you unlock a deeper, steadier source of strength?

- Are you willing to quietly do the inner work, even if no one else sees it?

Remember, your best self emerges not when you shout your greatness, but when you quietly keep digging deeper.

November 01

Real strength isn't about having an audience, it's about having a purpose. And a purpose, when you live it fully, will always attract both praise and scorn.

Sometimes you'll be hated, misunderstood, or criticized even when you're doing the right thing.

True humility isn't about chasing approval. Your role is to do what's right, even if it means being unpopular. Humility is knowing your value doesn't come from applause. It comes from alignment, from character, and from showing up with purpose, not ego.

Lean into the discomfort. Stay grounded in your values. Whether you're leading a team, a family, or just your own life, don't flinch when your efforts go unseen. Do good anyway. That's the mark of a true leader.

At the end of the day, what matters is the good you do, and not the noise around it.

Your Takeaway

If you need to be praised for every good thing you do, you're not leading, you're performing. If you focus too much on what others think, you'll lose yourself. Real greatness is doing what's right, even when it costs you the approval of others.

November 02

Stop complaining about the mess that comes with growth.

Life is messy. You're going to come across ego, discomfort, dysfunction, and disappointment. We all want the finished product – the successful project, the healthy body, the peaceful day – without the inevitable mess, but humility is knowing you're not above it all.

Stop taking it personally. You wouldn't get furious that your new car became a little dirty on a cross-country road trip, you'd see it as a natural part of the journey.

Treat all the noise and chaos of daily life with the same practicality. We don't have to like it, but we can stop wasting our energy complaining about it.

Your Takeaway

Stay centered, stay kind, and stop expecting life to always smell like roses. Accept the grime, but don't let it stick to you.

November 03

The world won't be saved by a single heroic gesture. It will be built one small, honest action at a time. Do your part without waiting for a parade.

The universe isn't waiting for your big speech. It's asking for your next right action. Stop trying to be the hero of the story and just be the person who shows up every day. You're part of an unstoppable current, and the most powerful thing you can do is align yourself with it.

Don't get caught trying to look important. Don't measure your worth by who's watching or how grand your role looks. You don't need to change the world in a day. You don't need to build a perfect society or play the hero. You just need to stay present and do what's *yours to do*.

It's okay if your contribution feels small today. Stay steady, do it well, and let humility be the proof that you're doing the work for the right reasons.

Your Takeaway

True greatness isn't found in a grandiose title, but in the quiet, consistent work you do when no one is watching. Life is about living simply, serving humbly, and being honest with yourself.

November 04

Stop trying to be an influencer and start trying to be an influence. The former is a performance, the latter is a legacy.

In a world obsessed with thought leaders and viral success, there's immense pressure to have all the answers. The simple truth is that you don't, and you never will. Acknowledging your own imperfections and accepting that you'll likely never be a celebrated mentor or leader is not a sign of weakness, it's a powerful act of liberation.

The true path to a good life isn't found in chasing a reputation or a title. It's found in the quiet, daily practice of living with honesty, moderation, courage, and self-reliance. A wise person isn't the one with all the answers, but the one who asks the right questions and lives with the courage of their convictions. The humble life is the good life because it's a life focused on what you can control, your character, not on what others will think of it.

Stop focusing on what others think about you. Start focusing on living true to who *you* are, right here, right now. Stick to those basics, and you're already winning.

Your Takeaway

None of us get to live the perfect life. If you're honest with yourself and with others, you know you're still figuring it out. The good life is in doing what your nature calls for and being honest, balanced, brave, and independent.

November 05

The voice inside you isn't a product of your environment, it's the environment for which all your thoughts and actions are accountable.

Your mind is the most powerful tool you've got. It can reflect, create, choose who you become, and make meaning out of everything. But it's all too easy to get lost in the noise of your own ego.

Take a moment to zoom out from your own life. Your projects, your successes, and your failures are just tiny blips on the timeline of the universe. This isn't meant to make you feel small, but to free you from the burden of trying to be everything to everyone. Your ultimate purpose isn't dependent on how long you live or how much you achieve. It's dependent on the quality of your character at this very moment.

True humility isn't a sign of weakness, it's the profound strength that comes from a clear-eyed perspective. Nothing is more valuable than your own integrity. It's a powerful understanding that your worth isn't found in your job title, bank account, or public reputation, but in the quiet, unshakeable virtue of your own mind. That is a strength no one can ever take from you.

Your Takeaway

Humility is remembering that no matter how much you've seen, you haven't seen it all and the universe isn't taking cues from your script. It's vast. Timeless. And you're a small, beautiful part of it. That perspective keeps the ego in check. It reminds you to keep learning, to keep loving people, and to let modesty be the quiet proof of your strength.

Reflect:

- How do you keep your ego in check when you know you're capable or skilled?

- In what areas of life could you listen more instead of leading with your opinion?

- Are you using your intelligence to elevate yourself or to lift others, too?

- How does remembering your small place in the vastness of time change your daily attitude?

Humility isn't downplaying your light, it's shining it in a way that warms others instead of blinding them.

November 06

Your victories and defeats are the common weather of a human life. Don't let either of them define you.

We're often convinced our successes are unique and our failures are a special punishment. Check that ego at the door and realize that the events of your life aren't a personalized script just for you. Nothing that happens to you is brand-new in the grand story of humanity. Breakups, job losses, sickness, gossip, success, and praise – they've all been on repeat for hundreds of years. They're part of the normal, recurring rhythm of existence.

Just as we accept seasons of sunshine and seasons of rain, we should accept the ebb and flow of fortune and misfortune. The key to inner peace is to stop taking it all so personally.

You're not the exception. Life's ups and downs happen to everyone. Stay humble, stay steady. By cultivating this humble perspective, you free yourself from the inflated pride of success and the crushing despair of failure. You learn that your true north, your inner compass, is the only thing that matters, and it's the only thing that remains unshaken by the common, impersonal chaos of the world.

Your Takeaway

Humility is remembering you're part of a much bigger cycle. When you accept that, you stop taking the highs too seriously and the lows too personally. You stay grounded and teachable. You stop chasing the illusion that life should be an endless summer. Ride the seasons with grace, knowing you're not in control of the weather, just your response to it.

Reflect:

- Where in life are you acting like your challenges or successes are completely unique?

- How would it change your mindset to see both good and bad seasons as equally normal?

- When things go your way, do you lead with gratitude or let ego take the wheel?

- When life turns difficult, do you respond with humility or resistance?

Humility keeps you steady in every season, because you know they're all just part of the same cycle.

November 07

Life's always in motion and you're just one chapter in a story that keeps rewriting itself.

Nothing stays the same for long. Seasons shift, trends fade, people grow, relationships change. The universe is based on reinvention. Every ending becomes the starting point for something else, whether you're talking about a career, a friendship, or even a past version of you from five years ago.

Humility is recognizing that you're part of this constant cycle. You're not the final product, and neither is anything you create. You're a seed, and so is your work, your influence, your legacy. And just like seeds, what comes next might look nothing like what you expected and that's okay.

When you accept that change is the default, you stop clinging to control or thinking you've arrived. You stop pretending you're the main event in a story that's been running long before you showed up and will keep going long after. Humility is letting yourself evolve without needing the universe to revolve around you.

Your Takeaway

Your story isn't the only one, and your time here is a momentary beat in an infinite song. Humility is the peace you find in accepting your place as a temporary, but vital, part of a much larger whole.

Reflect:

- Where in your life are you resisting change because you want to stay in control?

- How might accepting that you're part of a bigger cycle make you more adaptable?

- Are you willing to see yourself as a seed, valuable, but not the whole story?

- How could embracing change help you let go of ego and grow with more grace?

Humility is knowing you're part of the flow, not the one directing the current.

Concept 27: Keep Your Death in Mind (*Memento Mori*)

You will die. Let that truth shape how deeply you live.

November 08

The true length of a life isn't measured in breaths, but in the weight of the moments you filled with purpose.

Some of us act as if our life runs on an infinite supply. We put off our goals, postpone difficult conversations, and waste time on things that don't matter. Others desperately indulge in clean eating, high-tech biohacks, or wellness trends in an attempt to cheat the inevitable.

The real question isn't "How can I live forever?", but "What will I do with the time I have left?" This awareness should be the ultimate motivator to live virtuously and with a sense of purpose. It reminds you that the only thing that truly counts is the character you build, not the length of the life you lived. When you remember that the clock is always ticking, the petty stuff suddenly matters less. You stop wasting time on grudges, on scrolling your life away, on chasing things that don't feed your soul. You start asking better questions like "Am I proud of how I'm showing up today? If this were my last week, would I be spending it like this?" You don't get to control how long the film of your life runs, but you do get to choose what you put on screen in every scene.

Your Takeaway

Leave the question of 'how long' in the hands of the universe. Your job is to use the time you have wisely.

Reflect:

- If you knew your time was shorter than you think, what would you stop doing immediately?

- What's one way you could make today count without waiting for the "right time"?

- Are you living a life that would make you proud if it ended tomorrow?

- How might keeping your death in mind help you live with more urgency and gratitude?

When you stop fearing the end, you start truly living in the present moment.

November 09

The biggest lie we tell ourselves isn't that we'll do it tomorrow. It's that 'tomorrow' is guaranteed.

Most of us are living for a future that's not guaranteed. We're constantly adding things to our reading lists, planning difficult conversations for 'someday', and saving our energy for a version of ourselves we hope to become.

That promised old age is not a certainty, and the plans you're saving for the future may never come to pass. The wisdom of keeping death in mind isn't about morbid fear, it's about a fierce urgency to live.

This realization is an act of liberation. By abandoning the vain hope that you'll have unlimited time, you are freed to focus on the only moment that truly matters: right now. You're the only person who can save you. Stop waiting for a future you to get their act together and start being that person today.

The true measure of your life isn't found in what you plan to do, but in the character you build with every choice you make in the present. This urgent awareness should be the ultimate motivator to live virtuously, because your time is a finite and precious resource.

Your Takeaway

Stop saving ideas for your future self. Start living like you're the one who has to carry this life forward, because you are. Abandon the illusion of *later*. Show up for yourself today.

November 10

Stop living like you have forever, your deadline's closer than you think.

The illusion that you'll 'get to it later' is how dreams die and relationships fade. You have a finite number of mornings to wake up, a finite number of chances to tell people you love them, and a finite number of opportunities to show up as the person you *want* to be.

Memento Mori isn't about fear, it's about urgency with purpose. It's remembering that the clock is always running and that every moment you waste on pettiness, procrastination, or living on autopilot is a moment you don't get back.

This realization is an act of liberation. It strips away all the non-essential things we might chase, fame, wealth, or pleasure and leaves us with one, most important task: to use the time we have to focus on our character. Your ultimate purpose isn't found in living forever, it's found in living with virtue and integrity right now. You won't be judged by the length of your story, but by the weight of every sentence you wrote.

Your Takeaway

Your time here is a precious, finite resource. Stop waiting for 'someday' to be kinder, braver, or more honest. Make an active choice to be the kind of person who'll look back with no regrets.

Reflect:

- What important thing have you been putting off like you have forever?

- If you knew your deadline was sooner than you thought, what would you do differently this week?

- Who needs to hear from you *today* and what's stopping you from saying it?

- Are you living in a way that would make you proud if tomorrow wasn't guaranteed?

Life doesn't owe you more time, so spend what you have like it matters.

November 11

Memento Mori is the thought that puts all your mental notifications on silent

so you can hear what's real.

We're constantly on a treadmill of notifications, emotional drama, and the demands of our bodies. We're pulled in a million different directions, and it feels like we're never truly in control.

Death strips away all the distractions. No more being yanked around by every notification, craving, or emotional trigger. No more mind racing through a thousand "what ifs" or obsessing over how you look, what you own, or how you measure up.

If the end frees you from all that noise, why wait until then to find peace? *Memento Mori* is a reminder that you can start releasing some of those chains *today*. You can choose not to get dragged into every impulse; to step back from constant comparison and overstimulation; to live lighter, calmer, and more on your own terms.

Don't wait for death to set you free. Practice that freedom now by releasing yourself from what doesn't matter. By doing this, you're not just preparing for the end, you're living a more focused, purposeful, and truly free life in the here and now.

Your Takeaway

Death is not an end to be feared, but is the ultimate form of freedom. It's the permanent release from the noise, the desires, and the physical demands that hold us captive in life. You can practice that freedom now by consciously detaching yourself from the things that distract you. You can't escape your physical body, but you can stop letting its fleeting desires and aches rule your mind.

Reflect:

- Which distractions or impulses feel like they're running your life right now?

- How would it feel to let go of one unnecessary mental weight starting today?

- Are you living with intention, or just reacting to whatever grabs your attention next?

- How can you create a little more stillness in your life before life forces it on you?

The peace you're chasing at the end is available now, if you're willing to let go.

November 12

Death doesn't discriminate. It doesn't care about your job title or how many awards you win.

Death is the ultimate equalizer, dissolving all our carefully constructed social hierarchies and titles – your job, your fame, your follower count – back into the elements from which they came.

This liberates you from the anxiety of chasing a status that is ultimately meaningless. It forces you to ask, "If my external achievements are all temporary, what is it that truly matters?" Your character, your integrity, and your virtue are the only things that cannot be taken from you.

Your Takeaway

Make your life count now. This is your shot to show up as your real self. Drop the comparison, drop the ego, and focus on the impact and presence you bring today.

Reflect:

- Where are you letting status or comparison distract you from what really matters?

- How would your choices shift if you remembered that everyone ends up equal in the end?

- What could you let go of, knowing that no trophy or title gets a free pass?

- Are you willing to use the reminder of your own mortality to live more fully, right now?

Know that greatness isn't about how long you're remembered, it's about how deeply you lived while you were here.

November 13

A life lived with the fear of death is a curse. A life lived with gratitude for every extra day is a blessing. The choice is in your hands.

We often get so caught up in the grind of daily life that we forget what a gift it is. We feel anxious about the future, procrastinate on our most important work, and take a guaranteed tomorrow for granted. Try performing a mental reset: imagine your life ended just a moment ago, and everything from this point forward is an unexpected bonus.

This isn't a morbid thought, it's an act of liberation. By letting go of the trivial anxieties and the feeling of entitlement, you are freed to live with a fierce sense of gratitude and urgency. Your focus shifts from the things you can't control, like the length of your life, to the one thing you can: how you choose to live this bonus time.

This perspective allows you to clarify your priorities and live with purpose and integrity in every single moment, because you know it's a gift that can be taken back at any time.

Your Takeaway

Memento Mori isn't about doom and gloom, it's about gratitude with teeth. It's using the reminder of death to strip away excuses and make the most of the time you've been gifted back.

Reflect:

- If today was truly a second chance, what's the first thing you'd do differently?

- Which grudges, fears, or hesitations would suddenly feel unworthy of your time?

- What joy, connection, or creation have you been putting off that belongs in your bonus round?

- How can you live today so that if it ended tomorrow, you'd say,

"I used it well"?

The quickest way to stop wasting your time is to realize that you're just borrowing it. Be a good borrower.

November 14

Your digital footprint will be swept away by time's algorithm. The only thing you can't delete is the character you built offline.

By accepting that your reputation will one day fade, you are freed from the anxiety of chasing it. This allows you to focus on the one thing that truly matters: your character. That is the only thing that can't be taken from you, and it's the only thing you have control over in this vast, impersonal cycle of life and death.

Ask yourself, "What am I doing with my life, and does it really matter in the end?" Are you spending it chasing approval, getting lost in petty arguments, or waiting for 'later' to matter? Or are you making choices you'd be proud of, whether or not anyone remembers your name?

Your Takeaway

Memento Mori strips away the illusion that legacy is about how long you're remembered. It's about how deeply you live while you're here. You can't control if your name ends up in the history books or disappears in the shuffle, but you *can* control whether you actually showed up for your life.

Reflect:

- If no one ever remembered you, would your life still feel worth living?

- What are you doing today that actually matters to you, not just to your image?

- Who or what are you neglecting because you think you'll have time later?

- How would you live differently if you knew your 'turn' was closer than you think?

In the end, it's not about being remembered, it's about being *awake* while you're here.

November 15

A life lived in the shadow of death is a life lived in the light of purpose.

Death is a transition just like every other stage of life you've gone through. Birth. Teething. Puberty. Love. Wrinkles. Letting go. Death isn't the enemy. It's just your soul outgrowing its body. You don't have to fear it, and you don't have to rush it.

A truly wise person doesn't fear death, they instead see it as a natural and inevitable part of life, no different from the seasons changing or a plant wilting at the end of its cycle.

Find peace in the relief that death offers. A person can get exhausted by the constant noise of a world filled with endless disagreement and shallow values. The weariness of living in disharmony can make the prospect of leaving this world easier to face. This practice isn't about being cynical, it's about using every possible perspective to free yourself from the fear of death, allowing you to live more fully and without anxiety.

Your Takeaway

Keeping your death in mind is a practice of embracing life's full cycle. By accepting death as a natural transformation, you can find peace in the understanding that an ending is a fundamental part of the journey.

November 16

Stop living your one-time performance as if it were a dress rehearsal for a play that will never open. Step onto the stage.

We can all get lost in the endless scroll of daily life, but the profound truth is that you are a creature of *one day*. Just like leaves in the wind, we all show up, flutter around for a while, and then we're gone. The tree keeps growing, but the leaves are replaced before long.

This isn't just about your life, it's about all the external things you cling to. When you realize how short life really is, the petty arguments, social media drama, and desperate chase for approval all loses its shine. The people who make you or break you will eventually be gone, just like you.

This awareness is a tool that breaks us out of the trance of procrastination and forces us to live purposefully. The only thing of true and lasting value is your internal character, so focus on that. Stop living for a future that isn't guaranteed and start living with virtue and purpose in the here and now, because your time is a finite and precious resource.

Your Takeaway

Memento Mori isn't meant to make you sad, it's meant to strip away the nonsense. Live fully, love deeply, and let the wind take you when it's time, knowing you didn't waste the season you were given.

Reflect:

- What are you clinging to right now that won't matter when you're gone?

- How would you treat people differently if you remembered they're all "leaves" too?

- What would you stop chasing if you knew your season was short?

- Are you living in a way that makes the most of your time in the wind?

Life's too short to pretend you're permanent, so live like a leaf and make your season count.

November 17

The goal isn't to live without fear of the end, it's to live with the quiet confidence that you're ready for it.

A truly admirable person isn't someone who ignores death. It's someone who has achieved a state of philosophical readiness for it at any moment. This preparedness isn't born of a rebellious or emotional attitude, but is the result of deep, rational thought and a conscious decision to live a life of virtue.

The goal isn't to live without fear of the end, it's to live with the quiet confidence that you're ready for it. This mindset comes from accepting that the ultimate outcome of your death, whatever it may be, is outside of your control. What you can control is your response to this reality. By focusing on living a purposeful life, you cultivate the courage to make virtuous choices daily, so that when the end arrives, there are no regrets.

Your Takeaway

Real readiness is quiet, honest, and rooted in reflection, not reaction. Live in such a way that if today was your last, you will have shown up fully in your life.

Reflect:

- If today were your last, what conversations or actions would you regret leaving undone?

- Is your readiness for death coming from genuine acceptance or just avoidance?

- What would it take for you to live in a way that would make you ready to leave at any moment?

- How can you start preparing without turning it into a morbid performance?

Readiness for death isn't about wanting the end, it's about living so well that you're not afraid when it comes.

November 18

The universe isn't a story with a single ending. It's an endless cycle, and your life is a single, beautiful sentence.

We can easily get caught up in the modern fear of death, seeing it as a personal tragedy. The gentle challenge is to reframe it. Death isn't a failure or an enemy, it's a natural, impersonal process as fundamental as birth itself. Think of it less as an end and more as a return. The same elements that form you are simply going back into the makeup of the universe, like a book being returned to a library. A truly rational person doesn't oppose this basic law of nature.

The wisdom of keeping death in mind lies in using reason to overcome our irrational fear of it. By accepting that this is an event you can't control, you can focus on the one thing you can: your attitude toward it. This acceptance of nature's cycle frees you to live fully without the anxiety of the inevitable, choosing to embrace life rather than fear its conclusion.

Your Takeaway

Death is as natural as birth. It's just the elements reshuffling, the same way they did the day you showed up here. There's no shame in it, no disgrace, only the mind's resistance to what it can't control. *Memento Mori* means remembering this so that you live without the illusion that you're exempt.

Reflect:

- How would your choices shift if you truly accepted that death is just part of nature's plan?

- In what ways are you resisting life by resisting the fact that it ends?

- How might accepting death as part of the universe's design help you live with less fear and more intention?

- If you stopped seeing death as a tragedy, what would you start doing differently today?

Death isn't the enemy, it's the reminder to live like your time actually matters.

November 19

The ultimate way to defy death isn't to live forever. It's to live so fully that when the time comes, you have nothing left to prove.

If a person chasing fleeting pleasure can live without a constant fear of death, then a person striving for a life of purpose and integrity has no excuse.

This realization is born from using reason to overcome our irrational fears. Death is the ultimate external event we cannot control. The only thing we can control is our response to it, our internal work. This frees you to pursue a truly meaningful life without being sidetracked by fear. The goal isn't to live forever, it's to live so fully that when the time comes, you have nothing left to prove.

Today, take a deep breath and remind yourself that death isn't the enemy, wasting life is. Start living fully, while you still can.

Your Takeaway

Don't give death more weight than it deserves. When you stop fearing the end, you start showing up for the now with more purpose, more presence, and more peace.

Concept 28: Practice Detachment from the Outcome

Do your best and let go of the rest.

November 20

Your online footprint is a sandcastle. The waves of time will erase it. The only thing you truly own is the ocean inside you.

In a world of constant digital updates, performance reviews, and the pressure to build a lasting reputation, it's easy to feel like everything is out of your control. Your online presence can be inconsistent, your follower count erratic, and your reputation uncertain, but all of these external things are fleeting and unreliable.

The only thing that can truly escort you safely on your way is your inner compass. *Detachment from the outcome* – or outcome independence – is the discipline of letting go of the results you can't control and focusing on the one thing you can: your character.

When you stop gripping so hard to the concept of winning, you move through life lighter. You stop spiraling when things don't go your way because you understand they were never fully yours to dictate. You start accepting what comes, good or bad, as part of the same natural flow you're made from.

Focus on how you play the game, with integrity, purpose, and all your heart. True freedom comes from this mindset, which allows you to accept what happens with a serene mind, knowing that your value isn't dependent on the success or failure of any single moment.

This isn't about being passive, it's about being powerful by choosing to be a person of virtue regardless of the external results.

Your Takeaway

Life is short, unpredictable, and full of variables you'll never control. If you're attaching your worth to how things *turn out*, you're setting yourself up for a lifetime of anxiety and disappointment.

Detachment from the outcome means shifting your focus to what *you* can control: your integrity, your intention, your effort. It's about showing up fully, playing your part well, and releasing the illusion that you can manipulate every result.

Reflect:

- Where in your life are you gripping so tightly to an outcome that it's stealing your peace?

- How would you show up differently if you cared more about your actions than the result?

- What would it look like to measure success by your integrity, not by the scoreboard?

- How would accepting the flow of events as in accord with nature change your daily stress?

Detach from the result. Master the moment. That's where the real win lives.

November 21

A life built on the approval of others is a house built on sand. Your foundation is your integrity, and it doesn't need applause to stand.

One of the fastest ways to lose focus and peace is to agonize about what other people are doing, saying, or thinking; wondering who they're with, what they're posting, or why they made that choice. Our energy is wasted doomscrolling social media, worrying about what a colleague said, or being jealous of someone else's success. All of this is a self-inflicted distraction from our own inner work.

The truly admirable person is one who finds peace and purpose by focusing on their own character, accepting their fate, and doing their own work well, all while remaining unbothered by the praise or criticism of others.

The wisdom of this approach is in the *dichotomy of control.* By detaching from the chaotic outcomes outside of your power, what someone else is doing, their opinions of you, or the lot the universe has dealt you, you free yourself to focus on the one thing you can control: your own rational mind.

This detachment isn't about being cold or indifferent, it's about making virtue a priority. It's the necessary tool that allows you to be a person of integrity, uncorrupted by fleeting praise or criticism. It also leads to the acceptance of fate, a profound peace that comes from knowing that you've done your best and can welcome whatever outcome comes your way.

Your Takeaway

When you stop measuring your worth by how others see you or whether they approve, their praise and criticism lose power over you. *Detachment from the outcome* means letting go of the need to monitor, predict, or influence other people's actions, especially when it has nothing to do with your growth or your responsibilities.

Reflect:

- How much of your mental energy is going toward things you can't control?

- If you stopped tracking what others were doing, how much more could you pour into your own work?

- Are you filtering your actions through your own values or through how you think others will react?

- What would your day feel like if you gave zero weight to praise or criticism from people who don't live by your standards?

Detach from their moves. Focus on your mission. That's where your real power lives.

November 22

You're not a victim of circumstance, you're a prisoner of your perspective. The lock is on your side of the door.

Most of the pain we carry isn't from what actually happened, but from the story we tell ourselves about it. Someone says something critical, ignores your text, or passes you over for a promotion, and instantly your brain writes a whole narrative: "They don't respect me. I've been wronged. This is unfair." And just like that, the wound grows. It's our belief about the event that creates the feeling of harm. The moment you change your mindset and remove that belief, the harm disappears with it.

This wisdom is rooted in the *dichotomy of control*. The external outcome is a fact you can't influence, but your internal response is a choice you can make. By using reason to challenge your initial emotional reaction, you can reframe a setback not as a personal tragedy, but as a neutral event. This frees you from the anxiety that disrupts your peace and allows you to live a more tranquil, purposeful life.

Your Takeaway

If you can remove the belief that you've been harmed, the harm itself loses its power. You can't control what happens, but you *can* control whether you keep replaying the offense and letting it define you.

Reflect:

- What "I've been harmed" story are you still carrying, and what would happen if you dropped it?

- Are you more attached to the event itself, or to the identity you've built around it?

- How would your day change if you could remove the personal sting from someone else's actions?

- What outcome are you holding onto so tightly that it's keeping you stuck in resentment?

When you stop feeding the story, you stop feeding the pain.

November 23

Stop fighting reality and trust that what's here is meant to be here.

Things don't just happen at random, they happen as part of a bigger flow you might not fully see yet. *Detachment from the outcome* means accepting that what's in front of you is *supposed* to be here because it belongs in the bigger picture that's shaping you.

This mindset isn't about blind optimism or being passive. It's about using this belief as a tool to focus all your energy on what you *can* control: your actions and your character.

By accepting the outcome of the game with *Amor Fati*, you are free to focus on playing your part well. In every circumstance, your sole focus should be on acting with integrity, courage, and wisdom. This is virtue in action, letting go of the result so you can be fully present in the process.

Your Takeaway

Every twist in the road plays a role in your growth, even if you can't connect the dots yet. Your job is to keep showing up as the best version of yourself *within* it. Act with integrity, stay aligned with your values, and refuse to let disappointment drag you out of your lane.

Reflect:

- Where are you resisting reality because it's not the outcome you wanted?

- How would your mindset shift if you believed this moment is exactly where you're supposed to be?

- Are you showing up as the person you want to be, even when things don't go your way?

- How can you focus more on *how* you act rather than *what* you get?

Detachment is letting go of "it should be different" and leaning fully into "this is my moment, how will I meet it?"

November 24

The key isn't to control the world, but to control what you let the world mean to you.

When things don't go our way, we internalize the concept that we've been wronged. This leads to us blaming everyone from the people around us to the system itself. But the root of our suffering isn't the external event, it's the mistake of assigning moral value – whether good or bad – to things that are outside of our control. When you attach your happiness to an outcome, and it doesn't happen, you inevitably get angry.

The external outcome is a fact you can't influence, but your internal response is a choice you can make. By using reason to challenge the belief that a bad outcome can genuinely harm you, you free yourself from hostile passions and the desire to blame others. When you measure life by what's *yours* to control, you stop riding the emotional rollercoaster of every win and loss outside your hands. Make virtue the only good by focusing on your internal choices, which is the key to both inner peace and acting with integrity.

Your Takeaway

Re-center your definition of good and bad around the only thing you truly own: your choices, your effort, your integrity. When you stop assigning moral value to things you can't control, you stop creating enemies out of people and villains out of circumstances, and start meeting life with steadiness instead of suspicion.

Reflect:

- What external results are you labeling 'good' or 'bad' that you actually can't control?

- How much energy would you get back if you stopped blaming people or fate for what happens?

- What would it look like to define success entirely by your own actions and values?

- Are you willing to release your grip on the uncontrollable so you can hold onto your peace?

Detachment isn't passive, it's power focused where it matters most.

November 25

You're not a victim of circumstance, you're the master of your mindset. The art of living comes with the ability to re-author your own story.

It might feel like your values are under constant threat from a chaotic world, but your core principles and integrity can't be taken from you.

They can only be extinguished if you stop thinking the thoughts that uphold them. Your foundation is built on your mindset and your ability to see things clearly, choose your perspective, and act from your values, no matter what's happening around you.

By distinguishing between what's in your mind and what's outside of it, you realize that your internal state is safe from all external outcomes. This is the essence of *detachment from the outcome*. It's the necessary tool that proves your character can't be corrupted by external pressures.

Reclaim the power of your mind by actively training your thoughts to be unconcerned with everything outside. That's how you will secure your inner freedom and peace.

Your Takeaway

What happens outside you isn't where your stability comes from. Remember who you were before fear, stress, or disappointment clouded your vision. Stand up straight, mentally and emotionally, by returning to the thoughts and principles that actually make you strong.

Reflect:

- Where have you let outside events pull you away from your principles?

- What thoughts or beliefs do you need to rekindle to feel steady again?

- How might your day change if you truly saw external events as neutral?

- What would 'coming back to life' look like for you right now?

Your mindset is your anchor, so don't hand it over to the tide.

November 26

Your peace is not a gift from the world, it's a choice you make, over and over, every time the world tries to take it. The quiet you seek is not in a silent room. It's in the mental habit of ignoring the noise.

At any given moment, you get to decide whether something actually harms you or if it's just an event happening outside you. Your peace, your clarity, and your sense of self-worth are not automatically up for grabs.

Detachment from the outcome is about remembering this choice in real time. You can look at what's happening, strip away the drama, and see it for exactly what it is; not what your ego, your fears, or your worst assumptions make it out to be. It's the practice of using reason to override your initial emotional reactions and see things objectively. By doing so, you protect your tranquility and your virtue, which is the only thing of true and lasting value.

Your nature gave you this ability to stand steady. Use it. You can always choose to keep your center.

Your Takeaway

Our inner peace is fragile and easily disrupted by the chaos of the day, but your emotional state is always within your control. This is a practice of deliberately reminding yourself that your peace isn't a gift from the world, it's a choice you make, over and over, each and every time the world tries to take it.

Reflect:

- Where in your life are you giving people or events too much power over your mood?

- How can you start seeing things as they are, without the extra emotional baggage?

- What would it look like to protect your inner peace like it's your most valuable asset?

- Are you willing to remind yourself, moment by moment, that your response is yours to choose?

Peace isn't taken, it's given away. Stop giving yours up.

November 27

Stop rehearsing your misery. Strip it down, see it clearly, and move on.

We are actors in our own drama, performing our frustration over and over until it owns us. We waste our energy complaining about things that go wrong, yet our misery isn't caused by the external event itself – but by our emotional reaction to it. You can regain your peace of mind by analyzing and breaking down what's upsetting you into its core parts. By reducing a problem to its objective facts, you can strip it of its emotional power.

Your misery comes from your internal complaints, which are within your power, and not from the external event itself. The practice of *detachment from the outcome* uses reason to override your initial emotional reactions.

This isn't a long, drawn-out process, it's a decision you can make now. The time to start living a better, more tranquil life is always the present moment.

Your Takeaway

Instead of ruminating on your feelings about an unpleasant situation, see things for what they are. The time to simplify your reactions always starts now.

Reflect:

- What's something you've been mentally rehashing that's keeping you stuck?

- If you looked at it without the emotional storyline, what would you see?

- How much of your current misery is from the event and how much is from reliving it?

- What could you let go of today to make space for more peace?

Detachment starts the moment you stop performing your pain.

November 28

The ultimate shield against adversity isn't a suit of armor. It's the conviction that nothing external can touch your core worth.

Life throws a lot at you: criticism, rejection, delays, changes you didn't ask for. But unless it actually makes *you* a worse person – less honest, less kind, less grounded – it hasn't really harmed you.

Detachment from the outcome means separating what truly matters from what only *feels* like it matters in the moment. That bad review stings, but it doesn't define you. That missed opportunity is disappointing, but it doesn't damage your integrity. The only real loss is when you let outside events drag your values down.

Your character is the core. Guard that, and you can move through storms without losing your balance. The world can take a lot from you, but if it doesn't take the person you're committed to being, you're still whole.

Your Takeaway

If you truly believe that your character is the only thing of ultimate value, then no external outcome can harm you. Detachment is the practice of honoring this distinction, strengthening your mind to be a fortress that no external event can corrupt.

Reflect:

- What's something you've been treating like a disaster that actually left your character intact?

- How would your stress change if you judged events only by whether they made you better or worse inside?

- Are you letting small external hits turn into internal damage?

- What's one value you'll protect no matter what outcome you face?

When you protect your character, the rest can pass through without breaking you.

November 29

Freedom isn't found in getting everything you want. It's found in not needing anything you can't control. Make your moves with intention, not impulse.

Detachment from the outcome starts with detachment from *every little impulse* that passes through your mind. Not every desire is worth chasing, and not every knee-jerk reaction is worth acting on. The art is in slowing down, checking the impulse, and asking, "Is this mine to act on? Does it help anyone, including me? Is it actually worth it?"

When you say yes without thinking, you hand your peace over to whatever random craving, fear, or desire shows up next. But when you learn to condition your impulses, align them with your values, and make them proportional to what's actually at stake, then you stop being a slave to outcomes you never even wanted.

Avoid pouring your energy into resisting or fearing things you can't control. Save your "no" for the stuff that's truly yours to push back against. That's how you stop getting dragged into emotional drama over things that were never in your lane to begin with. By letting go of the future, you ground yourself in the present moment, where your integrity can be fully expressed. A life of peace and purpose comes from mastering your impulses and judgments.

Your Takeaway

Start focusing on things that are in your power, such as the strength of your character. Your actions are conditional, guided by reason and virtue, not by passionate desires for a specific result.

Reflect:

- How often do you say "yes" to an impulse without stopping to question it?

- What's one recurring desire or reaction you could pause and evaluate before acting on?

- How would your life feel different if you only acted on impulses that aligned with your deeper values?

- Where are you wasting energy resisting things you can't change?

Detachment is power because it's the freedom to choose your moves instead of letting your impulses choose them for you.

November 30

The path to peace isn't paved with a perfect world. It's built with the one decision to stop letting the world define your inner state.

The world around us is a constant storm of bad news and difficult circumstances, but the true nature of any event lies in your personal judgment or perspective. This judgment is always within your control. By choosing to eliminate the negative beliefs you hold about a situation, you can find inner peace and tranquility.

The only thing standing between you and calm is your own internal take on things, and that's entirely up to you. It's the practice of using reason to override your initial emotional reactions. The outside may continue to rage, but by actively exercising the power of the mind, you can find a perfect stillness in the unruffled bay within.

Your Takeaway

You decide on the meaning of your life. *Detachment from the outcome* means owning that power. If your belief about a situation is fueling your stress, you can choose a new perspective.

Reflect:

- What's one situation right now that's stressful mainly because of the meaning you've given it?

- How could shifting your perspective calm the waters?

- What beliefs are you holding that are keeping you in constant rough seas?

- If peace is one thought away, what thought would you choose?

You can't always calm the storm, but you can always steer toward stillness.

December 01

Your life is a blink in the endless span of time. Zoom out. None of this is as big as you think it is.

We live with a constant sense of anxiety – worrying over our careers, social standing, and the fleeting circumstances of our lives. Take a different perspective by contemplating your own tiny scale in the vastness of time and space. The stress you're feeling is a single pixel in a satellite photo of the earth. In the face of such cosmic insignificance, there's no reason to be attached to anything external.

This is the essence of *detachment from the outcome*. It's the direct application of the *dichotomy of control*: your sole focus should be on acting with integrity and purpose, the one thing you can control.

By serenely accepting whatever the universe brings your way, the things you can't control, you practice *Amor Fati*. This isn't about being passive, it's about making virtue a priority by directing all your energy toward building your character, free from the anxiety of results.

Your Takeaway

Don't waste your breath on things you were never meant to control. Use the fraction of time you *do* have to live in a way that would make you proud, no matter how long or short your run is. The only thing that really matters is living aligned with your nature, being honest, being kind, acting with integrity, and then rolling with whatever the universe sends your way.

Reflect:

- What outcome are you focusing on that won't matter in the big picture of time?

- How does remembering your small place in the universe actually give you freedom?

- Are you more focused on clinging to results, or on living true to your values in the moment?

When you zoom out, the pressure to control everything fades. What's left is the freedom to live well.

Concept 29: Find Joy in Simplicity

Peace isn't in having more, it's in needing less.

December 02

Face what comes with grace, courage, and justice. Do each act like it's your last, free of distractions, ego, or regret.

Every time something comes your way, tackle it with real grit and genuine kindness. Be scrupulous, generous, and just, and don't waste a second on distractions that don't matter.

Treat every action as if it's the last thing you'll ever do. That means no stray thoughts, no emotional sidetracks, no letting your passions pull you off course. Ditch the hypocrisy, the selfishness, and the constant "Why me?" mindset.

Master living with grace, love for others, fairness, and staying true to your reason, and you have everything it takes to live a content, meaningful life.

It's not complicated, it's about showing up fully, honestly, and with your heart in the right place.

Your Takeaway

Whatever today throws at you, meet it with integrity, not performative grace nor forced positivity. Let go of the mental noise. Let go of self-pity. Let go of pretending.

December 03

True beauty and goodness don't need an audience, they simply are. The work isn't for applause. It's for the quiet satisfaction of knowing you built it well. The craft is the reward, not the praise.

The heart of simplicity is finding joy in what *is*, without needing praise or validation to prove its worth. When something is genuinely good, true, or beautiful, it stands complete in itself. The same goes for you. Your integrity, your kindness, your quiet daily choices, none of that becomes more valuable just because someone notices, and none of it becomes worthless if they don't.

Joy in simplicity means learning to love yourself and things without the extra noise. Let the emerald just be an emerald. Let the flower just bloom, and let yourself live without constantly asking, "Does anyone see me?" or "Does anyone approve?"

Life gets lighter when you stop performing and just *are*.

Your Takeaway

Anything of true worth is beautiful and complete in itself, and your inherent worth doesn't depend on what anyone else thinks. Focus on your internal, controllable qualities rather than the uncontrollable, complex world of opinions and praise.

Reflect:

- Where in your life are you waiting for applause before you believe something has value?

- How would it feel to enjoy the simple goodness of something, even yourself, without outside validation?

- What everyday things already carry beauty or worth, even if no one talks about them?

- How might you free yourself by letting things and people just *be enough as they are*?

Happiness is found in what doesn't need to be proved.

December 04

Do what's necessary with intention, not excess. Cut the distractions both in your actions and in your thoughts.

If you want to feel content, sometimes the best move is to just do less. Most of what clutters your day, your calendar, your conversations, and your thoughts isn't necessary. You don't need to chase every task, weigh in on every debate, or run yourself ragged to prove you're productive. Busyness isn't the same as meaning. Every unnecessary thought breeds unnecessary actions, and every unnecessary action steals time, energy, and peace.

Doing what truly matters means taking the actions your reason and your role in this social world demand. Nothing extra, nothing wasted. Doing less *with purpose* isn't about giving up. It's about making space for the good stuff: your focus, your energy, and your peace. Whenever you're about to speak or act, ask yourself, "Is this helping me live with intention?"

Your Takeaway

Simplicity is asking, "Is this really necessary?" before you act or spiral. The joy is in trimming the excess so you can focus on what actually matters, showing up for your people, doing the work that aligns with your values, and leaving space to breathe. When you cut the noise, you not only do less, you feel more alive doing it.

Reflect:

- What actions in your day are just filler and not necessary?

- How would your life feel lighter if you cut half your unnecessary thoughts?

- Where are you confusing busyness with meaning?

- What would it look like to live with fewer actions, but deeper purpose?

Joy comes when you stop chasing more and start living with enough.

December 05

Life gets simpler when you stop asking, "Will this keep me safe?" and start asking, "Is this the right thing to do?"

Many of us think a person's worth is tied to their success, the number of followers they have, the size of their paycheck, or their job title. But a person's true worth is only measured by their moral character and the integrity of their actions. It's not about winning or losing, but about whether what you're doing is right or wrong, regardless of the consequences.

Focus on your choices, the only thing that's truly within your power. By detaching from the outcome, you gain the freedom that comes from knowing you're doing the right thing, even if no one is watching. The true win isn't a viral post or a promotion, it's the inner peace that comes from a clean conscience.

Your Takeaway

Most of our stress comes from overthinking, but that mindset keeps you trapped in fear. Instead, ask yourself one simple question, "Is this the right thing to do?" Living with simplicity brings a kind of peace that safety and approval can't buy. It's the joy of knowing you're anchored in what matters most.

Reflect:

- How often do you overcomplicate choices by chasing outcomes instead of asking, "Is this right?"

- Where in your life are you prioritizing safety or approval over integrity?

- What would change if your main filter for decisions was simply: *good or not good, right or not right?*

- How might joy return if you stopped living in fear of results and started living in alignment?

This isn't about doing less, it's about cutting through the noise to what truly matters.

December 06

The ambitious chase praise. The pleasure-seekers chase feelings. But the wise focus on their own actions.

Some people live for applause, constantly refreshing their feed, desperate for likes, validation, and recognition. Others live for the next hit of pleasure, food, sex, shopping, the quick fix that never really lasts. Both paths are exhausting because they depend on things outside of you. You don't need to be ruled by external validation or fleeting highs. True satisfaction lives in focusing on being intentional and acting in alignment with your values.

For a grounded, intelligent person, the question is simple: "What am I doing right now? Am I showing up with integrity? Am I proud of the work I put into the world?" That's it, just the quiet satisfaction of living aligned with your values.

Joy shows up when you stop outsourcing your worth, when you don't need applause or indulgence to feel alive. You just do the work, live the life, and let that be enough.

Your Takeaway

Your power isn't in what people think of you or how things feel in the moment. It's in what you do: how you show up, the choices you make, and the way you treat yourself and others.

Reflect:

- Where are you still chasing approval or quick pleasures instead of grounding in your own actions?

- How would it feel to let go of outside validation and find joy in simply *doing well?*

- What would shift if you measured your life not by recognition or feeling, but by integrity?

- Can you be content knowing your worth isn't up for public vote?

Take pride in your own actions, nothing more, nothing less.

December 07

Peace isn't stolen, it's surrendered by the stories you tell yourself..

Your mind is built to be steady. It doesn't get shaken unless *you* hand it over to fear, desire, or drama. Your body might ache, you might get stressed, and it may raise the alarm, but your deeper self only suffers if you let it write a story that says, "This is unbearable. This is who I am."

Simplicity is remembering that you don't have to pile extra meaning on top of pain or setbacks. A headache is a headache, it doesn't have to be a crisis. A rejection is a rejection, it doesn't have to mean you're unworthy. When you strip life down to what actually is, without layering it with judgment, you find calm.

Protect that inner stillness and refuse to create problems where there don't need to be any. Life gets lighter when you stop adding your own weight to it.

Your Takeaway

Our calm mind doesn't panic, spiral into worry, or chase every craving. Your mind only *needs* what you let it need. Simplify, stay calm, and let your mind run the show without the chaos. That's where peace lives.

Reflect:

- What stories are you layering onto challenges that make them heavier than they really are?

- How might your stress shrink if you stopped telling yourself it *had* to mean something about you?

- Where could you practice saying, "This is just what it is," and let that be enough?

- What would it feel like to live with a mind that didn't disturb itself?

Let your mind stop adding drama and just rest in the truth of the moment.

December 08

Your calm rational mind is your fortress. Build it, live in it, protect it.

Nothing on the outside can touch you if your inside stays steady. Your rational mind isn't invincible because the world is easy, it's invincible because you decide to anchor yourself, to withdraw from the noise, and to act from clarity instead of chaos.

Simplicity shows up when you realize you already have the strongest refuge within you. Not in possessions, not in other people's approval, not in external wins. Just in your ability to pause, think, and choose your response. That's your citadel, your inner stronghold where peace can't be invaded unless you open the gates.

The real tragedy isn't that life gets messy. It's knowing this truth and still refusing to use it, still letting every comment, every curveball, every inconvenience shake you when you could've stood firm in your own calm.

Remember that you already have the safest place to retreat. It's inside you, use it.

Your Takeaway

Your rational mind is strongest when it's backed by clear thinking, when you take time, reflect, and make a rational call. When the noise outside is loud, come home to your calm, clear center. A simple life isn't about having less, it's about having clarity. And clarity is freedom.

Reflect:

- Where are you looking outside yourself for safety that you could actually create within?

- What would it feel like to make your inner calm your go-to refuge instead of anger, worry, or distraction?
- How often do you forget that you already have this citadel, and what reminder could keep it front of mind?

- What might your life look like if you trusted your calm as your strongest defense?

Find joy in the quiet fortress of your own steady mind.

December 09

The most valuable things you can own are found in the quiet moments of a life well-lived. Your inner peace is the daily practice of turning off the noise you don't need.

Life is moving fast. It's like a river after a storm: everything's rushing, swirling, and half the time you're just trying not to get swept under. But your job isn't to control the whole river or design the perfect dam, your job is to show up for the part right in front of you and do it well. That's where simplicity lives.

We get caught chasing the big win, the flawless business, the dream body, the perfect relationship, or the Instagram-worthy life. Let go of that impossible standard. The work of finding joy is much simpler – it's about being satisfied with making even the smallest, most honest progress and doing what's right without needing a round of applause.

A life of true purpose isn't found in the acquisition of fame or power, it's found in the simple act of living virtuously. True contentment is the reward for doing the right thing, not for getting recognized for it. Stop chasing the noise and start finding joy in the quiet, simple work of becoming a better person.

Your Takeaway

Just moving the needle a little today is a victory worth celebrating. Real joy comes from knowing you did what was needed, honestly and without ego. Choose modest progress over flashy performance and watch your peace grow.

Reflect:

- Where are you making life harder by chasing perfection instead of progress?

- What's the next right thing in front of you today, and can you let that be enough?

- How much of your energy goes to impressing others instead of living simply for yourself?

- What small, unglamorous wins could you start celebrating as big victories?

Don't shrink your dreams, cut out the noise so you can actually live them.

December 10

Your peace only breaks if you let outside noise inside.

Your body can be hurt, your impulses can get blocked, your plans can get messed with. That's life. But your mind, your core intelligence, and your ability to choose how you see and respond can't be touched unless *you* give it away.

Obstacles only hurt when you meet them unprepared, when you demand life always go your way. But if you expect obstacles as part of the deal, they stop being personal attacks and just become bumps in the road.

Your mind is built to be untouchable – fire, insults, rejection, and loss can't reach it unless you let them define you. When your inner self stays whole, you stop getting knocked off balance by every little thing.

Joy shows up when you strip life down to this simple truth: nothing outside you has the power to obstruct your peace, unless you hand them the keys.

Your Takeaway

When your expectations aren't realized and when your desires aren't met, that undermines your motivation. Simplify. Expect that sometimes you will fail, sometimes you will lose, but stay focused. That's real strength.

Reflect:

- Where are you letting outside circumstances hijack your peace?

- How might expecting obstacles ahead of time make them easier to face?

- What's one place you could stop taking things personally and just keep moving?

Find yourself in the unshakable strength of your own steady mind.

December 11

Stop complaining about the luxuries of life, you don't need them to be happy.

It's easy to look at life's perfect moments, the luxuries, the milestones, the stuff that looks good on social media, and think that's where happiness lives. But true joy is never found in status or sparkle, it's found in the ordinary things you do and the gratitude you bring to them.

Complaining about what you *don't* have, or even what you *do* have, just because it doesn't match the dream in your head, is a recipe for constant dissatisfaction. The people who sleep best at night are the ones who love their morning coffee, appreciate a quiet walk, and can find magic on a regular Tuesday.

If you catch yourself complaining about your life, no matter how perfect it might look from the outside, pause. Go back to the basics. Let yourself be present, notice the little wins, and choose to find contentment where you are, not just where you hope to end up.

Embrace what you have without judgment. Find joy in the simple moments beneath the shiny exterior. Real contentment isn't about where you live or what you own, it's about how you show up.

Your Takeaway

Luxury isn't the problem, your mindset is. If you're always finding fault with indulgences, it's simply a sign you're stuck in scarcity, not peace.

Reflect:

- Where are you letting your idea of a dream life steal your joy from the simple stuff?
- How can you flip the script on comparing and find beauty in your everyday life?

- What's one ordinary thing you could appreciate more today?

- Are you willing to give up chasing the hype for the kind of happiness that actually lasts?

Joy lives in simplicity. Choose it, every day.

December 12

Strip it all back. Your peace lives in your mind, right here, right now.

You're made up of three parts: body, spirit, and mind. You care for the body and spirit, but they're not fully yours: they break down, get tired, crave things, and shift with the seasons of life. The only part that truly belongs to you is your mind. Real freedom looks like a mind that's clear, calm, and focused on doing what's right. A mind that accepts whatever comes, tells the truth, and lives fully in the present.

Train yourself to live like a peaceful, whole, centered and steady person.

When you do, you'll spend the rest of your life with a calm heart, kindness toward others, and a spirit at peace. Live this one moment fully, with kindness toward others and peace within yourself.

Your Takeaway

Unclutter that mind. Let go of obsessing over what other people say or do, stop dragging around your past mistakes, quit rehearsing your future worries. Even the aches and pulls of your body don't define you unless you let them.

Reflect:

- What's weighing on your mind right now that isn't even yours to carry?

- How much energy do you lose replaying the past or rehearsing the future?

- What would your inner life feel like if you focused only on this moment, right here, right now?

- How can you train your mind to be steady, simple, and whole?

Live fully present, with a mind unshaken by the noise.

December 13

Complexity is a choice you make when you're afraid to face a simple truth. The joy is in the ruthless clarity.

Life feels overwhelming when everything looks like one giant, tangled mess. But when you break things down into a situation, cause, and purpose, you clear the fog. "What's it made of?" is the situation. "What set it in motion?" is the cause. "What's the point of it?" is the purpose.

Declutter your mental space. Instead of getting lost in confusion or overwhelm, you'll see the pieces clearly; understand the facts, the reasons, and the real purpose behind what's going on.

That clarity is freedom. It's the kind of simple joy that comes from knowing you don't have to guess or panic. You just see the truth, plain and simple, and you move forward from there.

Next time life throws something your way, pause. Ask, "What's this made of? Why is it here? What's it for?" Keep it simple. That's where real peace lives.

Your Takeaway

Simplicity and the joy that comes with it stems from breaking things down into their essentials, into the simple categories of matter, cause, and purpose. Joy in simplicity is learning to look at life without the extra stories, labels, or exaggerations. Just the truth of what's in front of you and from there, peace.

Reflect:

- What's one problem in your life right now you can break down into matter, cause, and purpose?

- How often do you complicate things by adding stories instead of sticking to the facts?

- What joy might open up if you trained yourself to see things as they are, not as your mind inflates them to be?

- Could simplicity be as close as asking, "What is this really, and what's it for?"

Simplicity starts when you stop dramatizing and start seeing clearly.

Concept 30: Return to the Present and Your Principles

When in doubt, come back to what matters most.

December 14

It's time to stop leaning on others for your happiness and start respecting yourself.

Every time you pin your happiness on other people's approval, you abandon yourself. You trade your principles for attention and validation that doesn't last. The cost is time, energy, and life. All three slip away while you forget that the only soul you're responsible for is your own.

Return to the present and your principles, and call yourself out, gently but honestly. You know better. You've wasted enough time caring more about their opinions than your own integrity. Life's too short to keep disrespecting yourself like that.

You don't control how others see you. You don't control what they give or withhold. But you do control whether you stand in your values right now, in this moment or whether you keep betraying yourself for applause that never satisfies.

Every time you come back to the present, you get another chance to live honestly. That's where dignity and freedom live, and where peace waits for you. Right here, not out there.

Your Takeaway

While you're busy depending on what others think to feel happy, you're slipping further away from the real joy that comes from owning who you are. Your happiness can't live in someone else's hands, it's time to claim it. Respect yourself first, because no one else can do it for you.

Reflect:

- Where in your life are you still letting other people's opinions dictate your happiness?

- How would it feel to stand in your own principles, even if no one else applauded?

- What's one way you can return to yourself today instead of outsourcing your peace?

- Are you willing to stop wasting time dishonoring yourself for approval that doesn't last?

The moment you return to your principles, you return to your power.

December 15

Life isn't random, it's connected. Every moment shapes the next, so live this one with intention.

Nothing in your life is just a one-off. We live on a loop, replaying past mistakes or fast-forwarding to future anxieties. Every choice, every thought, every word ripples forward. What comes next isn't a coin toss, it's connected to what you've already set in motion.

Returning to the present and your principles means owning that connection. You can't change the past, but you *can* shape the present moment, which means you're also shaping the next one. Like a playlist you've curated, each track sets the vibe for the next.

When you live aligned with your principles right now, you're not just doing the 'right' thing at the moment, you're stacking your future toward harmony instead of chaos. You stop feeling like life is random or unfair, because you see the thread connecting it all.

The present isn't separate from the past or the future, it's the bridge. Stand firm here, and the rest will line up.

Your Takeaway

By understanding that everything is part of a rational timeline, you're freed from the burden of fighting reality. Don't waste energy on the plot twists you can't control, just focus on being a person of integrity, knowing that your character is the only part of the story you're in charge of.

Reflect:

- Where are you acting like your choices today don't connect to your tomorrow?

- What ripple are you creating right now with your thoughts, words, and actions?

- How would life feel different if you treated each moment as part of a larger design instead of a random blip?

- What principles do you want today's choices to carry forward into your future?

When you return to the present, you don't just steady yourself, you set the tone for everything that follows.

December 16

Stop obsessing over what drives them, come back to what drives you. Don't let their choices define your reaction. The space between their action and your response is where your character lives.

We waste so much energy analyzing other people: why they act the way they do, what they like, what they hate, and what their hidden motives are. It's a mental quicksand. The more you sink into their world, the further you drift from your own.

Returning to the present and your principles means letting their concerns be *theirs.* You don't need to decode every personality quirk or chase validation by figuring out what makes them tick. Their opinions, their drama, their preferences are not your business.

Your only concern is this moment you are living, your values, your choices and your integrity. Every time you return to it, you reclaim the energy you've been leaking into everyone else's lives.

Stop playing detective in people's inner worlds. Stay rooted in what is your concern

Your Takeaway

When someone annoys or frustrates you, your first impulse is to react, but their behavior isn't about you. The practice of returning to the present and your principles is an internal guidance to pause and analyze what's driving them, whether it's their insecurities, their fears, or their misguided goals.

Reflect:

- Where are you losing yourself by overanalyzing someone else's thoughts or motives?

- How would it feel to stop trying to manage their likes and dislikes and focus on your principles instead?

- What's one way you can redirect that energy back into living your values right now?

- Are you willing to stop drifting in their headspace and return to your own?

When you return to the present and your principles, you stop being pulled by everyone else's currents and steer your own ship.

December 17

Stop living your life on default settings. Your power is in the ability to walk your path with awareness.

Everything is in motion and nature is made up of countless cycles. When you're checked out and not paying attention, that flow can seem chaotic and strange.

So wake up, stop drifting through your days like you're half-asleep, treating life as background noise or autopilot. Stop living like a child who blindly accepts the beliefs, habits, and scripts handed down to you. This is your life, your path. Forgetting that, forgetting where you're headed and why is how you lose yourself.

The simplicity is in awareness: noticing the change, staying rooted in your principles, and walking forward with your eyes open. No denial, no excuses, no sleepwalking. Just conscious living.

Joy doesn't come from clinging to permanence. It comes from embracing change while standing firm in your own values.

Your Takeaway

Your character is the only constant in a world of variables. By consciously choosing to be present and by living according to your core principles, you find your anchor in the storm.

Reflect:

- Where are you resisting change that's actually just part of life's natural flow?

- Are you moving through your days awake and aware, or half-asleep on autopilot?

- What old scripts have you accepted without question that no longer fit your principles?

- How can you return, right now, to your own path, instead of drifting along someone else's?

Return to the present, live by your principles, and let change remind you: you're alive, and this moment is yours to shape.

December 18

Success is what you get. Integrity is who you become. Only one of them lasts.

The world loves a power trip. It's easy to get swept up in your own importance, but that's just a fast track to forgetting what actually matters.

The antidote is to return to your core. Stay humble, stay real, and show up for your responsibilities, not for applause, but because that's who you are at your best. Strip away the extra and live by your principles, right here, right now. Justice, kindness, and honesty should be your signature.

Life is short, and no one gets extra credit for being complicated or important. A real win would be to look back and know you kept your values at the center of everything you did. Be the person your future self will thank you for being: present, purposeful, and anchored in what's true.

Your Takeaway

Life is short. The only real harvest from your time here is a respectful heart and actions that actually help people. Live with balance and wisdom. Tackle problems with calm and focus, don't rush, handle criticism without bitterness, and ignore gossip. Stay patient and be open to better ideas.

Reflect:

- Where are you letting ego or ambition pull you away from your core principles?

- How can you return to the basics and focus on doing what's right, today?

- What would your days look like if you cared more about meaning than image?

- Are you ready to drop the performance and live out your real values, one choice at a time?

Forget the hype. Return to your principles, stay present, and build a legacy that actually matters.

December 19

The only company you're truly in charge of is your own mind.

It's so easy to get caught up in what other people think, want, or chase. Their opinions, drama, and distractions pull you off course if you're not careful, but your job isn't to live their lives, it's to live *yours*.

Stay locked in on your lane. Nature guides you through what happens and through what you're built to do. For us as human beings, that means serving the bigger picture, living in a way that contributes to the common good, not just feeding every craving or impulse.

Your senses will scream for comfort, your emotions will try to drag you into shortcuts, and your impulses will demand quick wins. But your deeper self – your rational, intelligent center – knows better. It was designed to use those feelings, not be ruled by them. And when you don't let yourself get tricked by appearances or swayed by every pull, you walk straight, steady, and fulfilled.

Simplicity is in that straight path: no detours into other people's chaos, no surrender to your impulses, just your principles guiding you forward.

Your Takeaway

Your focus is the most valuable currency you have, and you're giving it away for free. Stop looking over your shoulder at what everyone else is doing and instead fix your gaze straight ahead on your own purpose. Return to the present and your principles.

Reflect:

- Where are you letting someone else's opinions or agenda distract you from your own path?

- What impulses or feelings are running your show instead of your principles?

- How would life feel if you stopped being reactive and started being intentional with each step?

- What's one way you can 'look straight ahead' today and live from your core values, not outside noise?

Return to the present. Root yourself in your principles. That's where fulfillment lives.

December 20

Changing your mind or learning from others doesn't mean you lose yourself, it means you're in charge of your own growth. The only thing more impressive than a strong opinion is the strength to update it.

We confuse a strong opinion with a strong character. We think that holding our ground, even when we're wrong, is a sign of integrity, but changing your mind or accepting a negative piece of feedback is not a sign of weakness. It's the ultimate expression of a mind that's truly free.

Returning to the present and your principles means knowing the difference. If you realize you're off-track and correct yourself, that's not weakness, it's wisdom. If someone calls you higher and you listen, that's not dependence, it's intelligence. You're still the one making the choice. You're still steering your own ship.

Self-reliance isn't about never rerouting, it's about owning the fact that you're the one who chooses to turn the wheel.

The present moment is always an invitation, "Am I willing to return to my principles, even if it means pivoting?" That's not losing yourself, that's proving you know who you are.

Your Takeaway

It takes a conscious choice to break a stubborn habit and align with what's true. By elevating virtue and the unwavering commitment to truth above a fragile ego, you're not surrendering your independence, you're actively strengthening it.

Reflect:

- Where are you mistaking stubbornness for strength?

- How might listening to feedback actually prove your self-reliance?

- What's one area where you need to start over and own that choice today?

- How would it feel to return to your principles without clinging to ego?

Your principles aren't chains, they're your compass. And a compass doesn't fail you when you adjust. It keeps you moving true.

December 21

You're not looking for a new city, you're looking for a new perspective. The scenery changes but your role, your principles, and your mind remain the same.

No matter where you are, whether it's a vacation destination, a new city, or another country, it's all the same. The world doesn't change just because your location does.

Sometimes we feel stuck, in a routine or even frustrated, but you're not stuck because of where you are. You're stuck because you're not fully present, not grounded in your principles, unwilling to change your mindset, or unwilling to accept change.

Stop chasing some ideal better place or time. The moment you're in right now – with all its messiness and chaos – is your *spot*. Own it, bring your best self to it. Come back to your center, your principles, and act from there.

Wherever you go, that's where your life happens. Build steadfast principles and virtues to guide you. They are your true home.

Your Takeaway

No matter where you are, life's challenges and opportunities don't magically change and the core of who you are is no different. Your focus should stay on your principles, your work, and your mindset. Wherever life takes you, lean into your role with steady purpose.

December 22

Don't just move through life on autopilot, live like every action is a step towards the person you want to be.

Too often, we coast through life. We scroll, we react, we say yes when we mean no, we do things just because "that's how it's done." That's not living, that's drifting, but every move you make matters.

Be intentional. Before you act, ask yourself, "Is this in line with the values I actually want to live by?" Your principles aren't just abstract ideas, they're your blueprint for how to live well and stay grounded when life tries to pull you off course.

Show up fully, act with purpose, and let your decisions reflect the virtues, morals and philosophy that guides you into the art of living.

No half-measures or excuses, just you being present, clear, and committed to what truly matters.

Your Takeaway

Every small action is training your character, casting a vote for who you're becoming. Every word, every decision, every habit is either in line with your principles, or it's not. When you act with purpose, anchored in what you believe, you return to yourself.

Reflect:

- Where in your life are you just moving on autopilot instead of acting with purpose?

- What principles do you want your daily actions to reflect?

- How would your choices change if you treated every action as a vote for the person you want to be?

- What's one small thing you can do today with full intention, not out of habit?

Return to the present. Root yourself in your principles. And live like it matters, because it does.

December 23

Your inner compass only works when you're continuing on ahead. The path to clarity is a straight line through the present. Stay centered and stand in your own light.

A lot of us feel like our minds are constantly being pulled in different directions, pining for something we don't have or running from something we don't want.

A mind scattered by desire and aversion is a mind that is never truly at peace. Your inner clarity isn't something you find, it's something you cultivate by letting go of the need to cling or to push away.

This wisdom is rooted in the practice of returning to the present and your principles. It's a powerful mental discipline that anchors you to the here and now. When you stop chasing external things or trying to escape them, you free up your mind's energy.

This state of equilibrium allows your internal compass and principles to function perfectly. The payoff for living with integrity and self-control isn't some external reward, it's the quiet power of a mind that is its own fortress, a mind that can see the truth of all things because it has no hidden agenda.

Your Takeaway

Chasing external validation inflates you. Shrinking back in self-doubt collapses you. Both throw you off balance. Your soul shines brightest when it's steady, when you're not grasping for what's out there or retreating in fear.

Reflect:

- Where are you overreaching, trying to grab for what's outside your control?

- Where are you collapsing inward, shrinking instead of standing in your principles?

- What would it feel like to be steady, not inflated or deflated, but centered?

- How can you return to your own light today and let it guide your next step?

Your power isn't in chasing or hiding. It's in showing up, right here, steady in who you are.

December 24

Their behavior is their own mess to clean up. Don't let their drama become a chore on your to-do list. The way they act is their responsibility, the way you respond is yours.

People are going to mistreat you, misunderstand you, or just plain disappoint you. That's their lane. Their choices reflect *their* values, *their* character, and *their* level of awareness. Don't drag that weight into yours.

Returning to the present and your principles means staying rooted in who *you* are, not who they are. If someone treats you poorly, you don't need to match their energy or let it rewrite your story. Your job is to act in alignment with your own nature, with integrity, strength, and self-respect.

Peace comes when you stop outsourcing your behavior to theirs. The present moment always gives you a choice: stay true to yourself or let someone else's actions hijack your values. Choose you.

Your Takeaway

Don't let someone else's bad behavior shake your peace or distract you from who you are. Stay rooted in your own nature, keep your focus, and keep moving forward with calm and clarity. Their actions don't define your story. You do.

Reflect:

- Where are you letting someone else's bad behavior dictate how you show up?

- What would it look like to respond from your principles instead of from their energy?

- How can you remind yourself in the moment, "That's their story, not mine"?

- What's one way you can return to your lane today and let their actions stay theirs?

You can't control their choices, but you own yours. Stay rooted. Stay present. Stay you.

December 25

Don't let struggle steal your voice, stay anchored in what matters most.

When you're in pain, when life is full of challenges, or when the online world is just a mess of noise, the first impulse is to complain or check out, but your peace isn't an external reward. It's an internal state you're responsible for. Even when your body's hurting, your mind can stay clear. Even when life feels heavy, you can keep your values light.

This wisdom is rooted in the practice of returning to the present and your principles. It's the conscious command to stop letting external circumstances, like physical discomfort or someone else's opinion, dictate your inner world. Instead, get back to the present moment and focus exclusively on the task right in front of you. Your mind is the most powerful instrument you own, and its job is to run your personal code – your core values – no matter how much chaos is happening in the world outside.

Your Takeaway

Returning to the present and your principles means refusing to let your circumstances define your spirit. Whether you're sick, struggling, or just worn out, don't abandon who you are.

Reflect:

- Where are you letting hardship pull you away from your values?

- What would it look like to stay rooted in your principles, even in difficult circumstances?

- How can you shift your focus from the struggle itself to how you show up inside it?

- What 'signal' (value, truth, or practice) do you need to stay connected to right now?

Your body and your circumstances will shift, but your principles are your anchor. Don't let go.

December 26

Your body feels, your emotions react, but your principles decide who you really are.

A lot of us think our feelings, our passions, or even our intelligence are what make us uniquely human. However, a person's character isn't defined by their raw intellect or emotional highs and lows. What sets you apart is your ability to return to your principles, right here, right now. To meet whatever comes — success, loss, praise, criticism — not with impulse but with calm, clarity, and truth. To refuse to poison your inner peace with lies, anger, or injustice.

The conscious act of filtering out the constant stream of impressions — social media notifications, the news cycle, the opinions of others — and staying grounded in the here and now. The only thing that truly matters is your integrity and the serenity of your own mind.

Fulfillment doesn't come from external validation or a perfect life, it comes from the quiet, steady work of being just, being honest, and embracing your life as it unfolds, knowing that your principles are the only true measure of your worth.

Your Takeaway

Returning to the present, feel the sensations, and notice the impulses, but choose integrity, justice, and peace. Living true to your principles is its own reward. At the end, you leave life clean, at peace and in harmony with what was yours to live.

Reflect:

- Where in your life are you letting emotions or impulses drive instead of your principles?

- What does it look like, in practice, to welcome each experience without losing your center?

- How can you keep your inner peace unshaken, no matter how others behave or judge you?

- If today were your last, could you say you lived in alignment with your truth—or would you regret handing the wheel to impulse?

Return to the present. Lead with your principles. That's what makes you more than just reactive, you become intentional, unshakable, and free.

December 27

Peace comes from progress. Keep your thoughts and actions aligned, and you'll never be stuck.

Contentment is about steady movement in the right direction. You don't need to have it all figured out, but you *do* need to keep walking in alignment with your principles. That's what progress is: beliefs and actions working together, moment by moment.

Return to the present and your principles, and you'll see that nothing and no one outside of you can block that. The only thing that derails you is abandoning your own reason, your own values. Over time, that consistency builds strength. The right thoughts and right actions, repeated steadily, bring you peace.

Stop obsessing about outcomes, applause, or how fast you're moving. Progress isn't about speed, it's about direction. And when your principles are your compass, you're never lost.

Your Takeaway

Peace isn't an external reward you earn, it's an internal state you build moment by moment. True contentment isn't a destination, it's the ongoing process of aligning your beliefs and your actions with what you know to be right.

Reflect:

- Are your current thoughts and actions aligned with your principles, or are they pulling in opposite directions?

- What does the concept of progress mean for you right now?

- How often do you let external roadblocks define your contentment instead of your own steady alignment?

- What's one simple way you can return to your principles in action before today ends?

Contentment isn't a destination. It's the reward of showing up, aligned, in this moment.

December 28

The true battle isn't with the person in front of you. It's with the person you are tempted to become just to beat them.

When someone wrongs you, the knee-jerk reaction is to match their energy. It feels good in the moment, but the second you mirror their behavior, you've let them pull you off your own path. The moment you respond in kind, you've allowed them to dictate your reality and lower you to their level.

The conscious, here and now choice is to break the chain of a toxic interaction. Their actions are an external event, completely outside of your control. Your only job is to focus on what you can control: your own response. Your personal code – your integrity, your honesty, your calm – is the only thing truly worth defending. By refusing to become like your opponent, you don't just win the moral high ground, you preserve the only peace that truly matters: your own.

Your Takeaway

Don't mistake restraint for weakness. You defend yourself best not by copying the enemy but by refusing to let them rewrite your story.

Reflect:

- Where in your life are you tempted to mirror someone else's negativity instead of rising above it?

- What would it look like to respond from your principles instead of your anger?

- How can you remind yourself in the moment: "Their actions are theirs, mine are mine"?

- What's one situation right now where you can choose strength over spite?

The world doesn't need another version of your enemy. It needs the truest version of you.

December 29

The space between what you know is right and what you're actually doing is the source of all your frustration. Close the gap.

Most of the stress you carry isn't from the situation itself, it's from the *judgment* you attach to it. The suffering comes when your mind starts spinning a story: "This is ruining everything. I can't handle this. My life is over if this doesn't work out."

Practice catching yourself in the middle of that spiral and asking, "Is this the thing or just my story about the thing?" You can change the story instantly. You can reframe, shift perspective, and choose a calmer, stronger response.

When the issue is internal, like when you know you're avoiding something important, the fix isn't to wallow in guilt, it's to act. If you can do what needs to be done, do it as soon as possible. If you can't because the obstacle's bigger than you, let go of the weight – it was never yours to carry.

The struggle isn't the weight, it's the way you're thinking about it.

Your Takeaway

If something is stressing you out, take the time to examine your issue. If it can be handled, stop procrastinating and take care of the problem. If it can't, let go of the guilt and worry. Find time to be kind and calm, even with what's standing in your way.

Reflect:

- What's one area where your stress is more about your story than the actual situation?

- How can you reframe it right now to bring yourself back to calm?

- Are you stuck in guilt over inaction when you could just take one small step?

- Where do you need to accept that an obstacle is bigger than you, and release the weight?

The power is always in this moment: your story, your principles, your choice. That's where your peace lives.

December 30

Change isn't chaos, it's the system functioning as intended.

We spend so much energy worrying about what's coming next: a new job, a new city, a new phase of life, but change is natural. The world isn't a static place, it's a dynamic system that's always in flux. Your peace isn't found in a perfect, unchanging state, but in a radical acceptance of the constant flow.

Returning to the present and your principles means remembering that you don't have to panic every time life shifts. Change is the universal nature of picking things up and setting them down in new places. The sooner you stop resisting, the sooner you see it for what it is: part of the flow, not a disruption.

You can't control the world's constant updates, but you can act with integrity in the present moment. Your character and your values are the only things that don't change. By focusing on them, you find your stability, not by trying to stop the world's inevitable cycles.

Your Takeaway

Life is built on change. When you return to your principles, change doesn't throw you off balance, it refines you. You can face it with steadiness, clarity, and the calm of someone who knows this isn't unusual, this is life doing what it's always done.

Reflect:

- Where are you fighting change as if it were abnormal instead of natural?

- How would your stress shift if you saw change as a system update instead of a personal setback?

- What principle can anchor you when the ground under your feet feels like it's moving?

- How can you practice embracing change today without fear?

Change isn't the enemy, it's the rule. Your peace comes from flowing with it, not fighting it.

December 31

The book of your life will end when it ends. You have no control over the final chapter or page count. Your only responsibility is the integrity of the page you're writing right now.

We worry about how much time we have left or feel cheated if it seems shorter than we'd like. The truth is that life isn't measured by its runtime but by its quality and the depth of the life you live.

Your wisdom is the hand on the helm of a ship that is always at sea. You didn't choose the ocean, you can't control the wind, and you can't calm the storm, but you can choose your bearing and adjust the sails in this very moment. Your principles are the compass, and the present is the only water you're currently sailing on.

The mark of a life well-lived isn't how long the voyage is; it's the integrity of your bearing, mile by nautical mile. Stop worrying about reaching the faraway shore and pour all of your energy into making this very moment an expert, purposeful adjustment of the sails and wheel.

Your Takeaway

Returning to the present and your principles means letting go of the illusion that you're owed a certain length of time. As long as you lived aligned, present, and principled, your life was lived with success.

Reflect:

- Are you more focused on how many stage acts you have left, or on how you're showing up in the act you're in right now?

- How can you return to your principles when fear of endings pulls you off course?

- What would it look like to live today as if the length of the play didn't matter, only the honesty of your performance?

- If you left the stage tomorrow, would you feel at peace with the role you played?

The present moment *is* your stage. Don't waste it worrying about the final curtain just play your part with everything you've got.

About the Authors

Lourdes Laifer is a Certified Life Coach and Mindfulness-Based Stress Reduction teacher who holds a B.A. in Psychology and a Positive Psychology Specialization Certification. She guides clients in cultivating awareness, emotional balance, and calm strength. Her work focuses on helping people diminish their inner noise and expand their inner wisdom so they can focus on what truly matters: building lives rooted in purpose and peace rather than pressure.

Maria Sabio is a Certified Clinical Hypnotherapist, Life Coach, EFT Coach, and practicing Stoic. She helps clients reframe limiting beliefs, release emotional weight, and cultivate resilience through conscious awareness and emotional mastery. Her philosophy is simple: once you learn to direct your mind, you can transform your life, no matter your past or current circumstances.

Our shared mission is to translate timeless wisdom into tools you can actually use to navigate adversity with grace, respond instead of react, and find stability in the middle of uncertainty. We believe in meeting life as it is, not as we wish it to be, and in discovering strength, freedom, and peace right there. This book is part of our mission to make philosophy practical, mindset work real, and resilience accessible to everyone. When you learn to steady your mind, everything else follows. Your peace depends on what you practice daily.

www.ingramcontent.com/pod-product-compliance
Lightning Source LLC
Chambersburg PA
CBHW060401130626
46555CB00005B/1967